Databases in the 1990s

Databases in the 1990s

Proceedings of the Australian Database Research Conference

Melbourne 6 February 1990

Editors

B Srinivasan
Department of Computer Science
Monash University
Australia

J Zeleznikow
Department of Computer Science
La Trobe University
Australia

World Scientific
Singapore • New Jersey • London • Hong Kong

Published by

World Scientific Publishing Co Pte Ltd
5 Toh Tuck Link, Singapore 596224
USA office: 27 Warren Street, Suite 401-402, Hackensack, NJ 07601
UK office: 57 Shelton Street, Covent Garden, London WC2H 9HE

British Library Cataloguing-in-Publication Data
A catalogue record for this book is available from the British Library.

DATABASES IN THE 1990s

ISBN-13 978-981-02-0276-7
ISBN-10 981-02-0276-8

Preface

The intellectual challenge and economic rewards of developing and implementing database systems have been well established and recognized. Although various data models have been proposed to capture the semantics of applications, a totally performance acceptable and user friendly system is still far from being fully evolved. For a decade and more, both practitioners and theoreticians in various fields of this commercially relevant area have been looking at the solutions to numerous such problems. This conference has made an attempt to bring forth various researchers within Australia and the world to meet and discuss the latest ideas, results and trends. We are confident that these exchanges have been valuable and will lead to further advances in database technology. The united effort of the organizers in bringing about this conference indicates the great significance of database research being carried out by Australian industry, research institutes and universities.

The organizers of the Australian Database Research Conference would like to thank all authors who submitted papers for consideration. They helped to ensure an excellent program. Finally, special thanks are due to Prof Chris Wallace of Monash University for his support in having this conference prior to the Australian Computer Science Conference and Prof Tharam Dillon of La Trobe University for providing resources in bringing out the pre-conference proceedings. We offer this publication as one of the lasting record of the database research in Australia.

February 28, 1990
Melbourne

B. Srinivasan
J. Zeleznikow

Table of Contents

The Road Ahead: Moving from Relational to Object Oriented Databases

B. Srinivasan
Department of Computer Science
Monash University
Australia 3168
email: srini@bruce.cs.monash.edu.au

J. Zeleznikow
Department of Computer Science
La Trobe University
Australia 3083
email: johnz@latcs1.edu.au

The concept of database can be viewed in many ways. For example, from an application point of view, it is a collection of related files; whilst from the management point of view it is a model of the corporate enterprise activity. Irrespective of both the views, a database supports certain common functions such as; a query language to query and update the database, a high-level interface, preferably machine independent for the user's interaction, and mechanisms to support static and dynamic aspects of data.

The current database management systems attempt to implement ANSI standard three schema architecture [1]. The ANSI architecture generates islands of automations. Commercial vendor databases fail to fully support one or more of the following principal database functions[5].

- High performance
- Richer semantic data model
- Flexible query mechanism
- Host language independence
- Guaranteed concurrent operations
- Fault-tolerant/recovery facilities
- Distributed database support

Persistent storage, which is a necessary but not a sufficient condition for database management systems, results in islands of automation that contribute to major data access problems for corporate entities. Current benchmarks on the performance of databases indicate that they are too slow for object oriented environments, at least by a factor of 2 [2]. A high performance object server which is semantically independent of any data model implemented at the physical schema level would improve the current database implementations. It is possible for the server to have in-built optimizing mechanisms for improving throughput by analyzing the transactions and providing automatic clustering of data. The current relational databases are relational to the extent that they try to satisfy the Codd's definition of relational model [3]. In order for the model to be useful, it should support the notion of objects in its data model. Any semantic data model such as property driven model, fully embodied in relational model or entity-relationship model may be appropriate for future object oriented databases.

Although commercial databases do provide support for reasonably complex ad-hoc queries, they do not provide sufficient support for integrity (apart from domain and referential), transitive closure and inferencing. The current relational model does not support logic based approaches for query languages, what we require is a fully functional knowledge based management system.

Although mathematically proven procedures exist to preserve the integrity of data during concurrent access, commercial systems are skeptical about fully implementing them because of performance factors. Although locking is provided at the physical level, locking on a logical basis at the object level may be appropriate. In particular, version and long transaction support are critical factors for any object oriented database systems.

Viewing database at any historical time may allow post-mortem of operations in the database. This would require versioning and a stable view of the database. Hence, advance fault-tolerant mechanisms and automated recovery procedures need to be provided.

Query servers are provided to support distributed databases. However, most often they are little more than address resolution mechanisms. What we require in the future is a message cascading system coupled with typical SQL based servers for supporting both object oriented and relational databases.

References:

1. American National Standard Institute Study Group on Database Management Systems: Interim Report, FDT, 7:2,*ACM* 1975.

2. Cattell., R. G. G., Object-Oriented DBMS Performance Measurements, *In Advances in Object-Oriented Database Systems,* Springer-Verleg, 1988, pp 364 - 367.

3. Codd., E.F., Is Your Database Management System Really Relational?, *Computer world* (Australia), Feb 1986, pp 18 - 24.

4. Liberman., D. R., DBMS Evaluation by the Rules, *Database Programming and Design*, Vol 1, No 12, 1988, pp 30 -38.

5. Ken J. McDonell, Commercial Database Performance - Do we know where we are, much less where we are going?, *Proc. of Australian Database Research Conference*, (in this proceedings), 1990, pp 123 - 132.

Design Considerations for a Document Database System*

R. Sacks-Davis
J. A. Thom
A. J. Kent
K. Ramamohanarao

Key Centre for Knowledge Based Systems
Departments of Computer Science
Royal Melbourne Institute of Technology and The University of Melbourne

email: {rsd, jat, ajk, rao}@goanna.cs.rmit.OZ.AU

Abstract

Document databases have very different requirements to standard transaction oriented business systems. This paper provides a description of some of the features of the database kernel for the `Titan+` information management system, a research prototype system designed for document support. A description of the text processing features of the data manipulation language, TQL, is given. Other design considerations for a document database system are discussed.

1 Introduction

Document database requirements are very different from those of conventional transaction oriented business database systems. For document databases, text processing becomes of paramount importance and the requirements to effectively support text are not properly met by standard relational database systems. These

*This work is funded in part by a GIRD grant supported by the IR&D board of the Australian Government Department of Industry, Technology and Commerce.

requirements include the need to support hierarchical data structures so that hierarchically structured documents can be treated as atomic objects by the database system, the ability to provide links between objects in order to effectively support browsing interfaces and the ability to efficiently index large volumes of text.

The `Titan+` Database Management System is a research prototype developed under funding from the Australian Government and has been designed to efficiently support text processing applications. In this paper we will briefly describe some of the text processing requirements supported by `Titan+` by providing a description of the data manipulation language supported TQL. We will briefly compare TQL with SQL, the de facto standard relational data manipulation language. We will also describe how `Titan+` can efficiently index large volumes of text and discuss some of the database design techniques for a system such as `Titan+`.

2 TQL

TQL is a data manipulation language designed for an information system supporting advanced features such as the ability to support nested tables, structured data types and reference pointers for linking database objects. None of these features are supported in relational systems.

A number of other query languages have been proposed for databases supporting nested tables (sometimes referred to as non first normal form databases) [1, 8, 9, 7]. TQL closely follows the syntax of a language called SQL/NF [9] designed at the University of Texas/Austin by Mark Roth, Henry Korth and Don Batory. A major difference between TQL and SQL/NF is the inclusion of text operations in TQL. TQL also includes the concept of references and implicit joins from SQL/W [7] designed at the University of Waterloo by Per-Ake Larson. Other concepts borrowed from SQL/W include the structured tuple type. A full description of TQL can be founded in [13] and [12].

TQL can be viewed as an extension to the relational query language, SQL [4]. SQL has become a de facto standard for relational database systems and is described in most standard database textbooks (see for example [2, 6]). Because of its prevalence in the database community, many of the languages proposed for post-relational systems, such as SQL/W [7], OSQL [3], NF^2 [1, 8] and SQL/NF [9], have been designed to have an SQL flavour.

To illustrate some of the design features for TQL, let us consider a fictitious database for office correspondence. A possible TQL schema is

```
Memo (From_list (f REF Person,
                 position TEXT),
      To_list   (t REF Person,
                 position TEXT),
      subject TEXT,
      date DATE,
      Contents (para TEXT),
      Keywords (term TEXT))

Person (pid INTEGER,
        name <firstname TEXT,
              Middle (name TEXT),
              lastname TEXT>,
        department TEXT)
```

The schema defines two *tables*, `Memo` and `Person`. A memo is sent by one or more people from the organization to a second set of employees. The memo consists of a number of paragraphs, a set of keywords (to be of use when retrieving documents) and has a subject and date. The `subject` and `date` attributes have atomic types, whereas the fields `From_list`, `To_list`, `Contents`, and `Keywords` are *nested tables*. The nested table type is designated by round brackets in the schema definition. It allows for the direct representation of hierarchically structured objects. The other structured attribute type supported by TQL is the *tuple* and in table `Person`, the names of employees are stored as tuples consisting of three components, the `firstname`, a set of `Middle` names and a `lastname`. Tuples are designated using angled brackets.

The ability of TQL to be able to provide a direct representation of hierarchically structured objects is important in a number of application areas. One such area is document database systems since documents are typically hierarchical (for example, a document consists of sections and each section consists of paragraphs).

An equivalent normalized relational schema for our example would consist of seven tables.

```
Memo1 (memo_no, subject, date)
From_list1 (memo_no, pid, position)
To_list1 (memo_no, pid, position)
Contents1 (memo_no, para_no, para)
Keywords1 (memo_no, term)
People1 (pid, firstname, lastname, department)
Middle1 (pid, name)
```

Note that the information about a single memo is *fragmented* over five tables and that two relations are required for the people data in the relational model. If the physical design reflects the logical schema definition (as is almost always the case in relational databases) then the data will be stored in seven physical tables. This will make many common queries expensive to evaluate. For example, to retrieve the information about a single memo, five relations rather than a single table must be accessed. In addition, the query on the relational database will require that four *join operations* be evaluated. The SQL query to retrieve information about each memo can be expressed as

```
SELECT From_list1.pid, From_list1.position, To_list1.pid,
       To_list1.position, subject, date, para, term
FROM   From_list1, To_list1, Memo1, Contents1, Keywords1
WHERE  From_list1.pid = Memo1.pid
AND    To_list1.pid = Memo1.pid
AND    Contents1.pid = Memo1.pid
AND    Keywords1.pid = Memo1.pid
```

The query is complex to express, the result of the query does not have the appropriate hierarchical structure and the join processing required is potentially expensive. With the TQL implementation, none of these problems arise and the TQL query to retrieve the information about all households is

```
SELECT ALL
FROM   Memo;
```

or simply

```
Memo;
```

In relational databases all join conditions must be provided explicitly such as in the previous example. TQL also supports such explicit joins but, in addition, through the use of reference attributes, TQL supports a powerful language facility called *implicit joins*. To illustrate this facility, recall that the nested tables From_list and To_list in table Memo contain attributes which are references to table Person. In formulating a query, the user is able to view the Person tuples as belonging to the referencing tables. For example, a query to list the subjects of all memos together with the names of the people who sent and received the memos could be expressed as

```
SELECT subject,
       ( SELECT f.name
         FROM   From_list ),
       ( SELECT t.name
         FROM   To_list )
FROM   Memo;
```

The implicit join is supported using the dot notation and an explicit join condition is not required. Implicit joins simplify the formulation of many commonly occurring queries.

A reference attribute (such as f or t) has a domain consisting of the key values of the referenced table (pid of Person in both instances). If the key to the table **Memo** was a combination of the two attributes **subject** and **date**, then a reference attribute whose target was table **Memo** would have a domain consisting of **<subject, date>** tuples.

The equivalent TQL query, expressed with an explicit join condition is

```
SELECT subject,
       ( SELECT name
         FROM   From_list, Person
         WHERE  From_list.f.pid = Person.pid ),
       ( SELECT name
         FROM   To_list, Person
         WHERE  To_list.t.pid = Person.pid ),
From   Memo;
```

For efficient processing of user queries, the actual address of the referenced tuple may be stored with the key value for a reference attribute but this is an implementation issue and would be done transparently to the TQL user.

Like SQL, the basic construct of a query is a SELECT-FROM-WHERE (SFW) expression. However, in order to support nested tables, TQL has a recursively defined syntax so that SFW expressions can contain nested SFW expressions as in the above query. An SFW expression can be used in a TQL query in any place that a table name can be used. As well as supporting SFW expressions, TQL queries can be expressed in an alternative functional notation and the query

```
SELECT subject,
       ( SELECT f.name
         FROM   From_list ),
       ( SELECT t.name
         FROM   To_list )
FROM   Memo;
```

can be expressed as

```
SELECT subject, From_list( f.name ), To_list( t.name )
FROM   Memo;
```

or alternatively,

```
Memo( subject, From_list( f.name ), To_list( t.name ) );
```

3 Support for lists

Nested tables are actually maintained as lists by Titan+, so that the ordering of tuples is maintained. This is important in the context of document databases since the order of paragraphs in a document or the order of authors of a paper obviously need to be maintained. ROWNUM returns the tuple number of the current tuple. Hence to list the subject and first paragraph of each memo, we can use the following TQL query:

```
SELECT subject, (SELECT para
                 FROM   Contents
                 WHERE  ROWNUM = 1)
FROM   Memo;
```

TQL supports the following alternative syntax for this query:

```
Memo (subject, Contents[1].para)
```

An alternative approach for supporting lists would have been two support two structured attribute types, namely nested tables and lists. However, this would in our view have unnecessarily added to the complexity of the syntax of TQL.

4 Support for text attributes

Since Titan+ is designed for applications supporting free text, a number of text operators are supported by TQL. In TQL text is treated as an atomic type.

There are a number of ways a word in a query can be compared to a word of text. For example, it is often useful to compare the stems of words so that a query containing `'computer'` would match a document containing `'computing'` or `'computers'`. Another form of comparison is based on the use of the soundex algorithm and results in matches if a query term sounds the same as a document term. Exact matching and case insensitive matching are also supported.

For free text queries, the default type of comparison used is that which is defined in the *database schema.* Typically, stemming is used for free text, while soundex is often required for names of people or places. Although the default form of comparison is defined in the schema, it is possible to specify a query in which the default is overridden. For example stemming algorithms sometimes result in unrelated words reducing to the same stem. It may therefore be necessary to specify exact matching in some free text or string expressions. To achieve this, TQL provides single postfix characters (transformation marks) to select the method of comparison. The possible transformations are:

- exact match (`=`),
- ignore case (`^`),
- stemming (`~`), and
- soundex (`@`).

The absence of such a postfix transformation indicates that the default comparison is to be used. If there is no default comparison "exact match" comparisons are done.

It is also possible to specify indexing using these transformations, this is described in the following section.

Any of the transformations can be applied to the equality and inequality operators. Thus `==` means the two text operands match exactly (that is they are identical), `=^` means the two text operands are equal if case is ignored, `=~` means the stems of the two text operands are the same, and `=@` means the two text operands sound the same. Similarly for inequality operators <>=, <>^, <>~ and <>@.

Query 4.1 *Find all people in the art department — ignore case.*

```
SELECT name
FROM   Person
WHERE  department = ^ 'art'
```

The specification of substrings in queries on text fields is supported (as in SQL) using the LIKE construct. The LIKE operator uses % and _ for pattern matching as in standard SQL — % matches zero or more characters and _ matches a single character.

Query 4.2 *Find all people whose firstname ends with the letter 'a'*

```
SELECT name
FROM   Person
WHERE  name.firstname LIKE '%a';
```

Only the = and ^ transformations can be applied to the LIKE operator.

TQL supports the searching of free text using the CONTAINS operator to specify that combinations of words have to appear within a string of text.

The CONTAINS operator returns true if a text field holds a word or word phrase. A phrase is built from a list a words that must be adjacent in the text field. Phrases can be combined with & (and) or | (or). In a free text expression, the control over which method of comparison should be used should be done on a per word basis. Each word can use either exact match checking or the LIKE operators for pattern matching, also transformations can be specified at the word level. so CONTAINS cannot be used as a join operator.

Query 4.3 *List those memos whose subject contains the word 'computer'*

```
Memo WHERE subject CONTAINS 'computer';
```

Query 4.4 *List those memos whose subject contains the word 'computer' together with either of the words 'program' or 'process'*

```
Memo WHERE subject
     CONTAINS ~ 'computer' & (~ 'program' | ~ 'process');
```

If the default matching transformation in the schema for the location attribute was ignore case then this could simply be written

```
Memo WHERE subject
     CONTAINS 'computer' & ('program' | 'process');
```

Query 4.5 *List those memos whose subject contains the phrase 'computer science'*

```
Memo WHERE subject CONTAINS ~'computer' LIKE 'sci%';
```

Given two subexpressions of type text, `+` concatenates the two expressions. Thus `'computer' + 'science'` is equal to `'computer science'`.

5 Indexing text

`Titan+` uses *signature file* methods for indexing the data stored in database tables. These methods have a number of advantages over traditional inverted file methods for indexing text. Signature file methods are economical of storage, provide efficient support for all query types, including substring searching and querying on word phrases and in addition, signature file methods support fast database loading. Signatures are formed using the method of superimposed coding. A description of these methods can be found in [10, 5].

To create an index on a global table, the `CREATE INDEX` command must be used. The superimposed coding schemes used to index the contents of tables require a number of parameters to be specified. To make life easier for users, the `ANALYSE INDEX` command analyses a table of data and the index currently defined and automatically selects appropriate parameters. The easiest way to construct an index for a table therefore is to design the index without any parameters and then to use the analyse command.

Consider the following command

```
CREATE INDEX People (
        =pid,
        @name.firstname,
        ^name.firstname,
        @name.lastname,
        ^name.lastname,
        @department,
);
```

This command will cause the fields pid, firstname, lastname, and department to be indexed. Notice that the field Middle.name is not indexed. Notice also that the firstname and lastname fields have been specified twice. Each column name is prefixed by a transformation character. This effects the actual value used for indexing. For example, =pid causes the exact value of the people number to be indexed. By specifying both ^firstname and @firstname, both the firstname mapped to upper case and the soundex version of the firstname will be indexed. There are are two ways that a text field can be indexed. The first way is to index the field as a single value which is used to support queries such as WHERE lastname = 'Kent'. The second is by indexing each word in the text field individually. This is done by specifying the word TEXT in the CREATE INDEX command. Every pair of adjacent words in text fields are also indexed to support phrase queries. The query optimizer then automatically determines which indexes can be used to support a query. For example, a query specifying an exact value for name can use both the indexes on name although additional checking is required to make sure the record contains the exact value of name specified in the query.

```
CREATE INDEX Memo (
        TEXT ^subject,
        date,
```

```
        TEXT ~contents.para,
        TEXT ~Keywords.term
);
```

Once the index has been created, data can be loaded into the table. The ANALYSE INDEX command can then be used to design the index parameters. The table must contain some data before the ANALYSE INDEX command can be used as it samples the data in the table to determine information such as the average number of index terms per record.

```
ANALYSE INDEX Person;
```

6 Discussion

Although the table Memo described above may provide the best logical description of the data, it may not represent the best physical design. Since the memo contents consists of paragraphs of text, a memo table can be very large. For queries involving attributes other than the Contents field (and such queries may be very common), it would be more efficient to store the memo as two physical tables. A separate table would be formed for the memo contents in order to avoid retrieving large amounts of unnecessary data for such queries. An alternative design for memos is given below.

```
Memo_header (From_list (f REF Person,
                        position TEXT),
             To_list   (t REF Person,
                        position TEXT),
             subject TEXT,
             date DATE,
             Contents (para REF Paragraph),
             Keywords (term TEXT))

Paragraph (pno INTEGER,
```

```
ptext TEXT,
mh REF Memo_header)
```

By maintaining bidirectional links between the memo header and the contents, efficient query processing can be supported. However, the bidirectional links will need to be maintained on update. The best physical design will depend on the relative importance of query costs, update costs and storage costs. A design procedure for nested relations is given in [11].

A user interface for a document database system will need to support document browsing. A number of browsing modes should be supported. These modes include *structural browsing* (given a document outline consisting of chapter and section headings, a user should be able to point to a particular heading and start browsing the document from that location), *intra document browsing* (browsing the current document by moving forwards and backwards from the current position), *inter document browsing* (following database links to a referenced document from the current document) and *content based browsing* (to link documents containing the same text specified in a user query). The design of the user interface is beyond the scope of this paper, but by supporting the text operators using efficient indexing techniques and by providing for links between database objects, the framework has been provided to support each of these browsing modes.

References

[1] P. Dadam, K. Kuespert, F. Anderson, H. Blanken, R. Erbe, J. Guenauer, V. Lum, P. Pistor, and G. Walch. A DBMS prototype to support extended NF^2 relations: An integrated view of flat tables and hierarchies. *Proc. ACM SIGMOD*, pages 356–367, May 1986.

[2] C. J. Date. *An Introduction to Database Systems*, volume 1. Addison-Wesley, fourth edition, 1986.

[3] R. Hull and R. King. Semantic database modeling: Survey, applications, and research issues. *ACM Computing Surveys*, 19(3):201–260, Sept. 1987.

[4] I.S.O. Information processing systems - database language SQL. draft international standard 9075, June 1986.

[5] A. J. Kent, K. Ramamohanarao, and R. Sacks-Davis. A signature file scheme based on multiple organizations for indexing very large databases. *Journal of the American Society for Information Science*, 1990. To appear.

[6] H. F. Korth and A. Silberschatz. *Database System Concepts.* McGraw-Hill, 1986.

[7] P.-A. Larson. The data model and query language of LauRel. 1988.

[8] P. Pistor and F. Andersen. Designing a generalized NF^2 model with an SQL-type language interface. *Proceedings of the 12th International Conference on Very Large Data Bases*, pages 278–285, Aug. 1986.

[9] M. A. Roth, H. F. Korth, and D. S. Batory. SQL/NF: A query language for ¬1NF relational databases. *Information Systems*, 12(1):99–114, 1987.

[10] R. Sacks-Davis, K. Ramamohanarao, and A. J. Kent. Multi-key access methods based on descriptors and superimposed coding coding techniques. *ACM Transactions on Database Systems*, 1987 (to appear).

[11] R. Sacks-Davis, W. Wen, A. J. Kent, and K. Ramamohanarao. Complex object support for a document database system. In *Proceedings of Thirteenth Australian Computer Science Conference*, pages 322–333, Melbourne, Feb. 7-9 1990.

[12] J. A. Thom, A. J. Kent, and R. Sacks-Davis. TQL: A post-relational query language. In *Proceedings of Far-east Workshop on Future Database Systems*, Melbourne, Apr. 25-26 1990.

[13] J. A. Thom, A. J. Kent, and R. Sacks-Davis. TQL: Tutorial and user manual. Technical report, Key Centre for Knowledge Based Systems, Department of Computer Science, Royal Melbourne Institute of Technology, 1990.

AN EXPERIMENTAL SYSTEM FOR CONCEPTUAL EVOLUTION IN OBJECT DATABASES

Qing Li

Department of Computer Science
Australian National University
Canberra, ACT 2601, Australia
qing@anucsd.anu.oz.au

Kwang June Byeon
Dennis McLeod

Computer Science Department
University of Southern California
Los Angeles, California, USA
byeon@cse.usc.edu; mcleod@cse.usc.edu

ABSTRACT

An experimental system to support conceptual database evolution for the non-expert user is described. This system supports dynamic changes to the structure of a database, and employs techniques from applied machine learning to actively support database evolution. A prototype of this system has been designed and implemented, embodying a low-level object data model, a high-level semantic model, a learning module, and an end-user interface. The results of constructing this prototype using a commercial object database development system are examined.

1 Introduction

Traditionally, database systems have been used for large "commercial" applications such as banking, reservations, personnel, and inventory systems, whose data management requirements are considered relatively static. Relatively smaller and more "specialized" applications are becoming more and more important, including those to support computer-aided design, software engineering, office automation, personal information management, and artificial intelligence. In these application environments, changes to the conceptual structure (meta-data) of a database are common [1, 3, 9, 13, 14]; these dynamics are not adequately supported by existing database systems. The research described here focuses on extending current object and semantic database capabilities to accommodate dynamic conceptual database evolution (CDE). As part of this research, we have developed an experimental database system called PKM (for Personal Knowledge Manager), which allows non-expert users to perform CDE, and which actively suggests evolutionary changes according to some metrics of improvement [7, 8, 9].

Figure 1 presents an overview of the PKM system's components and their interrelationships. Conceptually, PKM has a layered architecture, consisting of a kernel model and a high level model for specifications of database objects and their relationships at different levels of abstraction, a machine learning module to actively support CDE for the user at various levels of granularity, and a high level end-user interface through which the user interacts with the database system. The prototype implementation of the PKM system has been greatly facilitated by current object-oriented programming and semantic database technology. In particular, we have used the Vbase system [2] as an implementation base for our prototype. The motivation was to gain insight into the use of a "real" object-oriented database tool for a specific "application" (a general-purpose approach to conceptual database evolution), by building our system upon existing technology to the extent possible. This also allows us to avoid building a complete database system from scratch.

The remainder of this paper is organized as follows. Section 2 specifies the PKM database system, in terms of its layered components. Section 3 describes the PKM prototype, and the kernel model and the high level model implementations in particular.[1] A

[1] Due to the space limitations, we present here only the kernel and high level model implementations; other parts of PKM shall be reported in subsequent papers.

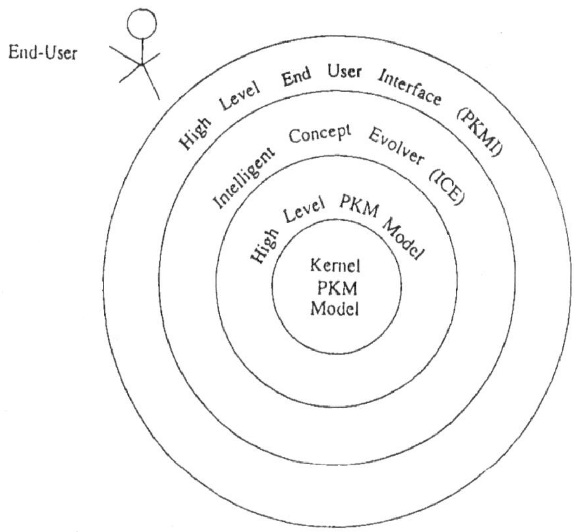

Figure 1: A Layered View of the PKM System Architecture

discussion of results, conclusions, and future research directions is presented in Section 4.

2 A Specification of the PKM System

As stated above, a principal purpose of developing PKM was to support various kinds of conceptual database evolution (CDE). This is provided by the underlying PKM model which supports rich "evolvability". As depicted by Figure 1, the PKM model consists of two levels: a kernel object model and a high level semantic model. CDE has been studied at each level [7, 8]. In this section, we present a brief review of these models and their associated CDE, as well as the other PKM components.

2.1 The kernel PKM model

The kernel PKM model is a simple, object-oriented database model which can be used as a foundation for constructing higher level semantic and object-oriented database models. It provides a small set of primitive operations that allow end-users to define, manipulate, and retrieve information objects. It also supports an important basic kind of conceptual database evolution that occurs in many application environments, object flavor evolution (OFE), as will be described below.

2.1.1 Structure and operations

A kernel PKM database is modeled as collections of objects and inter-object mappings which are used to associate objects. An object has a flavor which determines the role it can play in the database. Flavors supported by this model include *atomic/symbolic*, *social/abstract*, *set*, *mapping*, and *procedural/behavioral* [8]. *Atomic* objects represent non-decomposable units of information, such as strings (e.g., "John Hoffman"), numbers, etc. *Social* objects represent entities and concepts that are described by their relationships with other objects. For example, a person entity can be described by the relationships with his/her name, address, age, etc. *Set* objects represent collections of objects, and *mapping* objects represent relationships among objects. Procedural objects represent the entities which are executable (i.e., operations/methods). Figure 2 shows a sample kernel PKM database, illustrating the environment of a "Student Affairs Office" of a university. In this figure, there are four *open social set* objects (i.e., **Persons**, **Students**, **Instructors**, and **Courses**), and two *open atomic set* objects (i.e., **String**, **Integer**) [2]. All are related to each other via some *mapping* objects (e.g., **has-subset**, **has-name**, **has-salary**, etc.). Notice that in the kernel model, there is no distinction between "meta-data" and "data" as in traditional database models; all objects are treated uniformly.

The kernel PKM model operations are embedded within a host programming language in which high level database applications can be written. The host language must support data types such as objects, sets and identifiers, and the usual set operations. Variables can then be declared (in programs written in the host language) to be of these types. The kernel model operations are themselves stored as objects in the kernel database. Thus, operations can be added and modified as needed. The kernel model operations allow a user to add new objects to a database (*pkm_create*), to remove existing objects from a database (*pkm_delete*), to retrieve objects from the database (e.g., *select*, *choose*), to invoke the procedural objects (*invoke*), and to evolve objects from current flavors to new flavors (*assign_flavor*). A complete summary of the kernel PKM model operations is given in **Appendix A.1**.

The kernel model provides limited integrity control. It is therefore possible to create meaningless relationships, and there is no built-in mechanism for object classification. The

[2] An open set object indicates that its members are not fixed (hence members can be arbitrarily deleted from or inserted into it).

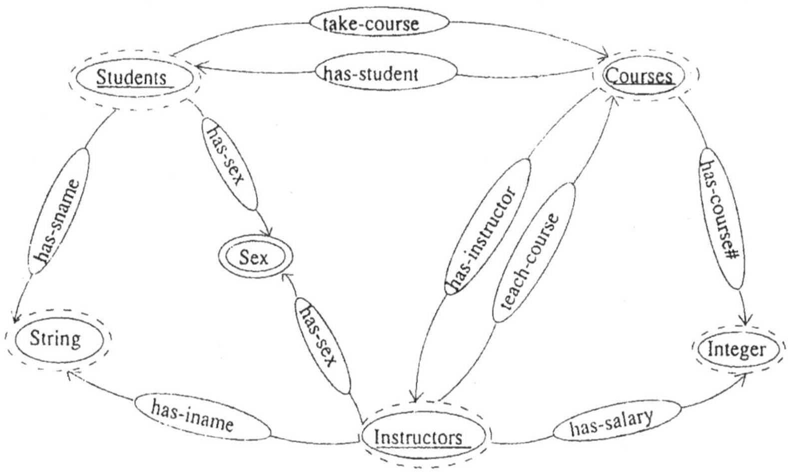

Figure 2: An Example Kernel PKM Database

main purpose of the kernel PKM model is not to introduce a high level data model, but rather to provide a basic framework for object database systems that support CDE.

2.1.2 Object flavor evolution

An important and innovative feature of the kernel PKM model is its support of *object flavor evolution* (OFE) [8, 9]. This kind of evolution concerns changes to the fundamental semantics of objects, vis-a-vis their nature as atomic, social, set, mapping, or procedural. For example, a real-world concept modeled in the database as an atomic object (e.g., "John Hoffman", a string denoting the name of a person) may later evolve to or be alternatively viewed as a social object (e.g., **John Hoffman**, a person entity whose name is "John Hoffman", whose occupation is a physician, etc.). This kind of evolution is essential in a database system in order to insure that the database presents a correct, accurate and useful model of its application environment. In the kernel model, 10 different object flavors are supported, and an object can evolve from one flavor to another if such an *evolution path* is defined. Figure 3 shows all the "legal" evolution paths supported by the kernel PKM model; each edge is bidirectional. The kernel system provides a mechanism that allows the user to explicitly conduct various such kinds of OFE gracefully [8].

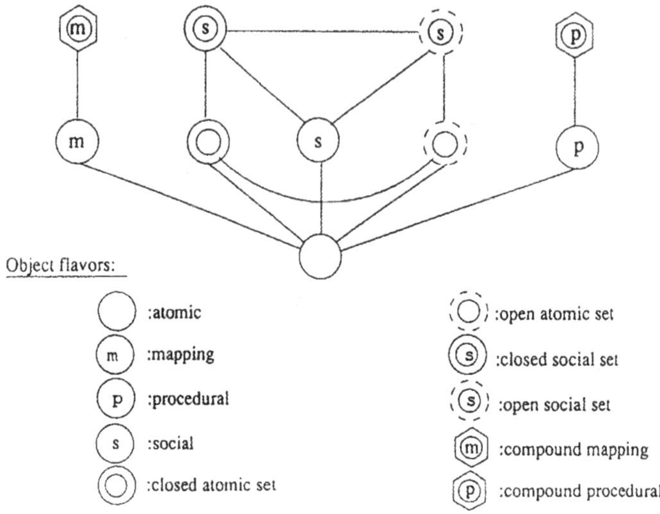

Figure 3: OFE Paths of the Kernel PKM Model

2.2 The high level PKM model

Although the kernel model provides a basis for low-level database evolution, it is too limited and primitive for an end-user to directly use. In particular, it provides no built-in mechanisms for object classification and only very limited integrity control; a higher-level data/knowledge base system that is based on a high level data model is more desirable and appropriate for the end-user. Such a high level data/knowledge base system has been built on top of the kernel PKM system. This approach not only makes the development of the high level PKM system easier, but also enables the high level system to support more sophisticated and higher-level types of evolution, with the "inherited" ability to accommodate OFE from the kernel system.

2.2.1 Basic constructs and operations

The high level PKM model is a simple, semantic (structurally object-oriented) database model [5, 10, 15] in which the modeling constructs type (**T**), sub/supertype (**S**), attribute (**A**), and instance (**I**) are supported.[3] Conceptually, a high level PKM database is modeled as a collection of *objects*; each object is an instance of some *type* object. A type

[3]By defining the high level PKM model to be a simple and generic semantic/object-oriented database model, it enables us to devise evolution principles and techniques that are applicable to most

object is itself a database object that carries the definitions of its instances' *attributes* (or *properties*).

An important difference between the high level PKM model and the kernel model is the concept of *inheritance*, which is defined by the *supertype* and *subtypes* properties of type objects. In the high level PKM model, every instance of a subtype is also an instance of and inherits the attributes from its supertype. A subtype can be defined by restricting via a *selection predicate* the values of one or more attributes of instances in the supertype [4], and/or by associating additional attribute(s) to the instances of the supertype.

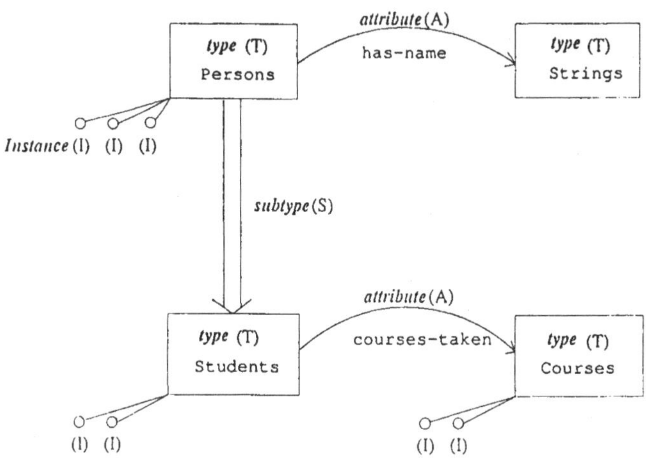

Figure 4: An Example High Level PKM Database

Figure 4 shows a portion of a database structure (schema) for the same "Student Affairs Office" environment described earlier, defined using this data model. In Figure 4, there are four type (T) objects: **Persons**, **Students**, **Courses**, and **Strings**. Type **Persons** has an attribute (**A**) **has-name** whose value range is the type **Strings**. Type **Students** is a subtype (S) of type **Persons**. In addition to the attribute **has-name** inherited from its supertype **Persons**, **Students** has the attribute **courses-taken** whose value range is the type **Courses**. Each type object has certain instances (**I**), and the

semantic/object-oriented databases.

[4]For example, the type **Honor_Students** can be defined from its supertype **Students** via **has_GPA** > "3.75".

instances of a supertype include all the instances of its subtypes.

The high level PKM system, built on top of the kernel system, provides a set of semantically simple yet functionally powerful operations. These operations invoke the primitive operations of the kernel model, and can be either embedded within a host programming language or used by the end-user directly. The operations allow a user (an application program or an end-user) to manipulate database objects at both type level (e.g., *CREATE_TYPE*, *DELETE_TYPE*) and instance level (e.g., *CREATE_INSTANCE*), and support retrieval (e.g., *SHOW_TYPE*, *SHOW_INSTANCES*). High level PKM operations also support conceptual database evolution cases; for example, *ATTRIBUTE_TO_TYPE* evolves an attribute (and its inverse) to a relationship object, as will be described below, and *RELATE_SUBTYPE* inserts a new type object in its appropriate place in the type hierarchy. **Appendix A.2** summarizes those operations.

2.2.2 High level evolution

An important goal of the high level PKM model is to support higher-level conceptual database evolution (CDE), based on the kernel OFE facilities [7]. Within the context of this model, kinds of important CDE have been studied, based upon the four basic modeling constructs (i.e., **T**, **S**, **A**, **I**), as depicted by Figure 5. Referring to Figure 5, an arrow

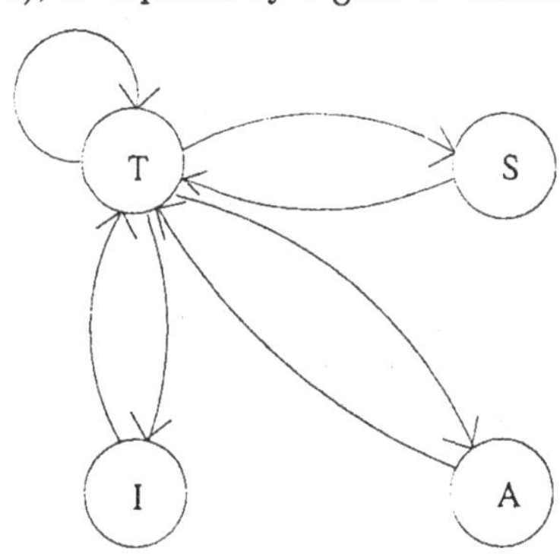

Figure 5: CDE Paths of the High Level PKM Model

indicates an evolution path of possible interest. For example, the evolution path from T to S may involve the decomposition of a type into two or more subtypes: in the "Student Affairs Office" environments shown in Figure 4, the type **Students** can be specialized into two subtypes **Undergraduate_Students** and **Graduate_Students**. Note that the supertype of these two types is **Students**. As another example, the evolution path from **A** to **T** involves the transformation of an attribute into a type object (in order to, e.g., evolve a binary relationship to a ternary relationship). In the same environment as shown in Figure 4, the attribute **courses-taken** of type **Students** with the range type **Courses**, can evolve to a type object **Enrollment** with the two attributes **has-student** (whose range type is **Students**) and **has-course** (whose range type is **Courses**). Such kinds of evolution concern various possible modifications of the database structure, semantic constraints, and derived data rules, and are termed as "high level" accordingly. The high level PKM operations supporting evolution cases (e.g., *ATTRIBUTE_TO_TYPE* for the above example) allow the user to explicitly conduct various kinds of CDE on a database.

2.3 The ICE module and end-user interface

The kernel PKM model and the high level PKM model together provide flexible and powerful facilities to allow the user to make changes to the conceptual database structure at various levels of granularity and abstraction. However, conceptual database evolution is in general a very complex problem-solving task, for which expert knowledge is needed. In particular, the user must know "what to evolve", "how to evolve", and "when to evolve". A truly useful database system should provide necessary facilities to actively support such CDE for the user. ICE (for *Intelligent Concept Evolver*) is a conceptual database evolution tool provided by the PKM system, which supports all kinds of evolution studied within the PKM model context. In particular, combinations of machine learning techniques [4, 11, 12] (i.e., *learning from instruction*, *learning from exception*, and *learning from observation*) are employed by the ICE module, with each aiming to cope with certain types of CDE cases for the user, based on a set of heuristics [7, 9].

In this approach, all the interactions between the end-user and the system are through a high level interface called PKMI (for *Personal Knowledge Manager Interface*). PKMI not only supports conventional database activities, but also supports the "evolution-through-learning" features of the ICE module. More specifically, PKMI is a graphics-and-menu based, window-driven interface, designed for relative novice users. Major facilities provided by this interface include: system-provided guidance and reminders, browsing functions, schema evolution facilities, stepwise type definition/derivation mechanisms, and multi-window features [6].

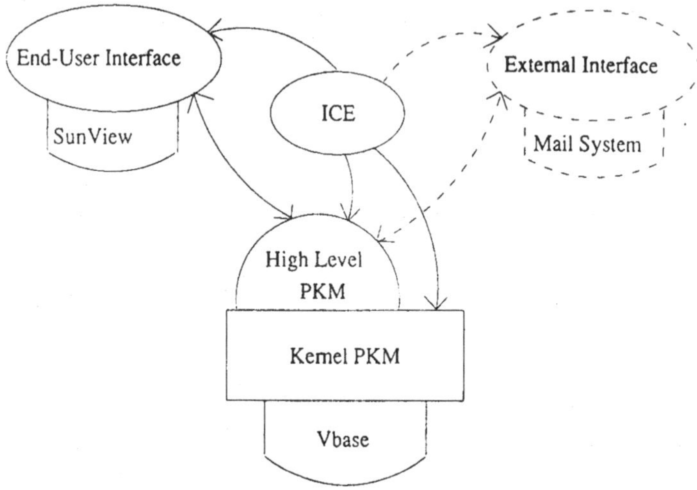

Figure 6: Overview of the PKM Prototype

3 An Implementation Prototype

The PKM database system uses the Vbase system for implementing the kernel and high level PKM models, and the SunView system for supporting the end-user interface, as shown in Figure 6. An inter-PKM sharing mechanism (the dashed line portion of Figure 6), based initially upon current mail system facilities, is under development. In this section, we summarize the experimental prototype implementation built on top of Vbase.

3.1 The Vbase implementation environment

Vbase is an object-oriented, semantic database development system [2]. It supports a type hierarchy in which a type can have only one supertype, the association of attributes and methods with a type, and the inheritance of attributes and methods down to subtypes along the type hierarchy. It also supports concepts of both the abstract datatype approach (e.g., strong typing and a block structured data definition language) and the semantic database approach (e.g., support for persistent objects, inverse relationships, and simple structural constraints). It uses two separate languages: **TDL** (for Type Definition Language) and **COP** (for C Object Processor). **TDL** is a block structured language, which specifies types and their associated attributes and methods. **COP** is an extension of the "C" language, which is used to write the actual code of methods specified in type definitions, and to implement application operations and programs invoking methods on objects [2].

The Vbase system has been utilized to provide an implementation base for the prototype of the experimental PKM database system, since it provides basic object-oriented and semantic database concepts. This has allowed us to avoid much low level database development that is not a main part of this research. However, Vbase has some significant limitations and problems vis-a-vis our needs. The most difficult problem involves the limited evolvability of a database schema. In Vbase, user-defined types are declared in advance using **TDL**, and are precompiled. Furthermore, changes to the structure of an application database (e.g., creating new types, changing the supertype of a type) require the recompilation of the associated types. Another significant limitation is the difficulty and cost of changing the database schema. The compilation of types is time consuming (e.g., recompiling a type after changing an attribute's specification takes about 10 minutes in the Vbase beta release 0.93 running on a Sun 3/60 workstation). Due to these problems, the type hierarchy mechanism provided by Vbase has been used only for the predefined types of the kernel and high level PKM models, which are relatively fixed.

3.2 Implementation of the kernel PKM model

The implementation of the kernel PKM model has been based upon the Vbase system. Although Vbase has significantly reduced the low level development effort required to construct an experimental prototype, it has some problems vis-a-vis our needs as described above. To work around these problems and actively support object flavor evolution (OFE) in the kernel model, a separate type hierarchy mechanism was built inside Vbase.

3.2.1 Predefined type hierarchy and operations

The various object flavors supported by the kernel model have been defined using Vbase types. Figure 7 shows the type hierarchy for the kernel model. Here **Entity** is a global system-defined supertype in Vbase. *PKM* is a root type of all predefined types in the PKM prototype, and has the four subtypes *AtomicSocial*, *AS_Set* (for Atomic/Social Set), *Mapping*, or *Proc* (for Procedural). Each object in a database is an instance of one of these subtypes. Since every object in the Vbase system has a system-generated unique identifier, the only difference between the specifications of atomic and social (set) objects is their flavor; hence separate types are not used for atomic and social (set) objects in this particular implementation hierarchy.

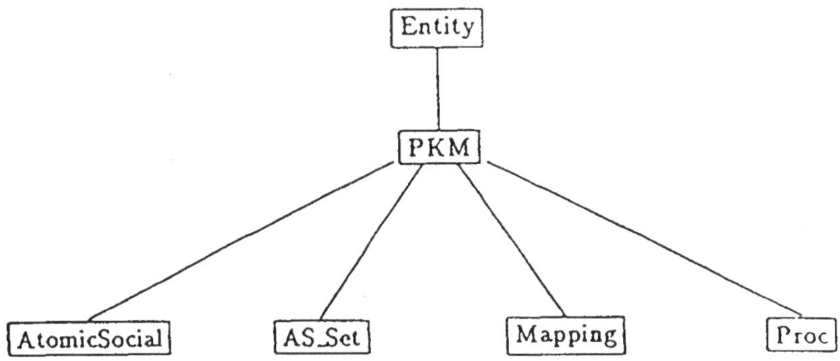

Figure 7: Type hierarchy for Kernel PKM model

The attributes "key" and "flavor" are defined for type *PKM*, and are inherited by the subtypes of *PKM*. The attribute "key" contains the external identifier of each object, and the attribute "flavor" indicates the flavor of this object. The attributes of other types are shown in Figure 8. For the type *AS_Set*, the attribute "members" contains all the members of a set object, and the attribute "constraints" specifies associated constraints to this set (e.g., a selection predicate which defines this set). The attribute "dr_pair" of type *Mapping* indicates the pairs of objects in the domain and range of a mapping via which these objects are inter-related. The attribute "body" of type *Proc* specifies a procedure body (an executable file name) for a procedural object.

Each PKM type has some associated methods for manipulating instances of that type; this is implemented using the Vbase method encapsulation mechanism. Methods are inherited by the subtypes of a type. Type *PKM* has the methods *create*, *delete*, and *lookup*, which create, delete, and find instances of this type (respectively). The method *delete* is not redefined in type *PKM*, but is rather inherited from type **Entity**. Each subtype of type *PKM* inherits these three methods, and has additional methods which can be divided into two categories based on their purposes. One category is for displaying the attribute values of an instance of the type. The other is to support specific evolution cases. For

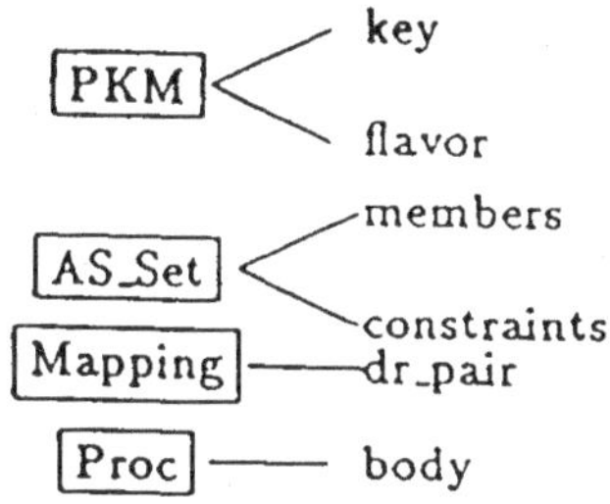

Figure 8: Attributes for type PKM, AS_Set, Mapping, and Proc

example, the type *AS_Set* has the method *chf_atss_ats* which changes the flavor "open atomic set" of its instance into a new flavor "atomic", i.e., which supports the evolution case from an "open atomic set" object of type *AS_Set* to an "atomic" object of type *AtomicSocial*. **Appendix B** presents the **TDL** code for the definition of a predefined type *AS_Set* shown in Figures 7 and 8; this includes the specifications of attributes and methods (e.g., *display_set*, *chf_atss_ats*) associated with this type. The actual code of methods is implemented in **COP**; an example COP code segment for the method *display_set* which is associated with the type *AS_Set* is shown in **Appendix C**.

A collection of the kernel model operations which support object retrieval and manipulation as well as object flavor evolution has been implemented using **COP**. These operations invoke methods associated with types, access attributes of objects, etc. For example, a kernel operation *pkm_create* invokes the method *create* associated with the type *AtomicSocial*; another operation *get_members* accesses the attribute "members" of a given set object and returns its value.

In the current version of the kernel PKM prototype, the kernel operations shown in **Appendix A.1** have been implemented. These operations consist of about 4,000 lines of **COP** code. The operations handling procedural objects (e.g., invoke a procedure, add/remove a procedure body) are under development.

3.3 Implementation of the high level PKM model

As shown in Figure 6, the implementation of the high level PKM model is based on the kernel PKM prototype and Vbase, in order to reduce the implementation effort yet assure the desired evolvability of the model. The general implementation architecture is similar to that of the kernel PKM model. In fact, the high level PKM model has been built as an application on top of the kernel PKM model.

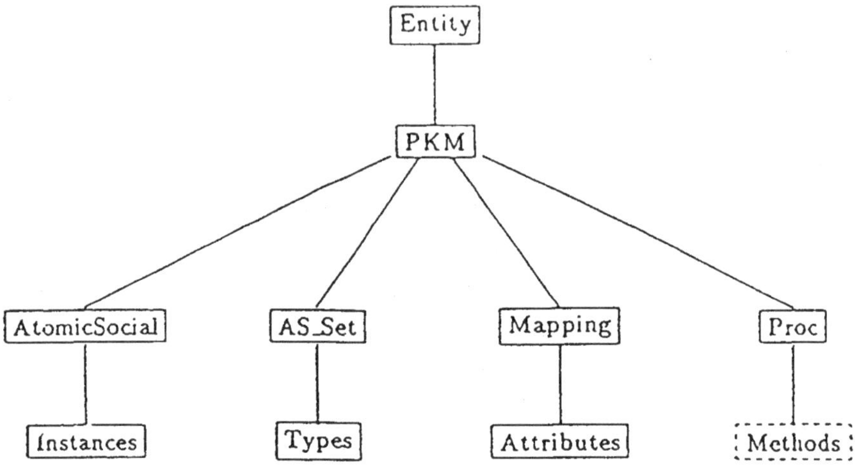

Figure 9: Type hierarchy for High-Level PKM model

3.3.1 Type hierarchy and high level operations

To support the modeling constructs of the high level model, the kernel type hierarchy (shown in Figure 7) is utilized. The resulting type hierarchy is shown in Figure 9, which is a direct extension of that of the kernel prototype. Three new PKM types are introduced for the high level model: *Instances*, *Types*, and *Attributes*. Each object in the high level model is an instance of one of these types. Since the implementation of type *Proc* is not yet complete, its subtype *Methods* (the dashed line portion of Figure 9) is not supported by the current version of the PKM prototype. Each of the types *Instances*, *Types*, and *Attributes* inherits all the attributes from its supertypes. For example, an instance of type *Types* has values for the attributes "key" and "flavor" which are inherited from type *PKM*. Additional attributes associated with these types are shown in Figure 10. The attribute "member_of" of type *Instances* indicates to which type object an instance object belongs. For type *Types*, the attributes "supertype" and "subtypes" indicate which type objects are the supertype and the subtypes of a type object (respectively). The attribute "attributes" contains the

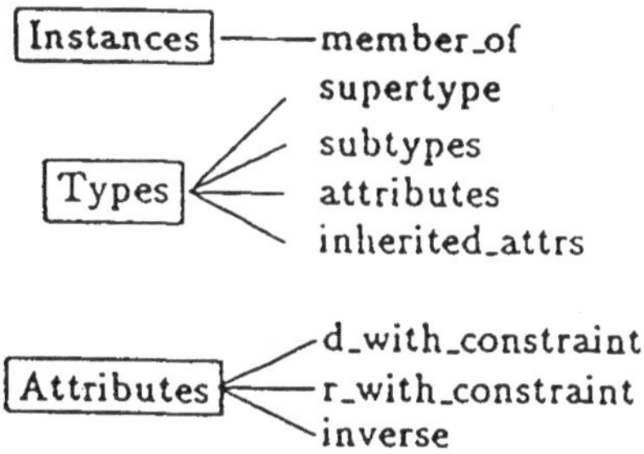

Figure 10: Attributes for type Instances, Types, and Attributes

set of user-defined attributes associated with a type, and the attribute "inherited_attrs" (for inherited attributes) specifies the set of attributes inherited from the supertype of this type. For type *Attributes*, the attributes "d_with_constraint" and "r_with_constraint" indicate the domain and range types of the attribute and specify the nature of the mapping (e.g., one-to-one, one-to-many). For example, (**Students**, "one") can be a value for the attribute "d_with_constraint". The attribute "inverse" indicates the inverse mapping for this attribute.

Each of the three types (*Instances*, *Types*, and *Attributes*) inherits all the methods from its supertype, and no additional methods are defined for it. For example, an instance of type *Instances* can be created using the method *create* which is defined in type *PKM* and is inherited by type *AtomicSocial*, and its attribute values can be shown by the method *display* which is defined for the type *AtomicSocial*.

It is important to note that the predefined type hierarchy shown in Figure 9 is transparent to the user. All user-defined types are instances of type *Types*. Because of the limited evolvability of Vbase schemas, the type hierarchy for user-defined types is constructed inside type *Types* using the attributes defined in/inherited by this type. In this user-defined type hierarchy, each type has only one supertype, and hence the multiple inheritance problem does not occur. The attributes "supertype" and "subtypes" of an instance (a user-defined type) of type *Types* shows the supertype and subtypes of this instance (respectively), which are also the instances (user-defined types) of type *Types*. The attributes inherited by an instance of type *Types* are specified in the attribute "inherited_attrs" of this instance. When a user-defined type is created, it inherits (from its supertype) the attributes defined in or inherited by its supertype in the user-defined type hierarchy. They are specified in the attribute "inherited_attrs" of the new type. If an attribute with the same name is defined in both a type and its supertype, the attribute in the supertype is not inherited by this type.

Suppose that **Persons** and **Students** are user-defined types (instances of type *Types*), and that **Persons** is a supertype of **Students**. Then the value of the attribute "subtypes" of **Persons** includes **Students**, and that of the attribute "supertype" of **Students** is **Persons**. If **Persons** has some associated attributes (e.g., **has-name, has-age**), and does not have any inherited attributes, the value of "attributes" of **Persons** is {**has-name, has-age**} (which is also the value of "inherited_attrs" of **Students**). When the user-defined type hierarchy is modified by operations such as create a type, insert a supertype, and add an attribute to a type, the PKM prototype changes the values of the attributes described above, so that the desired effect is achieved [5]. In consequence, users can dynamically change the schema of their application databases.

The high level object manipulation operations shown in **Appendix A.2** have been implemented in the PKM prototype system. These operations consist of approximately 4,000 lines of **COP** code. Each high level operation invokes some of the kernel operations and methods. For example, the high level operation *CREATE_TYPE* for creating a new type first invokes the kernel operation *pkm_create* to create a new object (with the flavor "atomic") in the database, and then calls another kernel operation *assign_flavor* twice, to change the flavor of the new object into "social" and then into "open social set". **Appendix C** contains the **COP** code for this sample high level operation.

4 Discussion

In this paper, we have described the fundamental aspects of an approach to conceptual database evolution as experimentally implemented utilizing the Vbase object-oriented system. In the PKM prototype system, users can dynamically build application databases and change the schemas of these databases, using the kernel and high level evolution operations. Experimental results indicate that such changes to the conceptual structure (meta-data) of application databases can be achieved with acceptable efficiency. For example, creating a new user-defined type takes about 8 seconds in the PKM prototype. The

[5]Changes to data (e.g., changing the values of attributes, inserting/deleting instances into/from a type), as opposed to meta-data (schema), are of course directly supported by Vbase.

size of the prototype system (without the end-user interface PKMI) is about 9 M bytes; this includes the Vbase beta release 0.93 system's rootarea (5.6 M bytes), the kernel PKM (1.8 M bytes), and the high level PKM (1.5 M bytes).

At the early stage of the construction of the PKM database system, we had choices between "starting from scratch" and "utilizing an implementation base" (i.e., the Vbase system). The former would likely provide more efficient performance for the PKM system, but would require substantial effort involving low level object-oriented database implementation. We chose the latter mainly for two reasons. First, utilizing an existing object-oriented development system permits us to focus on conceptual database evolution and learning techniques, rather than having to construct extensive object database management facilities, that is not a main part of this research. Second, diving into a "real" object-oriented software system provides us a practical opportunity to compare and contrast our model with others. This by itself is an interesting and valuable research experience, and has resulted in some significant insights into both PKM and Vbase.

In implementing the type hierarchy for user-defined types in the high level PKM model, which supports conceptual database evolution, we had two options: using the type hierarchy mechanism provided by the Vbase system, and providing our own type hierarchy mechanism. In the former approach, Vbase would automatically handle the inheritance of attributes and methods via the type hierarchy, and keep the database consistent before and after each evolution step. But it is very difficult and expensive to make changes to the database structure (i.e., type hierarchy) in Vbase due to the evolvability limitations. In the latter approach, all the tasks, which are automatically done by Vbase in the former case, must be explicitly handled by PKM, but changing the type hierarchy can be accomplished more easily. The latter approach was used for the PKM prototype since the main purpose of the PKM database system is to support conceptual database evolution actively and efficiently.

Another important implementation issue in developing the PKM system involved the strategy of supporting conceptual database evolution: "instant propagation" vs. "deferred propagation". In the former case, changes to the conceptual database structure are instantly propagated to the underlying database, thus a consistent database is maintained. In the latter case, changes to the conceptual database structure are deferred (possibly indefinitely); the representations of objects are corrected or filtered as they are used (this is effectively a late binding on the representation of objects) [13]. For this prototype, we have chosen the former approach due to its simplicity.

Analysis, testing, and extensions of the research described in this paper are currently under study. As mentioned earlier, we are still in the process of investigating the implementation of the procedural objects at kernel level, as well as the specification and implementation of the methods at the high level model. Another step to be taken is to test our experimental system on large-scale real databases (e.g., VLSI/CAD databases), and to evaluate and refine our system therefrom. Finally, a distributed version of PKM has been planned (see the broken line part of Figure 6). The goal is to provide a personal knowledge management environment that allows users of highly autonomous databases to communicate and share information. The CDE capabilities of a PKM system can contribute significantly to such database interconnection [7].

Appendix A.1

Kernel Level Object Manipulation Operations

1. **Object Level Operations**

   pkm_create(object-id): object-key : generates a new object of "atomic" flavor in the database. Note that *object-id* is a user-defined identifier for the new object, and *object-key* is its system-generated identifier.

   pkm_delete(object-id) : removes a given object from the database.

   relate(domain,mapping,range: object-id): object-key : creates a relationship among objects, and its inverse relationship (**range,mapping^{-1},domain**).

   detach(domain,mapping,range: object-id) : removes the specified relationship and its inverse.

2. **Set Level Operations**

   define-cse-set(object-id [, m_1,..,m_n: object-id]) : defines a specified "closed atomic/social set" object by enumerating its members (if any).

   define-csp-set(object-id, selection-predicate) : defines a specified "closed atomic/social set" object by indicating a selection predicate that its members should satisfy.

   add-to-set(set-id [, m_1,..,m_n: object-id]) : adds members to a given "open atomic/social set" object.

remove-from-set(set-id [, $m_1,..,m_n$: object-id]) : removes specified objects from a given "open atomic/social set" object.

get-members(set-id) : returns all the members of the specified set.

3. **Object Flavor Evolution Operations**

   assign-flavor(object-id, flavor): object-key : evolves an object (from its current flavor) to a new flavor. The object flavor evolution can be achieved only by this operation which invokes the methods associated with types (e.g., the method *chf_atss_ats* defined in the type *AS_Set*).

4. **Retrieval Operations**

   select(domain, mapping, range: object-id): set of triples (d, m, r) : retrieves relationships satisfying input parameters; each parameter can be "*" which can match all objects (domain/mapping/range) in the database.

   choose({D,M,R}, set of triples): set of object-ids : operates on a set of triples and returns a set of domain/mapping/range objects, based on its first parameter (D/M/R). For example, *choose*("R", *select*("Tommy", "courses-taken", "*")) returns all courses which **Tommy** has taken.

Appendix A.2

High Level Object Manipulation Operations

1. **Type Level Operations**

   CREATE-TYPE(type-id, supertype-id): object-key : generates a new type object with all attributes inherited from the specified supertype.

   DELETE-TYPE(type-id) : deletes the specified type object if it does not have any subtype.

   ADD-ATTRIBUTE(type-id, {one, many}, attribute-id, range-type-id, {one, many}): object-key : creates a new attribute to the named type, with the specified mapping constraint (e.g., one-to-many). The attribute will be inherited by the subtypes of the type.

DELETE-ATTRIBUTE(type-id, attribute-id): object-key :
deletes an attribute from the named type.

STORE-TYPE(type-id): object-key : makes a temporary type a permanent one.

2. **Instance Level Operations**

   CREATE-INSTANCE(instance-id, type-id): object-key : creates a new instance object of the specified type. The user is prompted to enter the values for all attributes of the instance.

   DELETE-INSTANCE(instance-id, type-id) : deletes a given instance from the specified type object; the instance is recursively deleted from all the subtypes

   MODIFY-INSTANCE-VALUE(instance-id): object-key : modifies the values of the specified instance. The modification takes place by prompting for the values of the attributes.

3. **Conceptual Evolution Operations**

   RELATE-SUBTYPE(type-id, subtype-id): object-key : relates a type (subtype-id) to another type (type-id) as its subtype.

   DETACH-SUBTYPE(type-id, subtype-id): object-key : detaches a subtype from the specified type T and makes it as a subtype of T's supertype.

   ATTRIBUTE-TO-TYPE(attribute-id, type-id): object-key : converts an attribute A to a new type object T. Also, see Section 2.2.2 for an example case.

   TYPE-TO-ATTRIBUTE(type-id, attribute-id) : inverse of *attribute-to-type.*

   PKM_ASSERT(set-id, Types*): object-key* : asserts (converts) a specified set object to a (user-defined) type object (i.e., an instance of the type *Types*). Note that *Types* is a predefined type in the high level PKM model.

4. **Retrieval Operations**

   SELECT-INTO-SUBTYPE(subtype-id, type-id, condition):
   object-key : defines a subtype by choosing from the specified type the instances that satisfy the condition C; C can be either a set of object identifiers or a selection predicate.

   UNION-INTO-SUPERTYPE(type1-id, type2-id, supertype-id): obejct-key : defines a supertype by union of the specified types.

SHOW-TYPE(type-id) : displays the name (identifier) of the given type, its supertype and subtypes, its attributes, and the number of its existing instances.

SHOW-INSTANCES(type-id) : displays all instances of the specified type.

Appendix B

Example TDL Code for a Predefined Kernel Type

As an example, the **TDL** code for a predefined type *AS_Set* of the kernel PKM model is briefly presented here. Note that Vbase uses terms "operations" and "methods", which are analogous to our terms "methods" and "code" respectively. Comment statements are attached to some blocks and statements for better understanding.

```
define Type AS_Set

   supertypes = {PKM};    /* Vbase does not support multiple
                            supertypes. */
   ClassType = $ExplicitClass;         /* An (explicit) class
                                       for storing instances */
   properties = {         /* Attributes defined in this type */
      members:     set [AtomicSocial];
      constraints: set [Selection_Predicate];
          /* A sample constraint is "(has-salary, >=, 30000)"
           where "has-salary" is a mapping, and ">=" denotes
           "greater than or equal to".          */
   };
   operations = {            /* Methods defined in this type */
      display_set (o: AS_Set)    /* Displays the members of */
      method (displaying_a_set); /*an atomic/social set (see*/
                                 /*Appendix C). */
      chf_atss_ats (o: AS_Set)   /* Supports evolution cases*/
      method (ChfAtSsAtS)        /*from atomic/social set to*/
      returns (AtomicSocial);    /*atomic/social objects. An*/
                                 /*example case is described*/
      ......                     /*in Section 3.2.1. */
```

```
   };
end AS_Set;
```

Appendix C

Example COP Code for a Method and a High Level Operation

Here we briefly describe one kernel method *display_set* as well as a high level PKM operation *CREATE_TYPE*, which are coded in **COP**.

As shown in **Appendix B**, the kernel method *display_set* is defined in the type *AS_Set*; it displays the constraints related to a set object as well as the members of it.

```
method    /* "void" means no return value specified. If some */
void      /*value (e.g., object of type "AS_Set") is returned*/
          /*then "void" is replaced by "obj $AS_Set".*/
displaying_a_set (aSet)
obj $AS_Set aSet;
{
   obj $AtomicSocial aMember;
   obj $Selection_Predicate aConstraint;
          /* "aSet.members" denotes the attribute "members"
              of a set object "aSet". */
   iterate (aMember = aSet.members) ......
          /* Iterate over the members of the set object
             "aSet" and print the key of each member.    */
   iterate (aConstraint = aSet.constraints) ......
          /* Iterate over the constraints to the set object
             "aSet", and print each one. See Appendix B for
             a sample constraint. */
}
```

The high level PKM operation *CREATE_TYPE* generates a new type object with all of the attributes inherited from the specified supertype, adds it to the database, and returns an integer flag. Notice this high level PKM operation is implemented by using several kernel PKM operations (i.e., *pkm_create*, *assign_flavor*) and other high level ones (i.e., *PKM_ASSERT*, *RELATE_SUBTYPE*). These operations are described in **Appendix A.1** and **Appendix A.2** in detail.

```
int
CREATE_TYPE (newtype_id, supertype_id)
char *newtype_id, *supertype_id;
{
   obj $AtomicSocial new_atomic_object, social_object;
   obj $AS_Set       social_set_object;
   obj $Types        newtype;

          ......

     new_atomic_object = pkm_create (newtype_id);
          /* Create a new atomic object with the identifier
             "newtype_id". */
     social_object = assign_flavor (new_atomic_object, "social");
          /* Evolve an atomic object to a "social" one. */
     social_set_object = assign_flavor (social_object, "oss");
          /* Evolve a "social" object to an "open social set"
             object. Note that the default flavor of a new type
             is "open_social_set". */
     newtype = PKM_ASSERT (a_social_set_object, Types);
          /* Convert a social set object to an object of type
             "Types". */
     RELATE_SUBTYPE (newtype_id, supertype_id);
          /* Place the new type as a subtype of the specified
             supertype. Note the 1st parameter of this operation
             is a user-defined identifier. */
     return (0);   /* The new type is successfully created. */
}
```

References

[1] R. Agrawal and N. Gehani. ODE (Object Database and Environment): The language and the data model. In *Proceedings of the ACM SIGMOD International Conference*

on Management of Data, pages 36–45. ACM SIGMOD, May 1989.

[2] T. Andrews and C. Harris. Combining language and database advances in an object-oriented development environment. In *Proceedings of the Conference on Object-Oriented Programming Systems, Languages, and Applications*, pages 430–440. ACM, 1987.

[3] J. Banerjee and W. Kim. Semantics and implementation of schema envolution in object-oriented databases. In *Proceedings of the ACM SIGMOD International Conference on Management of Data*, pages 311–322. ACM SIGMOD, May 1987.

[4] A. Borgida, T. M. Mitchell, and K. Williamson. Learning improved integrity constraints and schemas from exceptions in databases and knowledge bases. In M. L. Brodie and J. Mylopoulos, editors, *On Knowledge Base Management Systems*, pages 259–286. Springer Verlag, 1986.

[5] D. Fishman, D. Beech, H. Cate, E. Chow, T. Connors, T. Davis, N. Derrett, C. Hoch, W. Kent, P. Lyngbaek, B. Mahbod, M. Neimat, T. Ryan, and M. Shan. Iris: An object-oriented database management system. *ACM Transactions on Office Information Systems*, 5(1):48–69, January 1987.

[6] Q. Li. *A Learning-Based Object-Oriented Framework for Conceptual Database Evolution.* PhD thesis, Computer Science Department, University of Southern California, Los Angeles, CA90089-0782, Nov. 1988. TR-CRI88-63, USC.

[7] Q. Li and D. McLeod. Conceptual database evolution through learning. Technical Report TR-CRI88-03, Computer Research Institute, University of Southern California, 1988. To appear in *"Object-Oriented Databases and Applications"*, Gupta, R. and Horowitz, E. (editor), Prentice-Hall, 1990.

[8] Q. Li and D. McLeod. Object flavor evolution in an object-oriented database system. In *Proceedings of the ACM Conference on Office Information System, SIGOIS Bulletin.* vol. 9, no. 3, 1988.

[9] Q. Li and D. McLeod. Supporting object flavor evolution through learning in an object-oriented database system. In L. Kerschberg, editor, *Expert Database Systems. Proc. 2nd Intl. Conference.* Benjamin/Cummings, 1989.

[10] P. Lyngbaek and D. McLeod. A personal data manager. In *Proceedings of the International Conference on Very Large Databases*. VLDB Endowment, August 1984.

[11] R. Michalski, J. Carbonell, and T. (Editors) Mitchell. *Machine Learning: An Artificial Intelligence Approach (Volume 1)*. Tioga Publishing Company, 1983.

[12] R. Michalski, J. Carbonell, and T. (Editors) Mitchell. *Machine Learning: An Artificial Intelligence Approach (Volume 2)*. Morgan Kaufmann, 1986.

[13] D. J. Penney and J. Stein. Class modification in the GemStone object-oriented dbms. In *Proceedings of the Conference on Object-Oriented Programming Systems, Languages, and Applications*, pages 111–117, 1987.

[14] A.H. Skarra and S. Zdonik. The management of changing types in an object-oriented database. In *Proceedings of the Conference on Object-Oriented Programming Systems, Languages, and Applications*, pages 483–495. ACM, 1986.

[15] K. Smith and S. Zdonik. Intermedia: A case study of the differences between relational and object-oriented database systems. In *Proceedings of the Conference on Object-Oriented Programming Systems, Languages, and Applications*, pages 452–465. ACM, 1987.

Conceptual schemas and relational databases

Terry Halpin

Key Centre for Software Technology
Department of Computer Science
University of Queensland
St Lucia 4067 Australia
email: halpin@uqcspe.cs.uq.oz.au

No matter how intelligent an information system is, there are two tasks for which humans are needed: specifying the universe of discourse (UoD); and querying the system about the UoD. This paper provides an overview of recent work by the author, aimed at simplifying these tasks. Definite descriptions and derivation rules are discussed in some detail, and related results from the application of formal logic are summarized.

Introduction

For reasons such as correctness, clarity, adaptability and cost-effectiveness, UoDs are best specified first at the conceptual level (ISO 1982). For commercial applications, relational database systems are currently the favoured targets onto which conceptual information structures are mapped. This is mainly because relational systems are simpler to use than the older hierarchic and network systems, are based on mathematical foundations, and are now efficiently implemented. Though post-relational database systems (e.g. object-oriented and deductive database systems) appear to offer promising advantages, their lack of a standard model and a design methodology, coupled with the research-to-production lag-time, indicates that the relational approach will remain dominant for the next decade. Designing appropriate conceptual and relational schemas for practical applications is a non-trivial task. Our main research objective has been to provide a formal basis for reasoning about conceptual schemas and for making design choices.

Although the process-oriented and behaviour-oriented perspectives of information system design are important, this paper focusses on the data-oriented perspective. Most conceptual modelling methodologies provide a graphical language for the high level specification of conceptual schemas. Of these graphical notations, the conceptual schema diagram language of NIAM (Nijssen's Information Analysis Method) is perhaps the most intuitive and expressive. A detailed introduction to this methodology is provided by Nijssen and Halpin (1989).

Partly because of its expressive power, the designer may experience difficulties in assessing various properties of and relationships between NIAM conceptual schemas, e.g. satisfiability, implication and equivalence. To help resolve these difficulties, we formalize NIAM conceptual schemas in terms of logic, thereby providing a rigorous and well-founded treatment of the formal semantics and proof-theory.

In this short paper we have space to consider only two topics in any detail. The next section indicates how knowledge expressed in the graphical notation of NIAM may be translated into logical formulae, with special attention paid to definite descriptions. The following section discusses derivation rules, using the distinction between biconditional and conditional rules to assist in making design decisions. The final section provides a summary account of related research by the author: this summary includes reference to results of greater significance (e.g. our formal account of constraint implication and schema equivalence). However, since details on this work are readily accessible (Halpin 1989c; Halpin 1990), we have chosen to emphasize in this paper results that are less accessible. For an in-depth treatment of the topics, see Halpin (1989b).

Definite descriptions

A given UoD is formally modelled in an information system by a knowledge base, comprising a conceptual schema (CS) and a database (DB). The CS consists of generic axioms, as well as specific axioms which spell out the elementary fact types of interest, constraints on their populations, and derivation rules. Each DB state is a set of stored facts. In a lengthy work (Halpin 1989b), the knowledge system (KS) is specified as a formal system based on first order predicate calculus, translation rules are provided between NIAM and KS, and proofs are set out in KS.

The domain of discourse is partitioned into five main sets: strings (lexical objects); numbers; *described objects* (e.g. lecturers, departments); pairs; and the garbage set containing nil. Described objects are always referenced by means of *definite descriptions* (e.g. "the Subject with code 'CS112'"); other objects are referenced by specialized individual constants or function terms (e.g. 'CS112', 3). The domain is closed under pairing. Pairs enable the efficient implementation of "objectified relationships".

The same string or number may be used within descriptions of different objects. For example, "Brisbane" may be used as a surname and a cityname within the same application. Of course the object referred to as "the Person with surname 'Brisbane'" cannot be the same as the object referred to as "the City with cityname 'Brisbane'", since our specific partition axioms would include an assertion that Person and City are disjoint object types. Nevertheless it is both meaningful and simple in our formalization to make indirect connections between objects of disjoint types via the strings or numbers used in their descriptions. For example, allowing any single lower-case letter as an individual variable in our primitive query language:

List the surnames of those who live in a city with the same name.
List {*n*: ∃*pc*(*p* has_surname *n* & *p* lives_in *c* & *c* has_cityname *n*)}

List the surnames of anyone whose mass in kg is numerically greater than his/her height in cm.
List {*n*: ∃*pmxh*(*p* has_surname *n* & *p* weighs *m* & *m* has_kg_value *x*
& *p* has_height *h* & *h* has_cm_value *x*)}

We now give a simple example of how NIAM diagrams are translated, and clarify our theory of definite descriptions. In Figure 1, a simple knowledge base diagram is shown: here a fact type from the CS is pictured, and a sample population added in tabular form below the relevant roles. The described object types Lecturer and Year are depicted as named ellipses, with their injective reference modes parenthesized: the underlining of "AD" indicates that Year injects to Real (numeric) rather than String (lexical). The binary predicate is shown as two contiguous role boxes, and the line below the left role box is a uniqueness constraint (a lecturer is born in at most one year).

A knowledge base diagram is translated in two stages: first the schema is translated; then the fact entries. Ignoring the generic CS axioms, the schema may be translated as shown. We use "~", "&", "∨" and "→" as operators for negation, conjunction, inclusive disjunction and material implication. The symbols "∃!" and "∃?" are existential quantifiers for "there is exactly one" and "there is at most one" respectively. The generic axioms define numeric and lexical operations for Real and String. Addition, subtraction and ordering are also defined for numerically referenced entity types (alluded to in line 11 of the schema translation).

Notice how the fact entries have been translated. Elsewhere (Halpin 1989b, pp. 5-30) we provide an algorithm for syntactically generating high level fact readings. For example, the first row of the fact-table in Figure 1 is read as:

F1 The Lecturer with surname 'Halpin' was born in the Year 1946 AD.

Instead of this definite description formulation, simple existential formulae have been used. For example, fact f1 may be read as follows:

Some object with surname 'Halpin' was born in an object with AD value 1946.

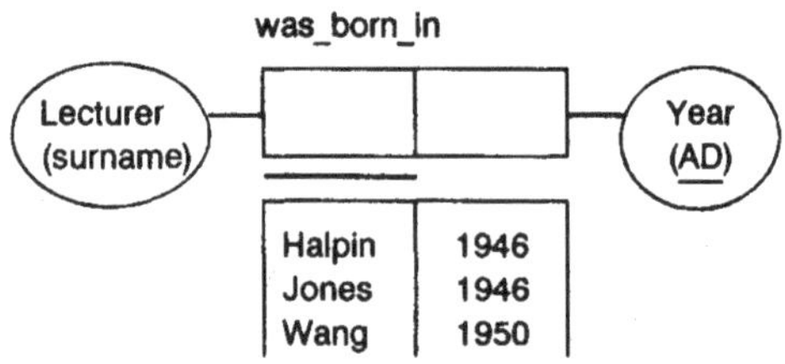

schema:

1 $\forall x(\text{ Lecturer } x \vee \text{ Year } x \rightarrow \text{ Described } x)$
2 $\forall x \sim(\text{Lecturer } x \;\&\; \text{Year } x)$
3 $\forall xy(x \text{ was\_born\_in } y \rightarrow \text{ Lecturer } x \;\&\; \text{Year } y)$
4 $\forall xyz(x \text{ was\_born\_in } y \;\&\; x \text{ was\_born\_in } z \rightarrow y = z)$
5 $\forall xy(x \text{ has\_surname } y \rightarrow \text{ Lecturer } x \;\&\; \text{String } y)$
6 $\forall x(\text{Lecturer } x \rightarrow \exists ! y \; x \text{ has\_surname } y)$
7 $\forall y \exists ? x \; x \text{ has\_surname } y$
8 $\forall xy(x \text{ has\_AD\_value } y \rightarrow \text{ Year } x \;\&\; \text{Real } y)$
9 $\forall x(\text{Year } x \rightarrow \exists ! y \; x \text{ has\_AD\_value } y)$
10 $\forall y \exists ? x \; x \text{ has\_AD\_value } y$
11 NRE+-$\leq$ for AD

fact table:

f1 $\exists xy(x \text{ has\_surname 'Halpin' } \& \; y \text{ has\_AD\_value } 1946 \;\&\; x \text{ was\_born\_in } y)$
f2 $\exists xy(x \text{ has\_surname 'Jones' } \& \; y \text{ has\_AD\_value } 1946 \;\&\; x \text{ was\_born\_in } y)$
f3 $\exists xy(x \text{ has\_surname 'Wang' } \& \; y \text{ has\_AD\_value } 1950 \;\&\; x \text{ was\_born\_in } y)$

Figure 1 Translating a knowledge base diagram

This is all that is required, since the schema (lines 3,5-10) provides the required context to ensure that there is exactly one object with surname 'Halpin' and that this object is a Lecturer, and that there is exactly one object which has AD value 1946 and that this object is a Year. This existential translation, in the context of our schema translation, provides the precise semantics for the definite description fact readings. This analysis generalizes straightforwardly to handle any *n*-ary elementary fact.

Our account of definite descriptions entails that such descriptions always succeed in referring (just as individual constants and ground function terms do). Earlier we included nil as a referent for garbage terms (e.g. "a"+2). In some analyses (e.g. ISO 1982, p. F-13) a similar referent is proposed for "impossible objects" e.g. square circles. With our approach, no described object can be nil. We place the onus on the designer to refrain from introducing impossible predicates; since the system has no formal means of detecting such absurdities, if they are used they will be taken to refer (e.g., "the Squarecircle with squarecirclename 'A'"). In practice, if such an unlikely predicate is introduced, to keep our formal system compatible with possible world semantics we can always interpret the predicate in such a way as to make it possible.

Of more relevance is the possibility of definite descriptions which do not refer to real world objects, e.g. "the President with surname 'Raygun'". Again, we demand that such descriptions do refer. We portray a UoD as a set of possible subworlds. In some possible worlds a president with this surname does exist. Our analysis of singular terms (including definite descriptions) ensures that there is at least one possible subworld in which such terms do refer. This is all we need. While the Conceptual Information Processor can ensure that the database is consistent with the CS supplied, it cannot ensure that the database is factual.

The treatment of definite descriptions is important, since our underlying formal proof mechanism (deduction trees) relies on successful reference. If instead we had adopted the Russellian theory of definite descriptions, and generated a branch formula such as $(\iota x)Ax \neq (\iota x)Ax$, this is merely equivalent to $\sim\exists!xAx$ and does not imply closure (e.g. see Rennie & Girle 1973, p. 215). Hilbert's analysis of ε could be used, since it guarantees reference and hence closure in this case. With our approach, no special operators for definite description are needed, and the non-identity of any ground term implies closure. Our earlier example of a KB diagram is typical, in that the ellipses depicted described object types. However, some or all of the ellipses may depict numeric or string types. Since our treatment of these possibilities differs from conventional NIAM, we discuss a few examples. Relationships between described and numeric objects must surely be admitted (e.g. F2-3), as well as relationships between described and lexical objects (e.g. F4-5).

F2 Person (surname) 'Jones' knows_the_kanji_for 3.
F3 Person (surname) 'Jones' has_IQ 120.
F4 Employee (emp#) '12345' has_employee_name 'Jones, E'.
F5 Person (surname) 'Jones' cannot_spell 'conceptualization'.

Falkenberg (1986) treats any relationship between a non-lexical object and a lexical object as a reference rather than as a fact. We feel it is more natural to treat examples like F4-5 as facts rather than as references.

Derivation rules

Basically, a derivation rule is a sentence which *defines*, at least partly, a predicate or a function. For example, we might define the derived predicate father_of in terms of the predicates parent_of and has_gender. Although in some contexts the term "derivation rule" is used as an alias for "transformation rule", we do not treat these terms as synonyms. Modus Ponens is a transformation rule but not a derivation rule.

Derived predicates and functions are often depicted graphically in terms of asterisked box-chains. In any case, they must be specified textually as derivation rules. In our formalization, a derivation rule must take the form of a universally quantified biconditional or a universally quantified conditional. In practice, *biconditionals* are typically far more common, so we examine these first. Consider Figure 2. This might be part of a schema used by a book retailer. The dots signify mandatory role constraints (for each known book, its cost and sales price must be known). Here the profit on a book is derived by subtracting its cost price from its retail price. *Braces* may be used with derivation rules to enclose *comments*: these are intended only for humans. We use "≡" as the operator for material equivalence. The term "w-z" is allowed since Money is a numerically referenced entity type.

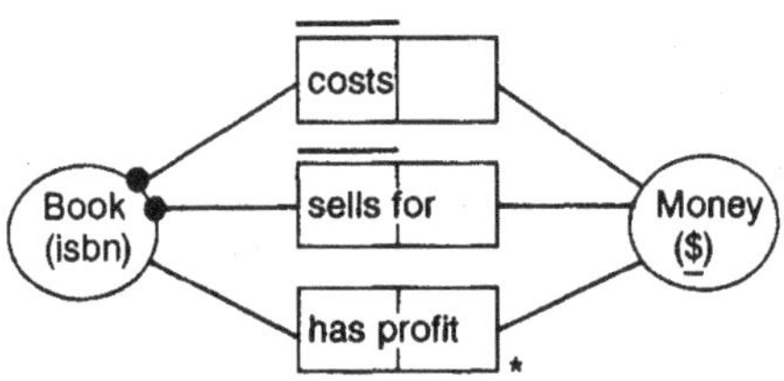

* { profit = sales price - cost price }
∀xy[x has_profit y ≡ ∃zw(x costs z & x sells_for w & y = w-z)]

Figure 2 Biconditional derivation rules are marked "*"

In rare cases, derivation rules may take the form of a *conditional* rather than a biconditional. As a simple example, consider the subschema of Figure 3. To enable the predicate being defined to be written first, we use "**if**" as the propositional operator for "is materially implied by", i.e. given any wffs α and $ß$, α **if** $ß =_{df} \alpha \rightarrow ß$. We also allow "←" as a variant for "**if**", and "**iff**" as a variant for "≡".

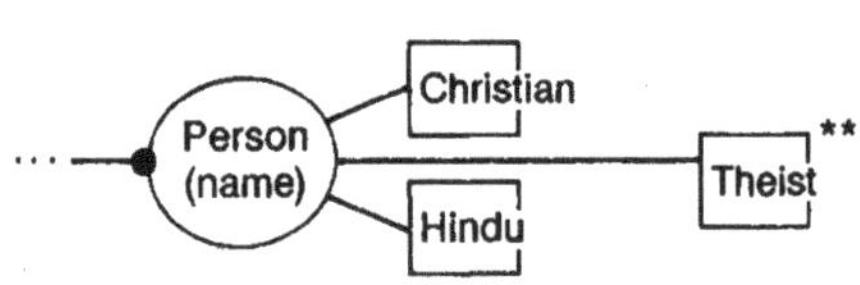

** ∀x(Theist x **if** Christian x ∨ Hindu x)

Figure 3 Conditional derivation rules are marked "**"

Note that *two asterisks* are used instead of the usual one. This new notation suggests that there is more being specified than just a simple derivation rule. Placing two asterisks besides a predicate indicates that the derivation rule provides only a *partial definition* of the predicate. This is reflected in the use of "**if**" rather than "**iff**". In this UoD it is possible that some people are known to be theists without being known to be Christian or Hindu (e.g. they might be Jewish, or we might simply not know what their religion is). With this schema, it is consistent to assert that a person is a theist without asserting that he or she is a Christian or Hindu. From the implementation viewpoint, this means that doubly asterisked predicates may be partly derived and partly stored.

On a CS diagram no predicate (asterisked or not) may appear more than once. However, when a derivation rule is specified textually, more than one formula may be used: in this case the derivation rule is the conjunction of these formulae. If the predicate is singly or doubly asterisked, each such formula must be a biconditional or conditional respectively. Unlike some systems (e.g. closed world Prolog), we do not treat the conjunction of conditionals as implicitly a biconditional. For example, if the derivation rule for Theist is ∀x(Theist x **if** Christian x) & ∀x(Theist x **if** Hindu x), this is not to be interpreted as ∀x(Theist x **iff** Christian x ∨ Hindu x). If the latter interpretation is intended, the predicate must be singly asterisked and defined as this biconditional.

With a typical derived fact type (the biconditional case), not only the predicate but its constraints must be derivable (this rule is sometimes needed to decide which of several related fact types should be derived from the others). In contrast, doubly asterisked predicates must have their constraints explicitly specified. From the implementation viewpoint, for any state of the knowledge base the constraints apply to the combined population of stored and derived instances of the predicate. Since the stored instances can affect the constraint satisfaction of this population, the constraints are not implied by a correctly formulated derivation rule (unlike the biconditional case). For example, consider Figure 4. The "1;4" is a frequency constraint (each person playing the role of having a grandparent must do so at least once and at most four times), and the "as,it" constrains the grandparent_of predicate to be asymmetric and intransitive.

The grandparent_of predicate is often used in Prolog texts as a paradigm case of a partly stored and partly derived predicate. Besides the grandparenthood information derived from parenthood facts, this approach allows the assertion of grandparenthood facts where the intermediate parents are unknown. The population of grandparent_of (including these stored facts) must obey the constraints.

In some, but not all, cases the same feature of a UoD may be captured by either a biconditional/conditional derivation rule or an equality/subset constraint. We now identify and provide design guidelines for these cases, beginning with *equality constraints*.

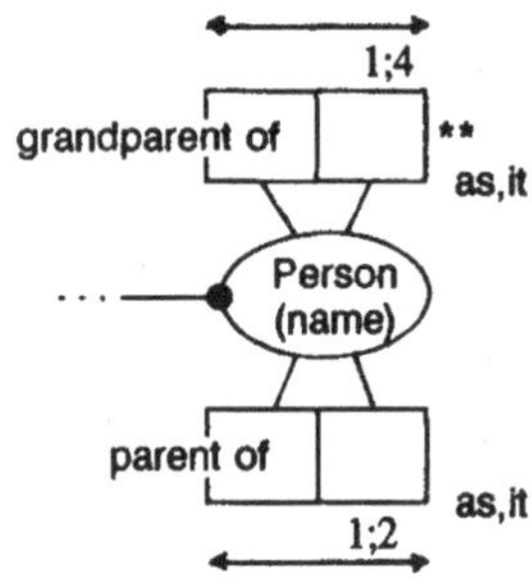

** ∀xz[x grandparent_of z iff ∃y(x parent_of y & y parent_of z)]

Figure 4 Constraints on stored part of ** are not implied

Figure 5 shows two equivalent schemas. In the left-hand version, an equality constraint is specified as a dotted line with two arrow heads. In the right-hand version, this aspect of the UoD is instead captured by the biconditional derivation rule. In this UoD we cannot know that a person was an Olympian in a particular sport unless we know one of the years in which this occurred.

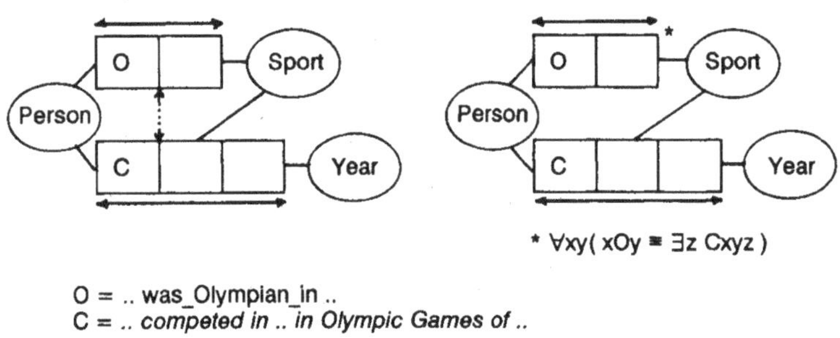

Figure 5 The right hand version is usually preferred

In cases like this, where at least one operands of the equality constraint is a *whole predicate* (here the binary), we generally recommend the derivation rule version since its implementation avoids the need to store this predicate. In the rare cases where both operands of an equality constraint are whole predicates, either predicate may be selected as derived. For example, suppose people own a car if and only if they drive it. If it is desired to use both predicates Owns and Drives, one could be stored and updated while the other predicate is derived from ∀xy(x owns y ≡ x drives y).

If neither operand of an equality constraint is a whole predicate, then we cannot recast this as a derivation rule. For example, if we want to know a person's resting heart rate if and only if we also want to know their reaction time then we specify this by means of an equality constraint between the first roles of has_resting_heart_rate and has_reaction_time (see Nijssen & Halpin 1989, p. 172). We cannot specify a derivation rule to enable a person's reaction time to be determined from their resting heart rate.

Let us now consider subset constraints. First note that, being uni-directional, a subset constraint cannot express a biconditionality. In situations where an **iff** is required, we must specify a derivation rule (or a subtype if subtype-specific knowledge is required). For example, suppose we want to know whether a person is a genius, and this can be precisely defined by the person's IQ. If there is something we wish to know only about geniuses then we create a subtype for Genius with this specific role attached. However if there is no such specific role we simply specify a derivation rule for Genius: this will be identical to the formulation of a subtype definition for Genius, e.g. $\forall$x[Genius x $\equiv$ $\exists$y(x has_iq y & y $\geq$ 150)]. We cannot handle this case with a subset constraint.

With a *subset constraint*, the role sequence which is the operand pointed to by the subset arrow is called the *target operand*. If the target operand is a whole predicate we generally prefer to represent this feature of the UoD by a subset constraint rather than using a derivation rule. For example, suppose we modify our Olympian schema by replacing the equality constraint by a subset constraint directed to the binary (omit the lower arrow-head from the dotted line). This means we can know a person was an Olympian in a sport without knowing when this happened. The binary may now be partly derived from the following conditional: $\forall$xy(xOy **if** $\exists$z Cxyz); but we also need to partly store the binary. The subset constraint approach is generally preferable to this partly stored/derived approach.

In an earlier work (Nijssen & Halpin 1989), we treated constraints as applying to the (stored) database. We now treat constraints as applying to the UoD and hence the knowledge base (what is known rather than what is stored). Which facts are stored and which are derived is not a conceptual issue: it makes no difference to the UoD. When it comes to implementing a conceptual schema, we must make a decision as to what is to be stored or derived. At this implementation level we treat the diagrams differently. Consider Figure 5: with the equality constraint, binary Olympian facts are actually stored and the constraint is enforced on relevant updates; with the biconditional derivation rule approach, the binary facts are not stored but are derived when relevant queries are issued.

In Nijssen & Halpin (1989), we classified relational properties as *positive* or *negative* according to whether the property could be used to deduce other (positive) facts or the negations of such facts. For example, reflexivity, symmetry and transitivity are positive whereas irreflexivity, asymmetry and intransitivity are negative. We suggested that negative properties be implemented as database constraints, but described how positive properties could be implemented as database constraints or conditional derivation rules.

The Olympian case that we have just examined fits within the general category of positive relational properties (though here two relations are involved). As a further implementation choice, it is always possible to replace a partially derived predicate by a stored predicate (used for updates) and a differently named fully derived predicate (used for queries), e.g. see our Synonym example (Nijssen & Halpin 1989, p. 186).

Further examples, and general rules for translating between constraints and derivation rules are provided elsewhere (Halpin 1989b). The general issue of whether to implement a feature by means of a database constraint or a derivation rule has been addressed by a number of researchers. A good overview of this research is provided by Gallaire, Minker and Nicolas (1984, pp. 173-5). We feel that our analysis has shed further light on this issue, by focussing on the nature of the derivation rule (biconditional vs conditional), identifying the cases where the design choice exists, and providing design guidelines for these cases. For NIAM in particular, our analysis adds a further class of conceptual equivalence theorems, which are formally provable in our system.

Summary of related research

One purpose of this paper is to provide an overview of recent research by the author. Because of space limitations, the following account is presented in summary form. Further details may be found in Halpin (1989a,b,c; 1990). Properties of, and relationships between conceptual schemas are analysed, with particular attention to satisfiability, constraint implication, and schema equivalence. The notion of "strong satisfiability" is introduced, leading to additional schema formation rules. One major contribution of our approach is its rigorous formalization of schema equivalence within NIAM, enabling transformation theorems to be precisely stated and formally proved. The notions of "contextual equivalence" and "contextual implication" are introduced to provide formal support for transformations between different world views.

The formalism is used to refine old results and to establish new theorems. The implementation of conceptual schemas in relational database systems is examined, focussing on the mapping of conceptual constraints into relational schemas and SQL systems in particular. The notion of conceptual tuning, whereby structures are manipulated by transformations at the conceptual level to achieve more efficient target structures at the relational level, is discussed both for conceptual schemas and query formulation. Selection guidelines are specified (e.g. the "overlap algorithm") with a view to minimizing the number of tables in the relational schema.

Two algorithms are introduced to facilitate the formulation of complex SQL queries based on set comparisons. The queries are first pictured in terms of logic diagrams, then translated into predicate calculus or set cardinality conditions, before being mapped onto SQL formulae. While the calculus mapping is more comprehensive in terms of its query capturing, the set cardinality approach is typically more efficient, leading to opportunities for query optimization.

The author acknowledges the useful advice of Professor John Staples concerning the formalization issues, and has benefited from numerous discussions with Dr G. M. Nijssen and Prof. E. D. Falkenberg regarding NIAM. Although cast in terms of NIAM, many of the results extend readily to other conceptual modelling approaches such as Entity-Relationship modelling.

References

Beeri, C. & Kifer, M. 1986, 'An Integrated Approach to Logical Design of Relational Database Schemes', *ACM TODS*, vol. 11, no. 2, pp. 134-158.

Bry, F. & Manthey, R. 1986, 'Checking Consistency of Database Constraints: a Logical Basis', *Proc. Twelfth International Conf. on Very Large Data Bases*, VLDB, Kyoto, pp. 13-20.

Chen, P.P. & Dogac, A. 1983, 'Entity-Relationship Model in the ANSI/SPARC Framework', *Entity-Relationship Approach to Information Modelling and Analysis*, ed. P.P. Chen, Elsevier Science Publishers B.V., North Holland.

D'Atri, A. & Sacca, D. 1984, 'Equivalence and Mapping of Database Schemes', *Proceedings of the 10th International Conference on Very Large Data Bases*, VLDB, Singapore, pp. 187-95.

Falkenberg, E.D. 1986, *Data Bases and Information Systems I: Lecture Notes*, University of Nijmegen, The Netherlands.

Gallaire, H., Minker, J. & Nicolas, J.-M. 1984, 'Logic and Databases: A Deductive Approach', *ACM Computing Surveys*, vol. 16, no. 2.

Halpin, T.A. 1986a, 'Conceptual Schemata and Predicate Logic', *Proceedings of the First Australian AI Congress*, Melbourne.

Halpin, T.A. 1986b, 'Logic Diagrams and Query Formulation in SQL', *Technical Report* 77, Dept of Computer Science, University of Qld.

Halpin, T.A. 1989a, 'Venn Diagrams and SQL Queries', *The Australian Computer Journal*, vol. 21, no. 1, pp. 27-32.

Halpin, T.A. 1989b, 'A Logical Analysis of Information Systems: static aspects of the data-oriented perspective', PhD thesis (submitted), University of Queensland.

Halpin, T.A. 1989c, 'Contextual equivalence of conceptual schemas', *Proc. of Advanced Database System Symposium '89*, Info. Proc. Soc. of Japan, Kyoto, pp. 47-54.

Halpin, T.A. 1990, 'Conceptual schema optimization', *Proc. 13th Australian Computer Science Conf.*, Melbourne.

ISO 1982, *Concepts and Terminology for the Conceptual Schema and the Information Base*, ed. J.J. van Griethuysen, ISO TC97/SC5/WG3, Eindhoven.

Kent, W. 1982, 'Choices in Practical Data Design', *Proc. of the Eigth Int. Conf. on Very Large Data Bases*, VLDB, pp. 165-180.

Kent, W. 1986, 'The Realities of Data: Basic Properties of Data Reconsidered', *Database Semantics*, eds T.B. Steel Jr & R.A. Meersman, Elseviers Science Publishers B.V., North Holland.

Kobayashi, I. 1986, 'Losslessness and semantic correctness of database schema transformation: another look at schema equivalence', *Inform. Systems*, vol. 11, no. 1, Pergamon Press, pp. 41-59

Leung, C.M.R. 1988, 'On Design and Implementation of a Fifth Generation Information System', PhD thesis, Dept of Computer Science, University of Queensland.

Mark, L. 1987, 'The Binary Relationship Model - 10th Anniversary', *Proc. VIM-47 EMDA Conf.*, Minneapolis, Nov. 1987.

Navathe, S.B., Sashidhar, T. & Elmasri, R. 1984, 'Relationship Merging in Schema Integration', *Proc. of the Tenth Int. Conf. on Very Large Data Bases*, Singapore, pp. 78-90.

Nijssen, G.M. & Halpin, T.A. 1989, *Conceptual Schema and Relational Database Design*, Prentice Hall, Sydney.

Olle, T.W., Hagelstein, J., Macdonald, I.G., Rolland, C., Sol, H.G., Van Assche, F.J.M. & Verrijn-Stuart, A.A. 1988, *Information Systems Methodologies - A Framework for Understanding*, Addison-Wesley, Wokingham, England.

Reiter, R. 1984, 'Towards a Logical Reconstruction of Relational Database Theory', *On Conceptual Modelling*, eds M.L. Brodie, J. Mylopoulas & J.W. Schmidt, Springer-Verlag, New York, pp. 191-233.

Rennie, M.K. & Girle, R.A. 1973, *Logic: Theory and Practice*, University of Queensland Press, Brisbane.

Teorey, T.J., Yang, D. & Fry, J.P. 1986, 'A Logical Design Methodology for Relational Databases Using the Extended Entity-Relationship Model', *ACM Computing Surveys*, vol 18, no. 2, pp. 197-222.

AN OVERVIEW OF INTEGRATION IN HETEROGENEOUS INFORMATION SYSTEMS

Peter Bernus
bernus@batserver.cs.uq.oz.au

Centre of Expertise in Distributed Information Systems
Key Centre for Software Technology, The University of Queensland
St.Lucia, QLD 4067, AUSTRALIA

ABSTRACT

Distributed homogeneous database systems are becoming commercially available but fulfill only partially the requirements typical of heterogeneous environments.

The paper [1] investigates the solutions that developers of heterogeneous information systems use and critically reviews the current situation. (Table 1. presents an overview of the heterogeneous systems under discussion.)

Our particular interest is in the data modelling aspects of information systems integration in order to assess the relevance of new data models (like the ones offered by object oriented or deductive databases).

We also outline the possibility of an object oriented data model based on logic, providing data abstractions through functions in a way similar to functional data models.

We draw our conclusions from previous work on integration[9] in particular on integration of CAD systems using AI techniques[4].

[1]This research was supported by Telecom Australia Research Laboratories.

1 INTRODUCTION

1.1 Distributed Versus Integrated Information Systems

The integration of existing information systems has specific problems somewhat similar to but not the same as the design of distributed information systems. Distributed databases for example ideally appear to their multiuser environment as a centralised database. In contrast, integrated heterogeneous information systems preserve the participant systems' autonomy, so that they can be further used independently. It is the task of the integrating platform to ensure a common access possibility, through which users can query (or in some cases update) the data stored in the participating subsystems.

Integration cannot usually be achieved by designing and then implementing the integrated system, rather integration is a process in which the systems become increasingly coupled.

In the *first* step of this process all we provide is a common query access facility (e.g. for management information purposes). Through this facility it is possible to issue queries in a uniform query language without knowing which subsystems are involved in answering them.

In the *second* step, updates through the common access facility become possible. The common access ensures that all the databases (possibly storing the same information in a redundant manner) become updated. The update transaction is disallowed if it is inconsistent with any of the constraints imposed by the involved databases.

In the *third* step, local updates become channeled through the integrating platform so that the effects of local updates can be propagated to other participant databases. Only in the third step can we speak of a *fully* integrated heterogeneous distributed information system.

Naturally, during all these steps, concurrency control functions need to be implemented just as in distributed database systems.

In the development process outlined, old databases become extinct, new ones are created and data are migrating from one database to the other.

It is not hard to foresee the conclusion: an integrated access facility has to model both the semantics of the data in the participant systems and the processes involved in the integration (read/write access, data translation, migration etc.)

1.2 Differences in the Systems to be Integrated

(1) The difference between the participating systems is in some cases small, and the task is to access and/or update relational databases which are implemented using different DMBS products but featuring SQL or SQL-like interfaces.

This problem is encountered in data processing applications within large organisations which have acquired different database products over the years and now want to use these as an integrated system. Here, the databases typically are based

Table 1: Overview of heterogeneous integrated database test-beds

name (originator)	Q/U	access language (I:internal)	acc.lang. based on	maintains global sch.	data models (G:global) (L:locals)
OMNIBASE[11] (U.of Houston)	Q	DOL	data model	yes (domain attr. KB)	not fixed
IMDAS[6] (NBS)	Q/U	GMDL (ŠQL) (+I)	ÕSAM conc. schema (I:G-table)	yes	G-table(G) +L
MERMAID[5] (Unisys)	Q/U	SQL or ARIEL (I:DIL)	data model	yes	relational
Gestalt[12] (MIT)	Q/U	Clisp	data model		functional
IRIS[7] (HP)	Q/U	logical	data model	no	obj.oriented functional(G) +L
MULTIBASE[13] (CCA)	Q	DAPLEX	data. model	yes	DAPLEX
IISS[14] (USAF)	Q	DML embedded in Cobol	?data model		relational
PRECI[15] (U.of Aberdeen)					canonical(G) +many L
MRDSM[16] (INRIA)	Q-s! U	MDSL (ŠQL)	conceptual schemata	multiple (not integrated)	relational
NDMS[17] (CRAI It.)		SQL (+I)	data model	yes	relational
DBPL[18]	Q/U	Modula embedded transactns	data model		relations as Modula types
IIICAD[8,9] (CWI)	Q/U	IDDL logic	data model	yes	obj.oriented logic+ functional(G) +L-s
HD-DMS[1] (UCLA)	Q/U	GCL	conceptual schema	yes	DIAM(G) +L-s

on the same data model. It is also customary that database vendors of nonrelational systems add an SQL interface to their products so they can be physically accessed in the same way as relational databases.

(2) Some systems create an integrated information system out of databases, in-memory tables, procedurally encoded data sources, control programmes etc. In this case there is no commonly accepted query language nor is there any common data model used by the participant systems.

(3) The kinds of applications mentioned before suppose that it is possible to carry out the integration by reconciling the differences in the participating databases' schemata pertaining to the same universe of discourse, by the design of a common integrated schema. This is not possible or desired in all cases; e.g. queries can have multiple answers and it is up to the user to interpret the results. While business applications or manufacturing information systems do need the resolution of conflicts this is not the case in public information services built to access large numbers of potentially overlapping databases. These kinds of services can tolerate the broadcast query approach resulting multiple answers rather than one. Apart from noting its existence we shall not deal with this type of application in this paper.

2 CHARACTERISTIC EXAMPLES OF TEST-BED SYSTEMS AND THEIR DATA MODELLING NEEDS

We have reviewed a number of experimental solutions to integrate information systems of different sorts.

2.1 Integration Based on the Relational Data Model

The assumptions are that the participant systems:

- are all based on the relational data model,
- use similar (but not identical) query languages,
- are used autonomously in addition to the integrated access,
- are accessed from the integration platform for queries only (no update),
- it is not allowed to redesign or alter the participant systems.

A prototype solution is Unisys's Mermaid system[5]. In Mermaid a common restricted relational query language is defined (called DIL).

The steps of integration are:

– Design an integrated global relational schema which is then stored in the system's DD/D (Data Dictionary/ Directory).

– Implement SQL query translation to DIL.

– Map global DIL queries to a DIL query tree. The mapping needs the DD/D to validate the query and plan its decomposition.

– Map local DIL queries to the local databases' data manipulation language (DML).

– Manage query execution and perform data translation (e.g. for dimension differences in domains) or schema translation (e.g. attribute renaming).

Unfortunately, the bottom-up integration of the participant systems' relational schemata in form of global relational views is more often than not infeasible. The integration can only take place on the conceptual schema level. For expressing the relationships between schemata, the DD/D would need to represent more semantics than is possible in the relational model.

Generalisation and aggregation of concepts needs to be represented and used for query translation. In addition, as Ceri et al.[21] point out there are still a row of problems in view integration which cannot be satisfactorily dealt with by static data analysis. The addition of ad hoc query modification procedures is awkward, error prone and is more a patching approach than good design.

Another problem is that in formulating global queries the explicit knowledge of the relational structure is necessary which is an unnatural requirement for the user.

The Mermaid system therefore has been equipped with a second interface language (ARIEL) and an alternative semantic schema in the DD/D database.

It is planned that on the basis of the semantic schema in the DD/D, Mermaid will be extended to support global updates.

Figure 1. shows the functional structure of a Mermaid query process.

Several lessons can be learned from this type of integrated system.

– Schema integration needs an extended schema language, expressing abstractions like generalisation and aggregation.

– There are cases which cannot be resolved by static schema integration but only by modelling the functions (behaviour) of the data and events.

– The integrated access facility does not deal with keeping the local databases consistent with each other, i.e. local updates in one database are not propagated automatically to others covered by the global schema.

2.2 Integration Based on Semantic Data Models

Typical assumptions are:

- The participant systems may not be based on the same or similar data models.
- No common query language is available.
- The participant systems may be modified slightly (extended or amended) in order to achieve consistency of local/global schemata.
- Autonomous use of the participant systems is allowed.
- The integrated access must support global queries and global updates. The propagation of local updates to the global level (i.e. turning the federated system into a heterogeneous distributed system) is a future option.

2.2.1 The IMDAS system and the OSAM semantic model

One of the important developers and users of information systems integration of this type is the CIM (Computer Integrated Manufacturing) community. This includes integration of Computer-aided Design systems as well as factory level integration.

A prototype of integration solutions based on semantic models is the IMDAS system[6] (Integrated Manufacturing Data Administration System) for the AMRF (Automated Manufacturing Research Facility) at the former US National Bureau of Standards.

IMDAS uses a very expressive conceptual schema definition language, OSAM[2,3,6] which allows generalised, aggregate, relation, set, bag, vector and matrix concepts to be defined.

The conceptual model is called "object-oriented semantic association model". The source available to date to us suggests that OSAM does not express the behavioural aspect of data. However, OSAM has an object concept (instead of entity and relationship), with object identity and rich forms of attribute inheritance.

The data model in IMDAS is an extended relational model, called G-relations. G-relations allow multiple valued attributes and a nested tabular structure.

OSAM conceptual schemas are implemented by (mapped to) G-tables so that:

– Every tuple in a G-table represents a set of attributes of an OSAM object. This object's unique object identifier is a primary key in that G-relation.

– Every object in the OSAM model is mapped onto one or more G-relations.

Figure 2. represents the functional structure of the IMDAS query process.

The DD/D in IMDAS is based on the OSAM semantic model. The query language (called GMDL) is translated into G-table manipulations using this semantic model of the data. Similarly, as happens in Mermaid using ARIEL, queries do not need to include specific access paths to attributes by explicit joins, e.g. attribute inheritance can be used etc.

Update requests can also be checked against the constraints specified in the OSAM semantic model.

Since there is no query language that is common to all subsystems, the G-table queries are translated to local DML requests. On the face of it, it appears that the situation is similar to the Mermaid solution where DIL queries have been translated to local relational queries. The biggest difference, however, in our opinion is the presence of object identifiers in G-tables because, without them, partial information could not be translated.

What is important to notice is that information in one subsystem can be complete about an object which, for the other subsystem, is an ambiguous description of the same object. G-relations on the surface look like slightly modified relational tables but the underlying knowledge representation principles are quite different. G-tables are extensional (based on object identifiers) while the relational model is intensional (based on sets of attributes). (Tomiyama and ten Hagen[10] treat the significance of this difference in more detail.)

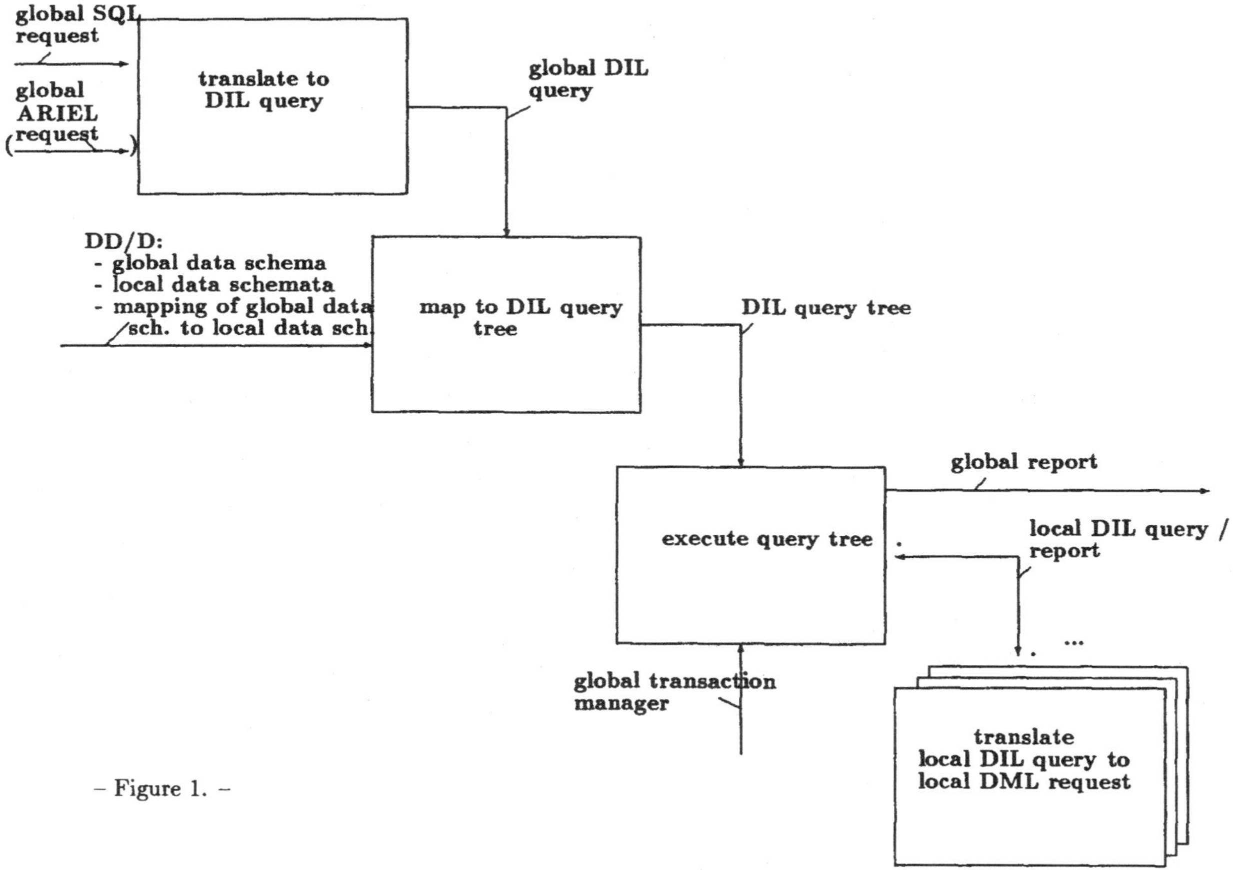
global SQL
request
global
ARIEL
(request)
translate to
DIL query
global DIL
query
DD/D:
- global data schema
- local data schemata
- mapping of global data
sch. to local data sch.
map to DIL query
tree
DIL query tree
global report
execute query tree
local DIL query /
report
global transaction
manager
...
translate
local DIL query to
local DML request

– Figure 1. –

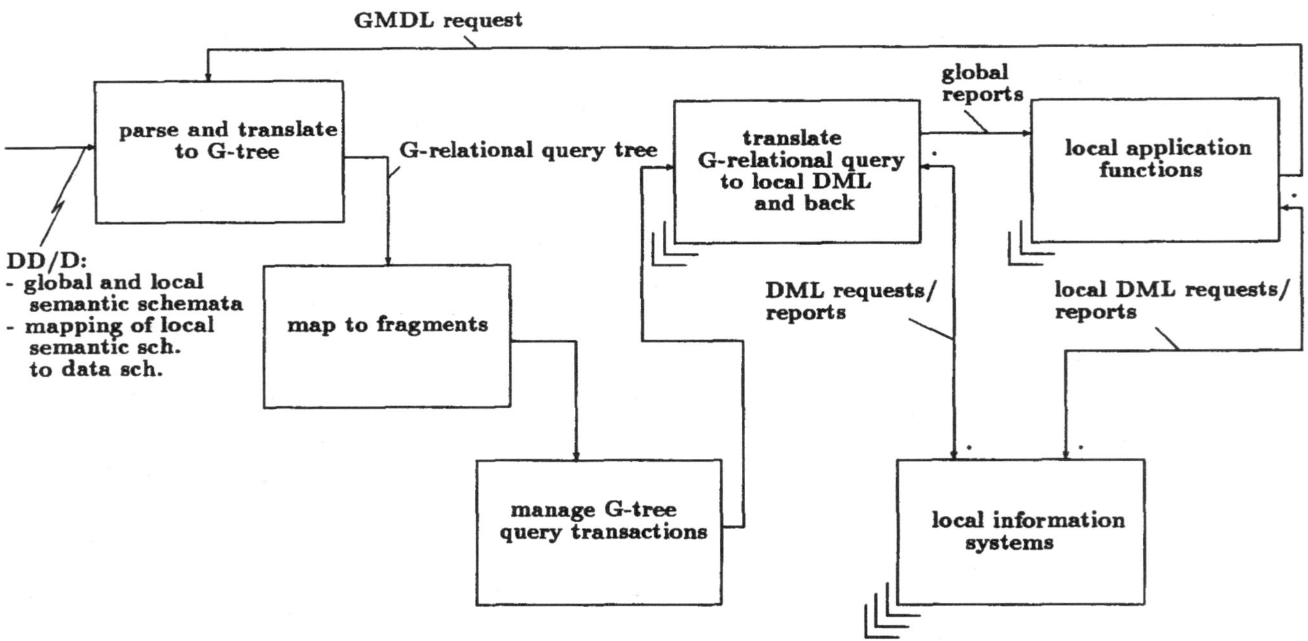
GMDL request
parse and translate to G-tree
G-relational query tree
DD/D:
- global and local semantic schemata
- mapping of local semantic sch. to data sch.
map to fragments
manage G-tree query transactions
translate G-relational query to local DML and back
global reports
local application functions
DML requests/ reports
local DML requests/ reports
local information systems

– Figure 2. –

A few comments:

- The OSAM model is a rich semantic data model. The static aspect of data is extensively covered.

- The lack of duality in the model between static and dynamic aspects is present in the OSAM model as well (to our knowledge of OSAM). In application domains where it is allowable to redesign the participating systems the problem may be smaller than in domains where local schema redesign or modification is not allowed.

2.2.2 The functional data model

The functional model of data as presented by Shipman[19] and Chan et al.[20] is a semantic data model based on objects (called entities in Daplex) and functions. Functions map objects to sets of objects.

The functional data model's modelling constructs are a strict superset of the relational data model[20].

Functions represent properties of objects. The value of a property is a single object or a set of objects. By convention, zero argument functions define object types, e.g. if we declare FUNCTION STUDENT() → PERSON then STUDENT() returns the set of person objects which are students.

The functional data model naturally expresses generalisation hierarchies and other abstractions. An important addition of the functional data model to the expressive power of conceptual modelling tools is the ability to represent conceptual abstraction (functional abstraction). Basically, the data abstraction mechanism of abstract data types is built into the functional data model.

Further features of the functional data model include: overloading of function definitions and disambiguation of multiply inherited functions with identical names, definition of derived data, definition of constraints and triggers, and – according to Chan et al.[20] – a natural solution to the maintenance of referential integrity.

2.2.3 Object-oriented data models

Other systems, like Hewlet Packard's IRIS system[7], also adopted a functional view of data but created an object-oriented database system based on it. In IRIS, declaration and implementation of functions is separated, by which means this system can be used to create a uniform global view of the participant systems data but can also implement the functions by whatever means are appropriate rather than resorting to simple value propagation. In particular, functions can be implemented by procedures, by reference to other objects functions or by immediate constant values.

IRIS's solution (as an example of the object oriented data model) allows functions with side effects. This is a behavioural modelling capability.

In using the object oriented data model for database integration the stress is on the semantic model stored in the DD/D database because this central model is acquiring a much more important role than it traditionally used to have. Within the integrating platform the DD/D is elevated from a dictionary position to a fully functional database system. There is no obstacle to using the object-oriented system for both semantic data modelling and implementation of the integration functions including query processing, transaction management etc.

Another project, called IIICAD[8] is aimed at the integration of Computer-aided Design. The specific modelling needs of design led to the conclusion that for integration of CAD systems, it is necessary to model both the static data aspect and the dynamic process (transaction, reasoning,...) aspect of design. Instead of using or extending data models developed for database technology, it was believed that we could use a logic language for modelling both data and processes. Static data — facts and constraints — are modelled by constants, terms, predicates and clauses while processes are modelled by forward reasoning rules (and meta-rules). Constructs for the semantic schema IDDS (Integrated Data Description Schema) have been added to the logic language IDDL[22,9]. The basic static notion of IDDL[2] is the object (represented by constants of IDDL). Functions in IDDL map objects to other objects (or sets of objects) and are implemented as evaluable terms.

In IDDS an object has two views. An outside view consists of a set of function names (corresponding to "properties" of objects). An inside view, on the other hand, is a collection of facts divided into three groups: facts about the object, constraints and function definitions. The inner view of an object is somewhat similar to a small deductive database; it contains facts, constraints and side effect free clauses. Functions can be local or exported. Exported functions connect the two views of an object.

The primitive dynamic modelling construct of IDDS is a rule. Rules are grouped into scenarios. Scenarios can be executed and can call each other. The facts that a scenario sees (i.e. the database the rules work on) is called the world of the scenario. A world can be considered the inside of an object. If it is, the scenario modifies the inside view of an object. If it isn't, the world may later be enclosed to form and object. Scenarios in IDDL are represented by scenario-type objects. The list of rules in a scenario object is simply one of the scenario object's properties.

Scenarios are useful constructs for modelling the processes that update an object's attributes or for modelling any type of behavioural knowledge.

It has also been recognised in the requirements analysis for IDDL that the expressive power of the logic language has to be gauged to the application domain (in IDDL's case Computer-aided Design). Nonclassical logic properties have been found necessary for the requirements of knowledge representation in CAD. One of the advantages of using a logic language for knowledge representation is that methods developed for logic programming can be used to precisely define the semantics of the language and analyse its properties.

---

[2]IDDL is still an evolving language so we can only give a personal view of the approach not a final evaluation

3 CONCLUSION

We have given samples of different approaches to the integration of heterogeneous information systems. It has become clear that whichever background we start from — databases or AI/ knowledge representation — the modelling tools to capture the global models for integration are similar.

In fact, semantic data models or knowledge representation tools converge in the sense that they expose similar features. These features are characteristic of object oriented data models. It has to be noted, however, that while object oriented data models pragmatically perform very well, still there is a lack of mathematical treatment of this model which would be similar to the relational model having its roots in relational algebra.

Implementation of semantic data models in computers is more debatable and will presumably result in application dependent optimal solutions.

For example, it is possible to map some of the semantic data models onto the relational model of data with stored procedures or to map the semantic model onto a logic programme. There may be many other solutions in between.

The advantage of keeping the structure of the implementation identical to the semantic model is that changes to the semantic schema can be made using the same method as changes to the data, thus not separating the design platform from the implementation platform in an integrated system. This approach favours the "logic programme approach" to the relational approach as far as the database of the integrating component is concerned.

REFERENCES

[1] Cardenas, A.F., Heterogeneous Distributed database Management: The HD-DBMS, *Proc. IEEE* **75**(5) (May 1987)pp588-600.

[2] Su, S.Y.W., SAM*: A Semantic Association Model for Corporate and Scientific-Statistical Databases, *Information Sciences*, No.29 (1983)pp151-199.

[3] Su, S.Y.W., Krishnamurthy, V.,, Lam, H., An Object-oriented Semantic Association Model (OSAM*), in AI in Industrial Engineering and Manufacturing: Theoretical Issues and Applications, R.L. Kashyap, S. Kumara and A.L. Soyster (eds), AIIE (1988).

[4] Bernus, P., Rigour and Permissiveness in the Design of CAD/CAM Systems, in*Integration of CAD/CAM*, D.Kochan (ed), North Holland, Amsterdam (1983)pp161-178.

[5] Templeton, M., et al, Mermaid — A Front-end to Distributed Heterogeneous Databases, *Proc. IEEE* **75**(5) (May 1987)pp695-708.

[6] Krishnamurthy, V., Su, S.Y.W., Lam, H., IMDAS — An Integrated Manufacturing Data Administration System, *Data and Knowledge Eng.* No.3., North Holland, Amsterdam (1988)pp109-131

[7] Fischman, D.H. et al, Iris: An Object-oriented database Management System, *ACM Trans on Office Information Systems* **5**(1) (January 1987).

[8] Bart Veth, An Integrated Data Description Language for Coding Design Knowledge, in *Intelligent CAD Systems 1 — Theoretical and Methodological Aspects*, P.J.W ten Hagen and T. Tomiyama (eds), Springer-Verlag, Berlin (1987)pp295-313.

[9] Veerkamp,P.J., Akman,V., Bernus, P. and ten Hagen,P.J.W.,IDDL: A Language for Intelligent Interactive Integrated CAD Systems, in *Intelligent CAD Systems II — Implementational Issues*, V. Akman, P.J.W. ten Hagen and P.J. Veerkamp (eds), Springer Verlag, Berlin, (1989)pp17.

[10] Tomiyama, T., Ten Hagen, P.J.W., Representing Knowledge in Two Distinct Descriptions: Extensional vs. Intensional, CWI Report No. CS-R8718,Centre for Mathematics and Computer Science, Amsterdam (1987); (also submitted for publication in *International Journal for AI in Engineering*).

[11] Czejdo, B., Rusinkiewicz, M., Embley, D., An Approach to Schema Integration and Query Formulation in Federated Database Systems, in *Proc. 3rd International Conf. on Data Engineering, Los Angeles, CA*, IEEE Computer Society Press (1987).

[12] Rusinkiewizc, W., Panel on Multi-database Systems, in *Proc ACM Sigmod Chicago, Ill., 1-3 June 1988, SIGMOD Record* **17**(3), ACM Press (1988)pp3-5.

[13] Landers, T., Rosenberg, R.L., An Overview of Multibase, *Second Symp. on Distrib. Databases, Berlin 1982*, North Holland, Amsterdam (1982)pp311-336.

[14] Integrated Information Support System, ICAM Materials Lab., AF Systems Control, Wright-Patterson AFB (February 1983).

[15] Deen, S.M., Amin, G.O., Ofori-Dwumfuo, Taylor, M.C., The Architecture of a Generalised Distributed database System — PRECI*, *Computer Journal* **28**(3) (1985)pp282-290.

[16] Litwin, W., Abdellatif, A., An Overview of the Multi-database Manipulation Language MDSL, *Proc. IEEE* **75**(5) (May 1987)pp621-632.

[17] Kaminski Staniskis, W., Kowalewsky, M., Krajewski, K., Mezyk, S., Turco, G., Architecture of the Network Data Management System, in *Proc. 3rd International Seminar on Distributed Data Sharing Systems, March 1984, Italy*, North Holland, Amsterdam (1985)pp57-74.

[18] Ge, L., Johanssen, W., Lamersdorf, W., Reinhardt, K., Schmidt, J.W., Database Applications Support in Open Systems: Language Concepts and Implementation Architectures, in *4th Int. Conf. on Data Engineering, Los Angeles, CA, 1-5 February 1988*, IEEE Computer Society Press (1988)p556.

[19] Shipman, D.P., Functional Data Model and Daplex, *ACM Trans. on Database Systems*, **6**(1) (March 1981)pp140-173.

[20] Chan, A., Dayal, U., Fox., S., An Ada-Compatible Distributed Database Management System, *Proc. IEEE* **75**(5) (May 1987)pp674-694.

[21] Ceri, S., Pernici, B., Wiederhold, G., Distributed Database Design Methodologies, *Proc IEEE*, **75**(5), (1987) pp 533-546.

[22] Tomiyama, T., ten Hagen, P.J.W., The Concept of Intelligent Integrated Interactive CAD Systems, Report CS-R8717, Centre for Mathematics and Computer Science, Amsterdam (1987)p29.

RESEARCH ISSUES IN KNOWLEDGE BASES

Robert M. Colomb
CSIRO Division of Information Technology
Box 1599 North Ryde NSW 2113 Australia
colomb@ditsyda.oz

ABSTRACT

The Knowledge Based Systems Engineering Program at CSIRO overlaps the database discipline in technologies employed, applications domains and in the scale of problem considered. We are specifically concerned with problems in the specification of the dynamics of information systems, the partitioning and integration of information models and the re-use of specifications; in the specification and maintenance of knowledge bases of various kinds, in the development of integrated knowledge management systems using hypermedia; in the use of the relational algebra as a programming paradigm; in persistent implementations of Prolog, in natural language processing and in the user interface to database and other kinds of system.

1. INTRODUCTION

The Knowledge Based Systems Engineering Program in the CSIRO Division of Information Technology is concerned with building tools for people to exploit knowledge. The Program is related to the database world in a number of ways:

- Use of database technology in knowledge base management;
- Extension of information modelling to knowledge modelling;
- Enhancement of information systems specifications;
- Management of large volumes of data not sufficiently structured for standard database technology.

In other words, we overlap in technology, methods of analysis, applications domains and in the scale of problem considered. This report considers the key database-related research issues as seen by the Knowledge Based Systems Engineering Program. It is based on present research, which is briefly reviewed, then relevant open questions are discussed.

2. INFORMATION SYSTEMS DYNAMICS

Specification of Process

Data base technology has substantially solved the problem of description and management of the data which forms the basis of information systems. A major component of these systems, however, is the set of processes in which the data participates. A significant challange is to be able to specify the processes along with the data, in an integrated way.

One direction is taken by Dampney (1989) in the specification of the possible states occupied by a data object and the permitted state transitions. The work represents the objects in a particular state as a subset of a domain containing all such objects. The subsets form a type hierarchy, which is represented by an extension of Entity-Relationship modelling. The transitions among states are modelled as finite state machines using an integrated graphical tool based on Jackson's Communicating Sequential Processes. The static ERA model can be transformed into the CSP model, and vice versa.

Another direction is taken by Rolland (Lingat *et al.* 1987a, b). The static objects are modelled by relations, and the dynamic aspects by operations, which are elementary actions on objects and events. An event is an elementary state change triggering one or more operations. Temporal aspects of the application are also taken into account.

Finally, processes can be modelled as explicit functional relationships between relations, expressed in clausal logic.

Partitioning and Integration

Highlighted by the integration of process into information systems specifications is the problem of partitioning and integration. Any system should have a specification which is simple at any grain of observation. If an aspect has no viewpoint in which it is simply specified, then it is very difficult to satisfy oneself that it is correct. (If you can't understand it, it is probably wrong.) The notion of hierarchical decomposition is highly developed in specifications of process, but it is very difficult to decompose data base schemas. If several analysts must cooperate in producing a schema, they normally are assigned to different parts of the organization being automated, each developing independent schemas, which then must be patched together.

Re-Use of Specifications

It is becoming clear that the main way software engineering can make significant efficiency improvement in the software development process is by facilitating re-use of elements of previous systems. Since it is becoming more and more possible to generate code from the specification of an information system, re-use is coming to mean re-use of specifications.

Suppose one has a library of a large number of specifications, and a new problem. How does one find which specifications in the library are relevant candidates for modification to suit the new requirement? The problem seems to be related to the partial match retrieval problem in data bases, and to the general information retrieval problem (Salton 1989). One would produce a partial specification which would form the basis for a query on the library management system, which would return candidates for adaptation.

There are at least two ways to match. One matches on the semantics: systems related to the customer relation, for example. The other makes a deeper match on the structure of the system, so that a system for processing an accounts payable relation might be relevant to an insurance policy management application.

3. SPECIFICATION AND MAINTENANCE OF KNOWLEDGE

Data base technology, embodied in the Knowledge Dictionary (Jansen and Compton 1988), has been very useful in the specification and management of propositional knowledge bases. Similar technology is applicable to the development of tools, based on the Debenham knowledge analysis method (Debenham 1989, Lindley 1990), to manage knowledge in Horn clause form. Knowledge can be added to conventional data bases by an enhancement of a data dictionary schema to accommodate knowledge expressed as rules and defined in terms of existing data base domains and relations.

Knowledge systems are software systems, so the traditional software engineering issues of partitioning, integration and re-use arise. Since we are using information analysis methods to analyse and manage knowledge, it would seem that these problems are closely related to the analogous problems in information systems specification engineering, as discussed above.

Another problem is the formalization of different knowledge representation schemes and their interrelation. For example, Jansen and Compton (1989) indicate how propositional knowledge can be expressed as production rules, then transformed to a frame system; while Colomb (1989) shows how to transform a set of propositional production rules into a decision table. The ability to perform transforms of this kind means that it becomes possible to express knowledge in a variety of ways for different purposes. In particular, it allows knowledge to be expressed in a form suitable for humans to understand and make changes, and then to be transformed into a form more convenient for computer processing.

4. SPECIFICATION OF HYPERTEXT

Hypertext systems are coming into use in the management of complex knowledge bases consisting of data, rules, numerical models and significant amounts of text. The knowledge base is not sufficiently structured that database technology can be directly used. One major research task is the identification and description of useful structure in the knowledge, and existing database and information analysis technology will be useful in that task.

Text based information retrieval systems assume very little structure. As a consequence, they are insufficiently reliable and do not support complex queries very well. However, the indexing and text management technologies used in information retrieval will be important in development of a knowledge management system.

Standard information retrieval systems have emerged from a library management culture, and so make very little assumption about the content of the information under management. In fact, the techniques work well for extremely heterogeneous text bases, such as the archives of a major newspaper. The knowledge to be managed by the system under discussion is more homogeneous in content, and should be of sufficient economic importance to justify a sort of editorial staff to add extra structure so as to be able to more reliably support more complex queries. An example of the kind of editorial input is that provided by publishers of taxation guides to accounting firms. The guides are based on the taxation legislation and records of cases decided by the Commissioner and courts. The publishers add extensive cross referencing, commentary and a controlled vocabulary index to make the metre-thick document usable. This additional structure will permit more complex queries.

The critical information technology research issues in the development of hypermedia systems to manage knowledge bases are:

- What questions are to be asked?

- What structures need to be built in the knowledge to support systems to answer those questions?

- What techniques are to be used to construct such systems economically?

In our work so far on this problem (Jansen 1989, Colomb and Jones 1989), we have been attempting to relate quite definite terms such as parameters in simulation models or questions in an expert system to the research papers which explain the meaning and significance of these terms in their scientific context. Since the semantic gap between the two is very great, we have introduced an intermediate form of knowledge consisting of the assertions (statements of fact or conclusion) made in the research papers. This intermediate form gives the system internal structure, so that we are able to link the definite terms to the assertions and then link the assertions to the research papers.

Conceptual models also appear to be an important element. A major research issue is how to specify the structure to be extracted from the knowledge so that systems can be built to make this knowledge accessible to people specialized in neither the knowledge domain or the access technology. In particular, the structure schemas must be independent of any particular implementation. It is probable that conceptual graphs (Sowa 1984, Garner and Tsui 1989) will have a number of uses in this area.

Assuming that the use of assertions and conceptual models turn out to be useful in creating the additional structure needed for these hypertext systems, a number of technological questions arise:

- How to economically produce these assertions. Techniques of automatic abstracting (Salton 1989, Jones 1989) may be useful.

- Application of knowledge analysis techniques (above) to the knowledge represented in the assertion tables.

- Use of text analysis tools (Salton 1989) to understand the structures of the documents and to find the important terms in them.

- How to relate the controlled vocabulary in the conceptual graphs to the actual text and to the structures derived from it.

- Investigation of the relation among the assertions, especially the results of the use of knowledge analysis methods, the conceptual graphs and conventional data dictionary technology applied to the definite terms and data in the system.

- These systems will necessarily be implemented in a highly distributed way, by many separate organizations which cooperate in different ways at different times. This is the domain of the new standards process of open distributed processing. An important question is how to manage the vocabulary used so that the different processes can agree on what they are communicating about (Colomb 1990b).

5. USE OF THE RELATIONAL ALGEBRA IN PROGRAMMING

The relational operations lend themselves to high speed implementations in specialized hardware (Allen *et al.* 1986, Colomb and Allen 1989, Jayasooriah *et al.* 1986). These implementations are particularly effective for relations with on the order of 10,000 tuples. If relational operations can be used to specify programs in areas not traditionally considered data base problems, there are gains both from the increased grain size of elementary operation and from rapid execution.

One area of research is the expression of algorithms as progressive refinements of sets with certain properties. Algorithms exist for searching tables on a wide variety of conditions (Kohonen 1980, Colomb 1987a), for complex relational operations (Colomb 1987b), and for pattern recognition techniques (Colomb 1988). We expect there to be applications of such algorithms in making of incremental changes in a complex structure.

Another application is set-at-a-time logical inference systems. A simple example is the transformation of a set of propositional production rules into a decision table (Colomb 1989). Most expert systems which have been produced to date use variations of propositional production rules. The transformation algorithm itself uses progressive refinement of sets, while the decision table product is a set-at-a-time logical inference system. A performance improvement of two orders of magnitude has been achieved and another two or three orders of magnitude are possible with assist from content-addressable memory.

We speculate that similar techniques can be applied to somewhat stronger logic systems, so that a large fraction of non-propositional expert systems presently coded in general-purpose inferencing systems such as OPS-5 and Prolog could be translated into very much faster implementations, perhaps not fully automatically.

6. PROLOG

Prolog is a programming language whose underlying theory is closely related to relational data base theory, both being based on the predicate calculus. In particular, the key operation of unification is a generalization of the query. Unification is not exploited nearly so much as is possible in principle because it is a computationally expensive process in existing implementations. The availability of fast implementations of relational operations means that it is possible to construct Prolog systems which make much more use of unification, leading to simpler programs which execute faster.

In addition, it is natural to wish to process large data and knowledge bases using the deductive capability of Prolog, but most current implementations do not support data which persists beyond a single execution of a program. Prolog and data base technology must be brought together by the development of persistent implementations of Prolog (Colomb 1990a). This requires implementation techniques to manage large, dynamic, shared, persistent procedures.

7. NATURAL LANGUAGE KNOWLEDGE

Much knowledge exists in the form of documents expressed in natural language. Most queries are expressed initially in natural language. CD-ROM storage, optical character recognition and speech recognition systems are becoming available which greatly increase the need to be able to process natural language. The need is partly in assisting humans to identify key structures in text data bases, and partly in assisting humans to make meaningful and accurate queries on the available knowledge bases.

8. USER INTERFACE TO DATA BASE SYSTEMS

Large and complex data bases are becoming much more available to casual users who wish to make *ad hoc* queries. These users need help in finding out exactly what is available (e.g the Australian Bureau of Statistics maintains 300,000 distinct time series), and how to formulate queries. Dialog management systems based on data dictionaries, with the help of conceptual graphs and possibly some natural language capability, are necessary to enable meaningful access.

REFERENCES

ALLEN, M.W., JAYASOORIAH, and COLOMB, R.M. (1986) "AIM: a New Form of Processor and its Application to Partial Match Data Retrieval", *Ninth Australian Computer Science Conference*, Canberra, pp. 347-355.

COLOMB, R.M. (1987a) *Table Searching Using Bit Map Operations* Technical Report TR-FB-77-04 CSIRO Division of Information Technology, Sydney, Australia.

COLOMB, R.M. (1987b) *Relational Operations Using a Bit-Serial Word-Parallel Content Addressable Memory* Technical Report TR-FB-87-05 CSIRO Division of Information Technology, Sydney, Australia.

COLOMB, R.M. (1988) *Artificial Intelligence Applications for Hardware Table Searching* Technical Report TR-FB-88-07 CSIRO Division of Information Technology.

COLOMB, R.M. (1989) "Representation of Propositional Expert Systems as Decision Tables" *Proceedings 1989 Australian Joint Artificial Intelligence Conference*

COLOMB, R.M. (1990a) *Implementing Persistent Prolog* Ellis Horwood, U.K.

COLOMB, R.M. (1990b) "Information Modelling Issues in ODP" *Open Distributed Processing Workshop* Sydney University.

COLOMB, R.M. & ALLEN, M.W. (1989) "Architecture of the Column Computer" *Conference on Computing Systems and Information Technology*, Institution of Engineers, Australia.

COLOMB, R.M. and JONES, M. (1989) "Managing the Knowledge Needed to Manage the Greenhouse Effect" *CSIRO Greenhouse and Energy Conference* Australia.

DAMPNEY, C.N.G. (1989) "From ERA to CSP Denotation, : A Synthesis of Information System Static and Dynamic Methods" *Third Annual Conference on Tools for Information Processing*, Nantes, France.

DEBENHAM, J. (1989) *Knowledge Base Design* Prentice Hall.

GARNER, B.J. and TSUI, E. (1989) "Acquiring Knowledge for Natural Language Interfaces to Expert Systems" *Proceedings 1989 Australian Joint Artificial Intelligence Conference*

JANSEN, R. (1989) *A Demonstration of Hypermedia Technology Applied to a Problem in the Wool Industry* Technical Report TR-FD-89-05 CSIRO Division of Information Technology, Sydney, Australia

JANSEN, R. and COMPTON, P.J. (1988) "The Knowledge Dictionary: A Relational Tool for the Maintenance of Expert Systems" *Proceedings of the International Conference on Fifth Generation Computer Systems,* Tokyo, Japan.

JANSEN, R. and COMPTON, P.J. (1989) "The Knowledge Dictionary: Storing Different Knowledge Representations" *Proceedings Fifth Australian Conference on Applications of Expert Systems* University of Technology, Sydney, Australia

JAYASOORIAH, ALLEN, M.W., and COLOMB, R.M. (1986) "Attached Index Machine: A New Form of Coprocessor for Manipulating Bit Encoded Index Structures", *Proceedings 2nd Australian Computer Engineering Conference,* Sydney.

JONES, R. (1989) "The Aida Project: Research into Automatic Document Analysis" *First Australia-Japan Joint symposium on Natural Language Processing* University of Melbourne, Australia

KOHONEN, T. (1980) *Content-Addressable Memories* , Springer-Verlag

LINDLEY, C. (1990) "An Integrated Conceptual Model for Data, Information and Knowledge"*13th Australian Computer Science Conference, Melbourne*

LYNGAT, J.Y., NOBECOUNT, P., and ROLLAND, C (1987a) "Rubis: an extended relational system managing events. Part I: specification" *Information and Software Technology* vol 29, No. 9, pp 503-510.

LYNGAT, J.Y., NOBECOUNT, P., and ROLLAND, C (1987b) "Rubis: an extended relational system managing events. Part II Implementation" *Information and Software Technology* vol 29, No. 10, pp 523-530.

SALTON, G. (1989) *Automatic text processing* Addison-Wesley

SOWA, J.F. (1984) *Conceptual Structures: Information Processing in Mind and Machine* Addison Wesley.

USING MULTIPLE KNOWLEDGE BASES TO MODEL THE PRAGMATIC ASPECTS OF SPEECH ACTS

Ruddy Lelouche, Ph. D.

Department of Computer Science
Laval University
Québec, CANADA, G1K 7P4

Telephone: (1) (418) 656-2597
Telex: 051-31621 UNILAVAL QBC
Fax: (1) (418) 656-5902
E-mail: c/o 1170054@LAVALVX1.BITNET

Abstract

The pragmatic aspects of speech acts still have not been paid much attention by researchers. However, these aspects are very important in natural language practice. This is why our system [1]*, named PILÉFACE, is being developed to take into account the pragmatic aspects of French, taught as a foreign language: in the generation mode, the system is to produce utterances consistent with given communication situation and intention; in the analysis mode, it is to determine whether a given utterance is consistent with some predefined particular communication situation and intention. This paper shows the main decisions that were made in the system design, and describes the system architecture as a series of three modules, each of them having its own external knowledge base(s). A complete example is then presented in generation mode. Finally, we detail some characteristics of the prototypes that are presently implemented.*

1. INTRODUCTION.

Among the various areas of natural language processing, *pragmatic aspects of speech acts* still have not been paid systematic attention by artificial intelligence researchers (see [Wilks 1985] for instance) or by people interested in computer-assisted language learning (see the review by Higgins [1984]). However, Diane Huot, a lin-

[1] This research has been financially supported by the FCAR Fund (Fonds pour la Formation des Chercheurs et l'Aide à la Recherche) of the Province of Quebec, Canada, thanks to the Grant 87-EQ-3506.

guistics and language didactics professor at Laval University, who is now an important member in our team, expressed a need for a computer program that could take into account the pragmatic aspect (i.e. the elements that reflect the social, spacio-temporal, cultural, relational, psychological, and affective aspects of a verbal exchange) of speech acts in foreign language teaching, in her case French as a second language. Independently of educational systems, pragmatic aspects are very important in natural language practice, since they usually allow a person to understand many things that are not explicitly said in a conversation, whether that person takes part in the conversation or not. Besides, *implicit information processing* can be viewed as a more general challenge in the development of artificial intelligence systems dealing with incomplete or imprecise knowledge [Zarri & al. 1983].

In order to try to fill this gap, we are developing a system, the exact purpose of which will be described in section 2. Section 3 will then present the data organization, i.e. how the problem at hand is specified, which will lead us in section 4 to describe how these various pieces of data and knowledge are handled, i.e. the program organization. In section 5, we show on a complete example how a given situation and a given intention are used to generate a semantically and pragmatically adequate production. Finally, the last section presents our implemented prototypes.

2. PURPOSE OF THE PILÉFACE SYSTEM.

Our system, named *PILÉFACE* for "Programme Intelligent pour les Langues Étrangères Favorisant l'Approche Communicative de l'Enseignement" (Intelligent Program for Foreign Languages Fostering the Communicative Approach to Teaching), is then being developed to take into account the pragmatic aspects of French, taught as a foreign language. Here, we shall focus our discussion on the linguistic goal of PILÉFACE, which is to take into account the pragmatic aspects of speech acts. The complete bases and goals of the expected system are presented in [Lelouche & Huot 1985]; they are derived from the communicative approach to language teaching and learning [Huot & al. 1984, Hymes 1984].

In the *generation mode*, the system is to produce *utterances* consistent with the *communication situation* (the speaker's or input context) as well as with the *communication intention* (greeting someone, asking something, excusing oneself, etc.); in the *analysis mode*, the system should determine and justify how an utterance, proposed by a student for instance, is consistent with some predefined particular communication situation and intention. Figure 1 illustrates these two modes (there is a third mode, the tutoring mode [Lelouche 1988], which is outside the scope of this paper).

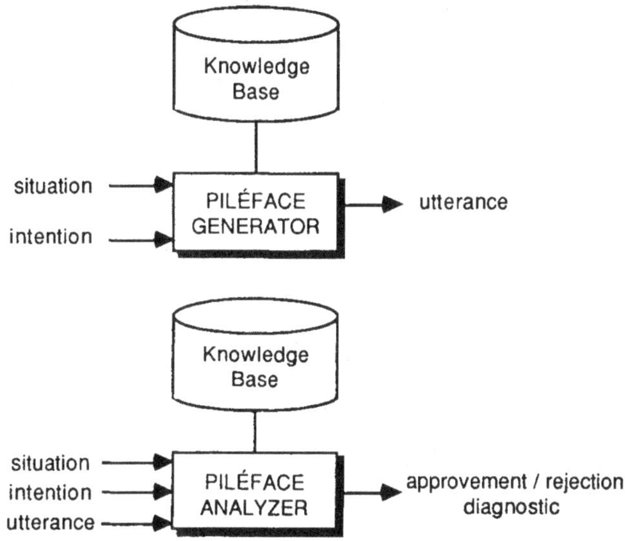

Figure 1. - Two uses of the PILÉFACE system

3. DATA ORGANIZATION: PROBLEM SPECIFICATION.

The first difficulty we had to address was the *specification* of the problem data , i.e. the complete description of the communication intention, the communication situation, and the corresponding utterance.

3.1 Communication intention.

The *communication intention* is clearly specified. Indeed, we had to restrict the expertise domain of our system [Hayes-Roth & al. 1983] and, in order to abide by the communicative approach principles, we chose the communication intention as the criterion used to do so. Therefore, in its first version we restricted our system to adequately deal with the intention of *greeting someone*, and the intention is presently a system constant.

3.2 Communication situation.

To describe the *communication situation*, we developed a model (the interested reader is refered to [Lelouche 1986] for more details) that:

- *separates* the elements describing the scene, hereafter called situation parameters, from the social, cultural, affective, psychological, and economic elements associated to it;
- *is adaptable* to describe various kinds of scenes, with various levels of precision or fuzziness, and various types of insights: each parameter may have a null, an approximative, or a structured value ;
- distinguishes *general parameters* (only one instance for a given particular situation) that are mostly spacio-temporal indications, from *individual parameters* (one instance per actor or character) that determine the identification and the social status of the character, as well as the various roles (real or fictitious) he might play; in particular, our model also takes into account situations involving roles like "X believes that Y thinks that ..." (loaned role) or "X wants Y to believe that ..."(borrowed role);
- takes into account the fact that *the role parameters are directed* in general: X may play a different role towards Y than towards Z.[2]

Indeed, the main interest of the proposed model is the first one mentioned, namely the separation it makes between the parameters used to describe the scene, that are fed into the system for each session, and the general knowledge associated to them, that is

---

[2] We are presently working on a model where this directivity is actually what distinguishes roles (directed towards another actor) from statuses (undirected, or directed towards every other actor).

independant from the scene and stored in external knowledge bases. This knowledge is necessary to fully interpret the implications of the scene parameters and to make proper inferences from them. Figures 2, 3, and 4 describe the parameters or groups or parameters we have identified to describe the scene, as well as the general external knowledge associated to each group.

PARAMETER	ASSOCIATED KNOWLEDGE
Continent	Links with cultures, traditions, etc. (for each continent considered in the application).
Country	Links with cultures, traditions, etc. (for each country considered in the application).
Region	Links with cultures, traditions, etc. (for each region considered in the application).
City or town	Links with cultures, traditions, etc. (for each city or town considered in the application).
Kind of building	Expected privacy level of the building. Socio-professional activities associated to it.
Site (room)	Expected privacy level of the room. Ex: office ≠ corridor ≠ cafeteria (even in the same building); kitchen ≠ living room ≠ bedroom.

Figure 2. - Spatial parameters

PARAMETER	ASSOCIATED KNOWLEDGE
Year	Events that may be associated with particular years.
Period of the year	Taxonomy of the year divisions (months and seasons). Corresponding climates and their socio-economical implications. Vacation periods, legal days-off, and their social implications.
Day	Day of the week. Working days and recess days.
Moment (hour of the day)	Working hours, coffee-breaks, ... Usual social activities (meal time, rest time, party time, etc.).

Figure 3. - Temporal parameters

PARAMETER		ASSOCIATED KNOWLEDGE
Identification (name, first name, ...)		Family or cultural meaning of the patronymic name (if any).
Statuses	Age	Socio-economical roles of the different age groups (*) ("young", "teenager", "elderly", etc.).
	Sex	Respective socio-cultural roles of men and women (*).
	Social status	Taxonomy of the various socio-professional categories (*). Social implications. Concept of "social level" (*). Definition of the links between a socio-professional categ. name, the corresponding work duty, ant the corresponding title (if any)
Roles	Relational role	Definition and taxonomy of family relationships. Definition and taxonomy of social and professional relationships (boss, employee, colleague, servant, teacher, etc.). Corresponding social implications (*).
	Affective role	Definition and taxonomy of feelings between two individuals - at a specified moment - in general (comradship, friendship, love, intimacy, hate, etc.).
	Psycho-logical role	Definition of various characters that an individual may exhibit - at a specified moment - in general (shyness, aggressiveness, tolerance, humour, etc.). Relationships between these characteristics (ex: introversion ≠ extroversion). Corresponding behavioral and psycho-social implications.
(*) may vary according to the culture specified by the spatial parameters		

Figure 4. - Individual parameters

3.3 Utterance.

The third and last component of the problem data is the *utterance* that is used to express the communication intention, here greeting someone. Utterances are described by a formal BNF-type grammar as well as by particular sets of rules of different kinds: *syntactic* (agreement rules for instance), *semantic*, and *pragmatic*, to make the utterance components relevant to the situation. For example, our grammar specifies three main components for a greeting utterance: a *greeting formula* like "good morning", "good evening", "hello", "hi", etc. (only the greeting formula is mandatory), an *addressing term* like "Sir", "Mr. Professor", a first name, "my dear friend", "honey", "you", etc., and an *inquiry* like "how are you?', "OK?", "How is your flu?", etc.. All this knowledge is stored in another external base that is independant from the current problem resolution. Finally, we also have an external dictionary, the structure of which is definitely beyond the scope of this paper.

4. PROGRAM ORGANIZATION: REASONING MECHANISMS.

The organization of the programs constituting the PILÉFACE system, i.e. its reasoning mechanisms, results from two fundamental decisions concerning the flow of information (or data, or knowledge) between the communication situation and intention on one hand, and the adequate corresponding utterance(s) on the other. In order to simplify this presentation, unless otherwise specified, we now limit our discussion to the generation mode of the system.

4.1 Exchange style.

One decision is theoretic. It consists in distinguishing the linguistic aspects of the problem from the other: sociological, cultural, geographical, and psychological aspects. We thus defined an arbitrary border, called the *exchange style,* as a compulsory intermediate step of the system cognitive process. Its definition is based on the following criterion: if we had been interested in the pragmatics of the English or Spanish language, the rules generating the exchange style from the communication situation description (e.g. cultural and social behaviour rules) would have been unchanged, as long as we still consider an occidental culture. However, the rules using the exchange style to generate possible utterances (such as the rules to address the person as *tu* or *vous*, or the various syntactic agreement rules) would have to be modified according to the selected goal language. That distinction led us to realize that some situation parameters influence the exchange style, whereas others do not.

At present, the exchange style is made of two ordinal variables:

- The *exchange style level* may take one of the following values:

- "polite", when the situation imposes some specific social behavior rules to be respected;
- "respectful", when in addition to politeness, further respect towards the addressee must be shown;
- "familiar", when free expression is possible, without unnecessary social constraints.

• The *personalization index* may take one of the following values:
  - "0": impossible to be familiar in the specified context;
  - "1": some familiarity is possible, without intimacy;
  - "2": possible reference to the addressee's intimacy.

4.2 Summarized context.

The second decision is *empirical.* It consists in extracting from the description of the communication situation (complete and possibly complex) some information that is perceived to be necessary and sufficient to define the exchange style. The main reasons for this decision are to describe the current situation with a higher, more general abstraction level [Lenat & al. 1979], and to circumvene the combinatorial explosion, which is a well known pitfall in the design of expert systems [Hayes-Roth & al. 1983]. The extracted information constitutes the *summarized context.* It is made of only four variables, each of which having a finite number of ordered values:

• the *degree of mutual acquaintance* between the speaker and the addressee: its value is 0 in case of poor or no acquaintance, 1 in case of good acquaintance, and 2 in case of very good acquaintance;

• the *degree of freedom* : its possible values are the same as the personalization index, with the same meaning;

• the *relative social level* of the speaker, which may take one of the following values:
  - "–" when the speaker's social level is inferior to the addressee's,
  - "+" when the speaker's social level is superior or equal to the addressee's, or when this variable is unknown or not relevant to the situation;

• the *degree of intensity* of the exchange; it may take one of the following values:
  - "-1" (negative): the speaker had rather not communicate, but is forced to by the circumstances,

- "0" (neutral): the intention to communicate corresponds to usual practice, but is not personalized,
- "+1" (positive): the intention to communicate is positively personalized.

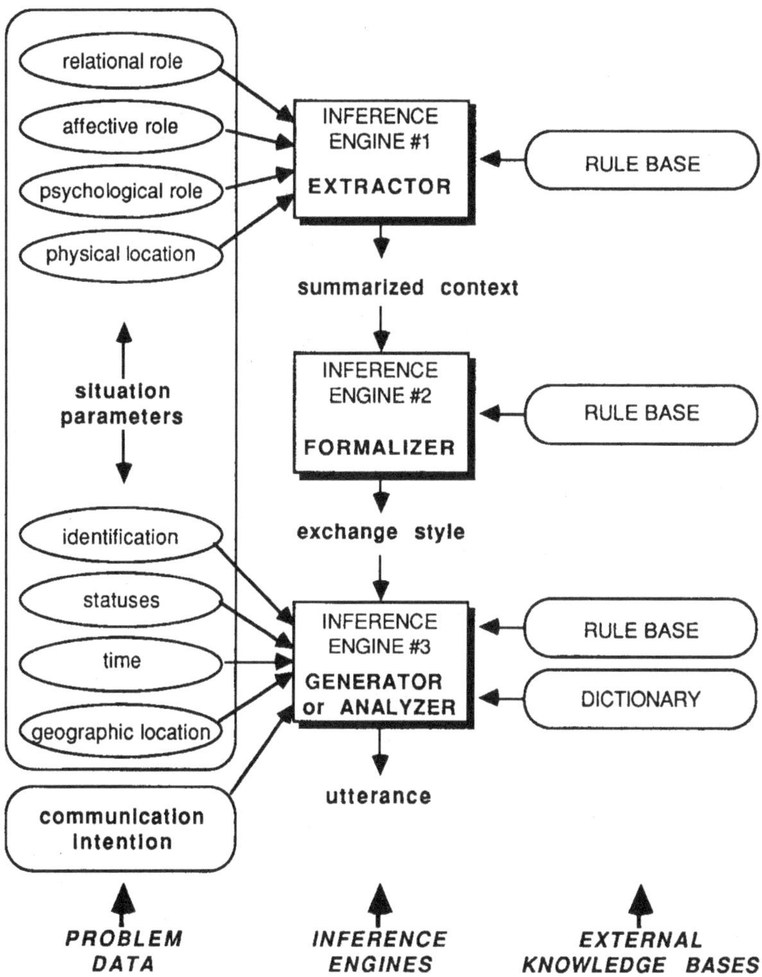

Figure 5. - The three inference engines

4.3 Three serial modules.

The existence of at least these two intermediate steps, i.e. the summarized context and the exchange style, between the situation description and the utterance to be produced or analyzed, led us to model the cognitive process of PILÉFACE as a serial set of three different *inference engines* as shown on figure 5. The first engine, the *extractor*, must produce the summarized context from the communication situation. The second engine, the *formalizer*, has to produce the exchange style from the summarized context. Finally, the third engine depends on the used mode: in generation mode, the *generator* has to produce utterances that are relevant to the situation, and in analysis mode, the *analyzer* has to diagnose whether the input utterance is relevant to the situation. At present, we only implemented the formalizer, the generator, and the analyzer. A fundamental theoretic study in linguistics is in progress to define and model the various situation parameters and their interrelations, so that we could, starting with a (possibly very complex) situation description, build automatically the summarized context.

5. A COMPLETE EXAMPLE.

In order to illustrate our approach, we now discuss a complete example in generation mode.

5.1 Problem statement.

In this example, the computer program acts as the addressee and presents the following situation description to the student playing the speaker's role:

> *I am your professor, French, male, strict, and distant. You are a freshman, quite shy, and you meet me in a hallway of the Computer Science Department building at Laval University, at the end of September* [3]*, on a recess afternoon. You are with friends whom you want to impress; you would like*

---

[3] In North-American universities, the academic year begins in September.

to greet me in order to show your friends that you already know me well, and that I also already know you. What would you say ?

5.2 Formal and complete description of the situation.

We can extract the following parameter values from the situation stated above. At present, this extraction is planned to be made manually, i.e. the situation will be directly expressed to the extractor in terms of these parameters.

Spatial parameters:

Continent:	North America (or Canada)
Country:	Canada, Québec
Region:	Québec City region
City:	Québec City (or Sainte-Foy, a suburb city of Quebec City)
Building:	Laval University, Computer Science Department building
Site:	hallway

Temporal parameters:

Year:	-
Period:	end of September
Day:	recess day
Moment:	in the afternoon

Addressee (character C1):

Identification:	Identity = addressee
	Name = -
Statuses:	Age = -
	Sex = male
	Social status = university professor
Absolute roles:	Relational role = professor (of C2), French
	Affective role = -
	Psychological role = strict, distant

Speaker (character C2):

Identification:	Identity = speaker		
	Name = -		
Statuses	Age = -		
	Sex = -		
	Social status = -		
Absolute roles:	Relational role = student (of C1), freshman		
	Affective role = friend (of C3)		
	Psychological role = quite shy		
Borrowed roles towards C3:		Relational role:	C2 knows C1 well
		Relational role:	C1 knows C2

Friends (passive character C3)

Identification:	Identity = friends
	Name = -
Statuses	Age = -
	Sex = -
	Social status = -
Absolute roles:	Relational role = -
	Affective role = friend (of C2)
	Psychological role = -

5.3 Description of the summarized context.

According to the model presented in section 2.4, the corresponding summarized context is the following:

degree of mutual acquaintance:	0 (weak) or 1 (good)
degree of freedom:	0 (no freedom)
relative social level:	"–" (inferiority)
degree of intensity:	1 (positive)

This summarized context will have to be generated by the extractor (when it is automated) from the complete formal situation description given in section 5.2. As it can be seen, the summarized context is made of a minimal information needed, in generation mode to force the semantic and pragmatic agreement of the generated utterances with the situation, or in analysis mode to diagnose whether the input proposed utterance agrees with the situation. We would have got the same summarized context if the situation had been one where the speaker is a job applicant taking an interview.

5.4 Description of the exchange style.

The summarized context stated above leads to the following exchange style:

exchange style level:	"respectful"
personalization index:	1 (some familiarity is possible)

This exchange style can actually be generated from the previous summarized context by our implemented formalizer (inference engine #2). In the present case, the exchange style level value results from the "null" degree of freedom and the "inferiority" relative social level, while the personalization index value results from the "positive" degree of intensity in the summarized context.

5.5 A possible utterance.

In the exchange style that is obtained, one might find some apparent contradiction between the exchange style level and the personalization index, which both are derived from the problem statement given in section 5.1. It is the responsibility of the inference engine #3 (the generator or the analyzer, depending on the used mode) to eliminate this inconsistency. Its implemented reasoning mechanism is the following. First, the exchange style level *requires* to use a relatively sophisticated language, as well as a respectful adressing term. The possible familiarity (personalization index) *may* therefore only be taken into account by an adequate inquiry (which then becomes compulsory). Consequently, the generator will only generate (and the analyzer will only accept) utterances that meet these two conditions. A possible utterance could thus be:

Bonjour Monsieur le professeur ! Comment allez-vous ?
Good afternoon Mr. professor! How are you?

6. IMPLEMENTATION ISSUES AND RESULTS.

6.1 Two prototypes.

So far, we have developed two prototypes (in Prolog). In both of them, the input situation is given as a summarized context; however, we are currently working on the linguistics study mentioned in 4.3 so that we can then implement the extractor and complete these prototypes. The first prototype, named *PILÉFACE-Generation*, generates utterances that are semantically acceptable and pragmatically plausible with respect to the information provided in the summarized context (in particular the speaker's and adressee's descriptions), as well as to the communication intention (here greeting the addressee). The second prototype, named *PILÉFACE-Analysis*, takes an utterance and a summarized context as input, and produces a diagnostic to determine whether this utterance is adequate or should be rejected; it also justifies its diagnostic, identifying syntactic, semantic, or pragmatic errors. The first results obtained with these two prototypes are fairly hopeful, and we believe that our approach is a promising one.

6.2 Weaknesses of the implementation.

However, our present prototypes still suffer from two minor drawbacks concerning modelling as well as implementation issues.

First, our model still does not deal correctly with *intimacy* : at present, we only identify intimacy with a strong mutual acquaintance (which led our prototype to generate unexpected and funny utterances). Also our model ignores the *speaker's mood* (humour, irony, desire to hurt, etc.) or the influence of his *personality* on the utterance to be generated. We shall soon redefine the summarized context components in order to explicitly consider these aspects.

Secondly, from an implementation point of view, our prototypes were developed for demonstration purposes: the dictionary was not an aspect to be focused upon, and thus we developed a small lexicon specifically for the greeting act. Therefore that lexicon cannot be used for other communication intentions. We are currently working on developing a dictionary independant on the intended intention. With such a dictionary, utterances referring to the greeting act would be identified by a particular syntax as well as particular semantic features, rather than by a specific ad-hoc dictionary or lexicon.

CONCLUSION: STRONG POINTS OF OUR MODEL.

In spite of the weaknesses of our present implementation, we believe that our model has definitely a few strong points.

A first strength is the introduction of the *exchange style*, that separates the pragmatic aspects about the world from the ones truly concerning the language used. As a result, the tasks to be performed by two engines out of three, namely the extractor and the formalizer, are independant of the selected processing mode (generation or analysis).

Secondly, by introducing the *summarized context* concept, we were able to obtain some significant results without needing to wait for the outcome of the theoretical study in fundamental linguistics that is still in progress.

Thirdly, by considering a *three-engine architecture*, we may easily adopt, if the need arises, a distinct representation language (and thus a different tool) for each engine as well as for its associated external knowledge base. Such a choice could be justified by the different nature of the knowledge used by each of the processes and of the types of inferences to be made.

Finally, another point to stress, which revealed to be a major strength in the modelling phase, is certainly the *interdisciplinary aspect* of the developing team. This is why I want to end this article in thanking my collegue Diane Huot, our expert in linguistics and in language teaching, for her fruitful collaboration.

REFERENCES.

Hayes-Roth F., Waterman D. A., Lenat D. B., eds. (1983): *Building Expert Systems*. Addison-Wesley (Reading, Mass., U.S.A.).

Higgins J. & Johns T. (1984): *Computers in Language Learning*. Collins ELT (London, England) & Addison-Wesley (Reading, Mass., U.S.A.).

Huot D., Girard C., Lussier D. (1984): "L'évaluation de la compétence de communication en classe de langue seconde" (Assessment of the Communication Competence in a Second Language Classroom). *Etudes de Linguistique Appliquée*, Nº 56, Octobre-Décembre 1984, pp. 77-87.

Hymes D. H. (1984): *Vers la Compétence de Communication* (Towards Communication Competence). Hatier (Paris, France), Nov. 1984.

Lelouche R., D. Huot (1985): *Fondements et objectifs d'un système intelligent pour l'apprentissage des langues* (Bases and Goals of an Intelligent System for Language Learning). Research report DIUL-RR-8506, Computer Science Department, Laval University (Québec, Canada), May 85, 42 p.

Lelouche R. (1986), "Quelques aperçus sur la modélisation de la description statique d'une scène" (Some issues on modelling a scene static description). *CIIAM 86, Proc. of the second International Conf. on Artificial Intelligence*, Marseille (France), 1-5 Dec. 1986, pp. 121-139.

Lelouche R. (1988) "Approches théorique et empirique dans la conception des systèmes d'E.I.A.O. - Une étude de cas: le système PILÉFACE" (Theoretic and empirical approaches in the design of intelligent tutoring systems - A case study: the PILÉFACE system). *ITS-88, Proc. of the International Conference on Intelligent Tutoring Systems*, Université de Montréal (Montréal, Canada), 1-3 June 1988, pp. 469-476.

Lenat D., Hayes-Roth F., Klahr P. (1979) *Cognitive Economy*. Working paper HPP-79-15, Stanford Heuristic Programming Project, Stanford University (Stanford, California), June 1979, 46 p.

Zarri G. P., Lelouche R., Ornato M., Faribault M., Meissonnier V., Leon J. (1983): *Réalisations pratiques et Développements théoriques dans le Cadre d'un Système I.A. pour Bases de Données biographiques* (Practical realizations and theoretical developments in the scope of an A.I. system for biographical databases). Rapport LISH/363, Laboratoire d'Informatique pour les Sciences de l'Homme (Paris, France), Juillet 1983.

Wilks Y. (1985) *Relevance, Points of View and Speech Acts: an Artificial Intelligence View*. Research Paper MCCS-85-25, Computing Research Laboratory, New Mexico State University (New Mexico, Arizona), 24 p.

On Enhancements of Semantic Methodologies for Relational Database Design

Maria E. Orlowska and Yanchun Zhang

Key Centre for Software Technology
Department of Computer Science
University of Queensland
St. Lucia, Q.4067
Australia

Email: maria@uqcspe.uq.oz.au

ABSTRACT

We describe a tool system (ESM) for detection of unwanted properties (such as implied fact types) of a conceptual schema and show how the system supports the design process. The system uses a rigorous, information-content-preserving approach to schema transformation, but combines it with heuristic and user interaction. We show how normalization techniques, particularly the synthesis method originally developed to produce an initial relational schema from functional dependencies, apply in the redesign of NIAM conceptual schemas. We present our approach for identifying redundant relationships and to show how relationship inference can be supported by user interaction which removes many of the unavoidable errors in the design process. The system is under implementation in the Key Centre for Software Technology at University of Queensland, using Turbo Pascal 5.5 on IBM PS2, and then it will be tested for large database design projects.

Keywords: NIAM Conceptual Schema, Fact Type, Functional Dependency, Synthesis approach, Transformation

1. INTRODUCTION

The problem of designing a relational database for an information system is a complex one; it involves the analysis of an informal, and often incomplete, statement about some enterprise and then formal application of the established theories.

In general, we focus on enhancements of existing information systems modelling methods by a development of computer-based tools for the design of conceptual schemata for large systems, and finally the design of high quality relational databases.

We describe a tool system (ESM) for detection of unwanted properties (such as implied fact types) of a conceptual schema and show how the system supports the design process. The system uses a rigorous, information-content-preserving approach to schema transformation, but combines it with heuristic and user interaction. We show how normalization techniques, particularly the synthesis method originally developed to produce an initial relational schema from functional dependencies, apply in the redesign of NIAM conceptual schemas. The redesign task is important in modifications of a schema towards minimization of knowledge representation for a particular application. We present our approach for identifying redundant relationships and to show how relationship inference can be supported by user interaction which remove many unavoidable errors in the design process. The system architecture is described in Figure 1.

In this paper, we provide an enhancement on the synthesis approach in Section 2 and review the structure of NIAM conceptual schema in Section 3. We consider the detection of the implied fact types in Section 4. The redesign of NIAM conceptual schemas and the design of relational database schemas are presented in Section 5, and conclusions presented in Section 6.

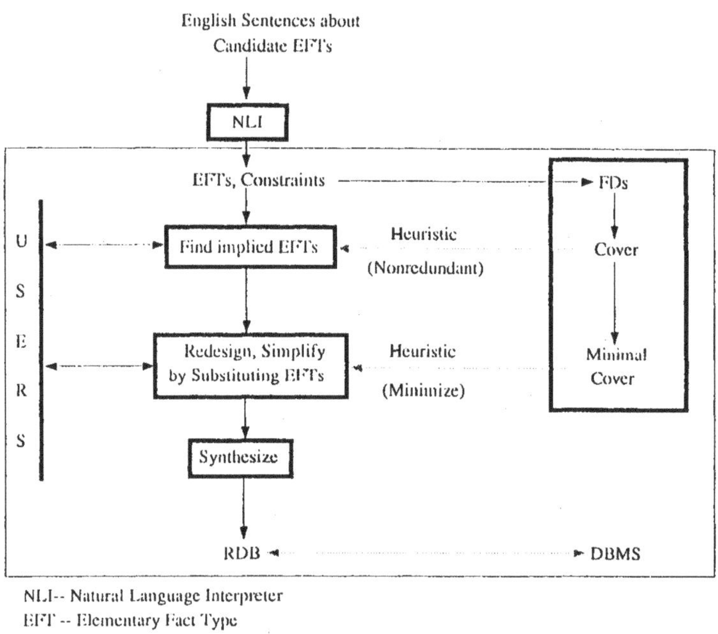

Figure 1: System Architecture of the ESM

2. The Synthesis approach to design relational database schemas

Normalization in many cases can be viewed as the next level of an analysis which is applied on some conceptual model like the Entity-Relationship model [3] or the Universal Relation [6]. Normalization is the process of removing redundancies from the initial Relational Data Base Model (RDB) which uses ideas from the relational theory such as functional dependencies (FDs) and multivalued dependencies (MVD) [6].

For relational database design, there are some synthesis algorithms available in the literature [1, 2, 7, 9-13]. In the synthesis approach pioneered by Bernstein, relations are created directly from the set of FDs. The core of the problem lies in determining the proper set of FDs that should be used. In general, this approach works well for FDs, but is not suitable for MVDs. The synthesis approach has been enhanced by several authors.

Most synthesis approaches produce one minimal cover and use it to generate relations in 3NF or in EKNF; however, the order in which the FDs are submitted to the synthesis algorithm may affect the minimal cover produced. In fact, different covers may be produced by reordering the FDs. To find some other minimal covers, the FDs need to be reordered in all possible distinct ways; however, this is extremely inefficient.

In this section, we briefly describe an enhancement of the traditional synthesis approaches. The notation used is adopted from [6]. X, Y, Z will be used to denote sets of attributes while A, B, C will be used to denote individual attributes. An FD, represented as $X \rightarrow Y$, describes a logical association between two sets of attributes, X and Y. Thus, FDs act as structure descriptors as well as integrity constraints.

Let R be a relation schema. If F and T are two sets of functional dependencies for R, we say that F covers T (and vice versa) if the closures of F and T are equal. The closure of a set of attributes X with respect to a set of FDs F will be denoted by $X_F{}^+$. It is the set of all attributes derived from X using the FDs in F and Armstrong's axioms. F, G, H will be used to denote sets of FDs.

Given a set of FDs, it is possible that some FDs are implied by others. Bernstein's synthesis approach tries to eliminate all such FDs. The final set of FDs thus derived constitutes a minimal cover, which is then used for synthesizing relations in 3NF. A minimal cover for a set of FDs is defined as follows [1]:

(1). every right side of a dependency in F is a single attribute;

(2). for no $X \rightarrow Y$ in F is the set $F - \{X \rightarrow Y\}$ equivalent to F;

(3). for no $X \rightarrow A$ in F and proper subset Z of X is $(F - \{X \rightarrow A\}) \cup \{Z \rightarrow A\}$ equivalent to F.

Intuitively, (2) guarantees that no dependency in F is redundant, and (3) guarantees that no attribute on any left side is redundant. Since every right side has a single attribute, no attribute on the right side is redundant.

However, a given set of FDs (F) may have more than one cover. In turn, differences between minimal covers may, in fact, produce different relation schemes.

Here we propose a modified approach SYNTHESIZER+, based on SYNTHESIZER[12, 13], to provide more minimal covers, and the tool also includes several heuristics to aid the design of relational databases. The algorithm, SYNTHESIZER+, is described as follows [7]:

Input: A set of FDs (F).

Output: 3NF relations.

Step 1: Eliminate extraneous attributes. Eliminate extraneous attributes from the left side of each FD in F producing the set G. An attribute is extraneous if its elimination does not affect the closure of the set of FDs.

Step 2: Check for redundant FDs. Delete duplicate FDs; delete FDs that have non-implied extraneous attributes on the LHS; mark all the FDs that are determined to be potentially redundant. Partition G into two sets H and H'. H is the basic cover that contains all non-redundant FDs and H' contains FDs that are found to be potentially redundant.

Step 3a: Create {M: {R}} sets. Consider the set H' which consists of potentially redundant FDs. Consider an FD, X→A, from the set H'. Determine the effect of removing X→A from the set G on the redundancy for all other FDs of the set H', thus creating the {M: {R}} sets. If removal of X→A has no effect on any of remaining FDs in H', remove it from G.

Step 3b: Partition the {M: {R}}sets. Once all the {M: {R}} sets are identified, they are partitioned into mutually independent sets using the direct graphs.

Step 3c: Choose one minimal cover. From each independent cluster of {M: {R}} sets we choose one FD belonging to the M type of FDs. Use heuristics for making the choice. The FDs thus chosen are added to the basic set H thus creating a minimal cover.

Step 4: Partition. Partition the minimal cover into groups such that all FDs in each group have identical left hand sides.

Step 5: Construct relations. For each group, construct a relation consisting of all attributes appearing in that group. Each set of attributes that appears on the left side of any FD in the group is a key of the relation.

Step 6: Combine the relations with equivalent keys. Check the equivalent keys among the different relations. If R1 = (U1, K1) and R2 = (U2, K2) have the equivalent keys $k1 \in K1, k2 \in K2, k1 \equiv k2$, Combine them into one relation R12 with the attributes $U12 = U1 \cup U2$ and key set $K12 = K1 \cup K2$. Furthermore, check the redundancy of attributes in R12. If an attribute in the new relation is redundant with respect to other relations, delete it from the relation. For each group, construct a relation consisting of all the attributes appearing in that group. Each set of attributes that appears on the left side of any FD in a group is a key of the relation. The set of relations constructed constitutes a schema for a given set of FDs.

As a result, SYNTHESIZER+ aids in efficiently determining more minimal covers. The expert design heuristics have been incorporated in the tool. The modified synthesis algorithm SYNTHESIZER+ can also guarantee the minimality of the final relational database schema.

Theorem 1 [7]. With a set of FDs F as the input, the final relational database schema **R** produced by SYNTHESIZER+ has following properties:

1). **R** preserves the FDs in F.

2). Every relation scheme Ri in **R** is in 3NF with respect to F.

3). There is no database schema with fewer relation schemes than **R** satisfying properties 1 and 2.

3. NIJSSEN'S INFORMATION ANALYSIS METHOD (NIAM)

There is another recent development in which databases are based on some conceptual or semantic data model and implemented directly. This trend will enable users to do the conceptual design of their database in a conceptual data model and implement it directly. It avoids the overload of mapping to a conventional model at design time.

NIAM is a semantic approach for the construction of a Conceptual Model (CM) of information, totally free of implementation technology constraints. Hence it is concerned only with analysis. A systematic procedure - NIAM Conceptual Schema Design Procedure (CSDP) has been designed in [4] which allows users of the conceptual model to arrive at a NIAM conceptual schema for any UoD. Its attempt to map between the real world Universe of Discourse (UoD) and the information system in both directions through the environment of users is commendable. A transformation algorithm has been developed to map a Conceptual Model into an Optimal Normal Form (ONF) of a relational data model [5].

In the NIAM conceptual model, a NIAM conceptual schema consists of Elementary fact types, Entity types and subtypes, label types, nested fact types, constraints and validation rules [4, 5]. We will assume that reader is familiar with the basic idea of NIAM. For details, see [4].

Constraints or validation rules are conditions that ensure the consistency and integrity of the conceptual schema. The declarative constraints found in the NIAM conceptual schema are uniqueness constraints, mandatory constraints, exclusivity constraints, equality constraints and subset constraints.

Elementary fact types (represented by a concatenation of boxes representing roles) are used to represent facts about entity types, or associations between two or more entity types.

However, from a NIAM conceptual schema and by the ONF algorithm, the final relational database may not have the minimality required. It may not result in the highest quality RDB design [8].

4. DETECTING THE IMPLIED FACT TYPES

Our system can be considered as a module of a larger system which includes a natural language interpreter (NLI) [16]. But the focus of this paper will be on the system as independent one. The NLI assumes as input a collection of natural language sentences - candidates for elementary fact types. The output is a collection of elementary fact types with semantic constraints on them.

There are some theorems relating the constraints in elementary fact types to the data dependencies of elementary fact relations [5]. One of them is that if an elementary fact type FT has an intra-fact type uniqueness constraint which does not cover all roles, then a non-trivial FD X→Y exists in the corresponding elementary fact relation FR, where X is the set of reference roles of roles covered by the constraint and Y is the set of reference roles which are not covered by the constraint.

For a given set of FDs, the synthesis approach can be used to find a minimal cover and then to construct 3NF or EKNF relational database schema. For a set of fact types (FTs) with uniqueness constraints, there is a collection of FDs. In these FDs, there may be some redundant FDs. Only those FTs whose corresponding FDs are redundant may be derived. So we can use the synthesis approach as a heuristic tool to find the suspect fact types for the further checking of the derivability of fact types.

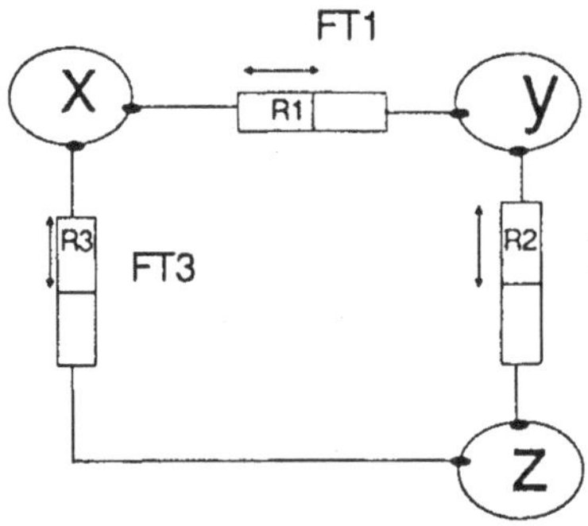

Figure 2: A NIAM Conceptual Schema

For instance, for the NIAM conceptual schema in Figure 2, there are three fact types FT1, FT2 and FT3.

FT1: Person X works in the Factory Y.

FT2: the Factory Y is located in the City Z.

FT3: Person X lives in the City Z.

Correspondingly, there are three FDs, X→Y, Y→Z, X→Z.

From the Armstrong axioms [1] and a purely formal approach, X→Z is redundant, since it is derivable from X→Y and Y→Z. In such a case, FT1 and FT2 are not derivable, since their corresponding FDs are not derivable. What we need is to check the derivability of FT3 since only FD3 (X→Z) is redundant. But the elementary fact type FT3 is not necessarily redundant, since it is not derivable from the other two fact types. In fact, another elementary fact type FT4,

Person X works in the City Z,

is redundant.

Since elementary fact types (EFT) carry more semantics than Functional Dependencies (FDs), the influence of semantic meaning is very important. In the relational theory, X→Z is only an indication of the functional dependency between X and Z, but there may be many interpretations of them. For example, X→Z may come from FT3 or FT4. Although X→Z is redundant, only FT4 is derivable. Therefore, we can use the dependency theory as a heuristic role to help designer/user to further check the derivability of fact types in the NIAM conceptual schema.

In order to generalize the above idea, given a NIAM conceptual schema, we first transform it into a graph G=(V, E) where V is a nonempty set of nodes and E is a nonempty set of arcs such that

(1) For every simple entity type A, there is a simple node labeled A,

(2) For every nested entity type X ($A_1A_2..A_n$), there is a compound node labeled X, and dotted arcs from X to A_1, A_2, A_n.

(3) For every n-ary fact Y ($A_1A_2..A_n$) whose uniqueness constraint covers whole roles, there is a compound node labeled Y, and dotted arcs from Y to $A_1, A_2,.., A_n$ and a full arc from Y to ϕ (ϕ is a new attribute),

(4) For every n-ary fact type whose uniqueness constraint covers n-1 roles ($A_1A_2..A_{n-1}$), there is a compound node (simple node if n=2) labeled X=$A_1A_2..A_{n-1}$), and a full arc from X to A_n.

From the transforming procedure above, the final graph has the same form of representation as that of an FD-graph. Correspondingly, if we treat the resultant graph as an FD-graph, we can use the synthesis algorithm to find redundant FDs. In this case, only those fact types corresponding to these redundant FDs may be derivable from other fact types. In order to find all the derived fact types in a NIAM conceptual schema, we can use dependency theory as heuristic tool, to identify the redundant FTs. Suppose that at the first stage, the set of information examples is significant and consistent. The consistency here means that if an entity is recorded in the examples, every role it plays in will be recorded. We devise an algorithm below to help the designer find the derived fact types in NIAM conceptual schema.

ALGORITHM DFT: Find derived fact types in NIAM Conceptual Schema.

INPUT: a NIAM conceptual schema NS and a set of information examples (fact type populations).

OUTPUT: a nonredundant NIAM conceptual schema (all derived fact types marked), and an FD-graph.

METHOD:

(1) Find the graph representation G for the NIAM conceptual schema.

(2) For every FDi (full arc <X, Y> in G (its corresponding fact type is FTi in NIAM conceptual schema), find the set S of all the FD-path from X to Y not including <X, Y>.

(2.1) If S = ∅, the Fact Type FT1 is underivable.

(2.2) If S ≠ ∅, let si ∈ S, si=[FD1, FD2, ..., FDn].

(2.2.1) For every si ∈ S, if $\prod_{j=1}^{j=n} pop$ (FTj)[X, Y] = pop(FTi), we present the fact path [X, Y] [FT1, FT2,..., FTj => FTi] (suspected deriving chain) to the user or designer and ask s/he to check the semantics to confirm whether it is derived or not.

If the user confirms it as derivable, we mark the fact type FTi derivable and simply delete the FDi in G.

Otherwise, the fact type FTi is underivable.

(3) Return the NIAM conceptual schema.

At the step 2, pop(FTi) represents the population of fact type FTi, $\prod$ is the natural join operation, T[X, Y] is the projection of fact type T on entities X and Y.

Example 1: For the NIAM conceptual schema in Figure 2, suppose the set of populations of Fact Types FT1, FT2 and FT3 below is significant and complete.

FT1

Person	Factory
s1	f1
s2	f2
s3	f1

FT2

Factory	City
f1	c1
f2	c2

FT3

Person	City
s1	c1
s2	c2
s3	c3

When we input a NIAM conceptual schema and its populations to the algorithm FDT, FT3 will be found underivable. Though FD3 is derivable from FD1 and FD2 (FD1, FD2 => FD3), pop(FT1) * pop(FT2)[Person, City] ≠ pop(FT3), FT3 is not derivable.

5. CONSTRUCT RELATIONAL SCHEMATA FROM niam CONCEPTUAL SCHEMATA

In the NIAM conceptual schema produced in Section 4, all fact types are elementary (reduced) and all derived fact types are identified. The next step is to design a relational database schema. In the synthesis approach, once a minimal cover for a set of FDs is found, the partition (or group) step is processed, and then a relation is constructed for each group. Coincidently, the group step of the ONF algorithm [3, 4] works in the same way as synthesis approach does for FDs.

The main steps of the ONF Algorithm are:

(1). For each fact type without a simple key, create a separate table. Select the shortest key of the fact type as primary key of the table.

(2). Group fact types with a simple key attached to a common object type into the same table with the primary key based on this object type.

(3). For each remaining fact type, create a separate table. Select a key of the fact type as the primary key of the table.

Example 2: Consider a UoD about a summer vacation course. The entities involved are students, courses, and computer accounts. Every student has an account, and every account belongs to a student. For every pair of student and course, there is a score indicating the student's grade for the course. The amount of time spent under a account for a particular course is also recorded. Let A stand for student names, E for course names, D for accounts, C for scores, B for computing time spent for every pair of account and course. Let R be a universal relation for this UoD, where U = {A, B, C, D, E } and F = { A→D, D→A, DE→B, AE→C}. Its conceptual schema in Figure 3 can be obtained through NIAM CSDP.

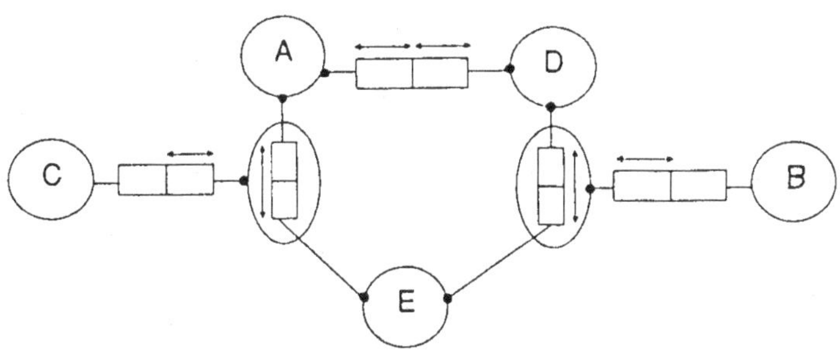

Figure 3: A Conceptual Schema of Example 2

From this conceptual schema, a relational database schema **R4** can be designed using the ONF algorithm, **R1** = { R1, R2, R3 }, where

R1 = (AD, {A, D}),

R2 = (DEB, {DE}) and

R3 = (AEC, {AE}).

Here, the relational database schema **R2** is in 3NF (in fact, in 5NF). In this example, the final relational database schema has 3 relations. When we reconsider the NIAM conceptual schema, we find the fact FT1 in Figure 4 has the same semantics as that of FT2 in Figure 5.

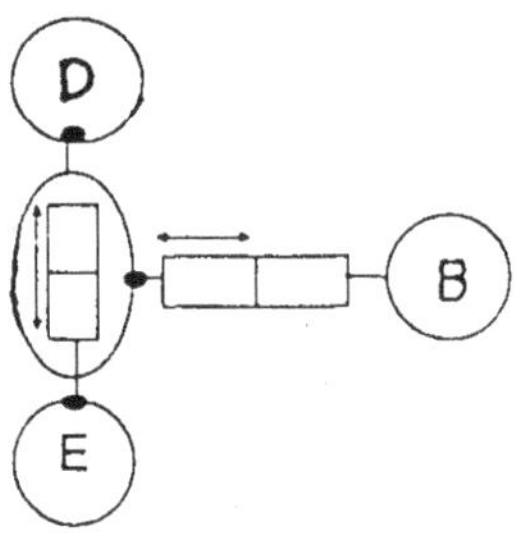

Figure 4: FT1

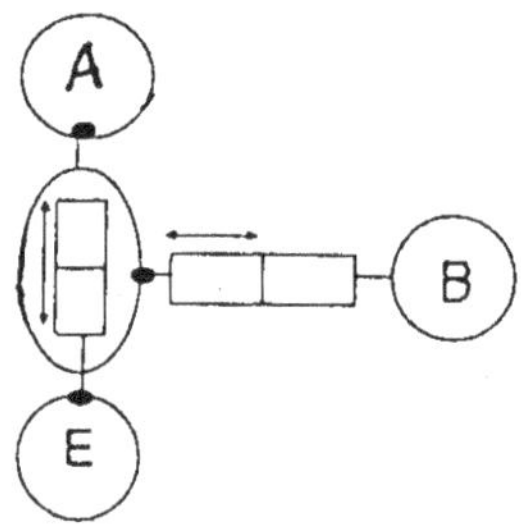

Figure 5: FT2

So, if we substitute the fact FT1 by FT2 in the conceptual schema, we will obtain another conceptual schema in Figure 6.

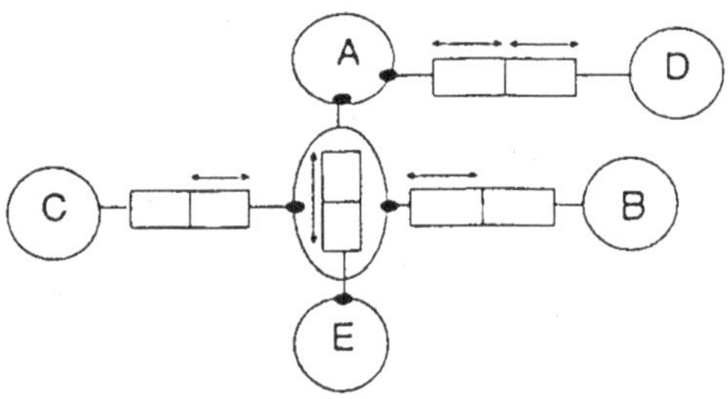

Figure 6: Another Conceptual Schema for Example 2

From this conceptual schema, by ONF algorithm, we can obtain the following relational database schema **R2**.

R1 = (AD, {A, D}),

R2 = (AEBC, {AE}).

This relational database schema has 2 relations. Obviously, it is preferred to **R1**, since it is minimal with respect to 3NF.

Our goal of schema design is to minimize the storage space that the base relations (files) occupy. Grouping of attributes into relation schemas has a significant effect on storage space. In order to design a relational database schema and to minimize the number of relations in the system, we consider the redesign of the NIAM conceptual schema by substituting some FTs by the new equivalent ones. Again, we use the synthesis approach as a heuristic tool to find the candidate FTs for substitution. And we also interact with the users since it will change some fact types. Finally, we use ONF algorithm to transform it to a 3NF relational database schema with fewer relations.

6. CONCLUSIONS

In this paper, we describe a system for enhamcements of semantic methodologies for relational database design. In order to design a well-formed NIAM conceptual schema, we can use dependency theory as heuristic tool to help the designer detect the derived fact types in the NIAM conceptual schema.

In order to design a minimal relational database schema, we can use dependency theory as a heuristic tool to find the candidate FTs for substitution and interact with the users to redesign the conceptual schema, then transform it into 3NF relational database schema with the minimal number of relations.

Currently, the proposed system is under implementation in the Key Centre for Software Technology at University of Queensland, using Turbo Pascal 5.5 on IBM PS2. The system is intended to be tested for large database design projects. For further research, we will investigate more constraints in NIAM conceptual schema to build systematic formulations for future implementation of the whole conceptual design procedure.

References

[1] P. A. Bernstein, Synthesising Third Normal Form Relations from Functional Dependencies, ACM Trans. on Database Design Systems 1, 277-297(1976).

[2] G. Ausillo, Graph Algorithms for Functional Dependencies Manipulation, JACM Vol 30, No.4, Oct 1984.

[3] P.P. Chen, The Entity-Relationship Model: Towards a Unified View of Data, ACM TODS 1, No.1

[4] G.M. Nijssen and T.A. Halpin, Conceptual schema and Relational Database Design: A Fact-Based Approach, Prentice Hall, 1989.

[5] C.M.R. Leung and G.M. Nijssen, Relational Database Design Using The NIAM Conceptual Schema, Inform. Systems Vol.13, No.2, pp219-227, 1988.

[6] Maier, D., Theory of Relational Databases, Computer Science Press, Rockville, MD20850, 1983.

[7] Y. Zhang and M.E. Orlowska, An Upgrade of the Automated Tool for Relational Database Design, Tech. Report No.136, Department of Computer Science, University of Queensland, 1989.

[8] M.E. Orlowska and Y. Zhang, Relational Database Schema Design: A Comparison Between NIAM and Synthesis Approach, Proceedings of the 2nd International Symposium on Systems Research Informatics and Cybernetics, August 11 - 16, 1989, Baden-Baden, West German.

[9] Y. Zhang and M.E. Orlowska, Some Properties of the Synthesis Algorithm, Proceedings of International Symposium for Young Computer Professionals, August 21 - 24, 1989, Beijing.

[10] Y. Zhang and M.E. Orlowska, Transform a NIAM Conceptual Schema into an EKNF relational Schema, Proceedings of International Conference on Databases, Parallel Structures and their Applications, Miami, March 7-9, 1990.

[11] C. Yang, Relational Database, Prentice-Hall, 1988.

[12] S. Ram and S.M. Curran, An Automated Tool For Relational Database Design, Inform. Systems Vol. 14, No.3, pp 247-259, 1989

[13] S. Ram and S. M. Curran, An Automated Tool for Relational Database Design, Information Systems Vol.14, No.3, pp.247-259, 1989

[14] J. T. Ullman, Principles of Database Systems, Second Edition. Computer Science Press, Rockville (1982)

[15] R. Elmasri and S.B. Navathe, Fundamentals of Database Systems, The Benjiamin/Cummings Publishing Company, Inc. 1989.

[16] L. Dunn and Maria E. Orlowska, A Natural Language Interpreter for the Construction of Conceptual Schemas, Tech. Report No.124, Dept. of Computer Science, Univ. of Queensland, Nov. 1989.

The R^2 Model: Database = Relations + Relationships

Fatma Mili[+] Hafedh Mili[*]
[+]: Oakland University, Rochester, MI48309, USA
[*]: Université de Québec à Montréal, Canada

Abstract

In this paper, we propose a model of databases based on the *relational* model, the *object oriented* paradigm, and an explicit representation of the *semantics* that define the participating entities and relate them to each other. This model benefits from the *logical independence* of the relational model, the *structure modeling* power of semantic data models, and the *behavior modeling* power of object oriented models. We extend the object oriented approach by relating the structure of database entities to their update behavior, and by representing structural and behavioral relationships by *explicit* database entities that carry their definitions and the procedures that maintain them.

1 INTRODUCTION

The database problem has traditionally consisted of developing a set of data modeling and data manipulation techniques that allow an efficient storage, retrieval, and modifications of real world data about individuals, facts, events, and transactions. Early database research was more concerned with typical data processing issues, such as file organizations and data structures, and with mathematical models of data such as hierarchical, network, and relational. The focus was more on the form of the data than on their contents. Semantic contents, often limited to integrity constraints, were treated in an ad-hoc fashion. The relational model [5], the last of what we call the *non-semantic models*, received wide acclaim for its simplicity, mathematical elegance, and logical independence, and became virtually the *de-facto* language of database research. However, it was still devoid of much semantic modeling.

The need for semantic modeling became more apparent for novel and complex database applications such as CAD/CAM [8], and office automation [19]. Researchers have since been actively trying to incorporate semantic information in data models. In one approach, semantic constructs were incorporated in existing data models. Examples of such constructs include entities, properties, and associations [7, 4, 25], classes [10], roles [1], is-a hierarchies [23, 9], part-of hierarchies [11], equivalence relations [12], ordered relations [24], and others. A second approach consists of applying the Object-Oriented (OO) paradigm to database modeling and management [15]. The first approach focuses on modeling the *semantic structure* of data, while the object-oriented approach focuses on modeling the *semantic behavior* of data [14]

In this paper, we propose a model that integrates both structural and behavioral modeling. Furthermore, our model uses the structure of data in order to explain and derive its behavior. In fact, the behavior often consists of propagating the changes in a way that preserves the structure of the data. The resulting model incorporates elements of the relational model, semantic models, and object oriented models.

In the next section, we present the behavior modeling problem, and show how existing database models fail to address it adequately. In section 3, we discuss our model of databases, the R^2 model. We conclude this paper by highlighting the advantages of R^2 and discussing issues still under investigation.

2 BEHAVIORAL MODELING

2.1 The Update Problem

The relational algebra and calculus were introduced soon after the introduction of the relational model [5], and were set as completeness standard for relational data sublanguages [6]. The completeness criterion became later an inherent part of the relational model. In fact, the initial purpose of the two languages is *data retrieval*, or, using Codd's words [6] *data selection*. This suggests that the relational completeness measures the retrieval power of a language and not its *update* power. The difference between retrieval and update lies in the scope of the operations. While retrieving can be seen as defining *one* relation function of the n given relations in the database, updating can be seen as defining n relations (the new state of the database) function of the n given relations (the old state of the database). As a result, existing data sublanguages are largely inadequate when it comes to update operations. They all have recourse to the notion of transaction, a "procedure" defined by the user, in which he must specify a sequence of *relation-level* update operations that is equivalent to his desired *database-level* update. We illustrate this aspect using an example borrowed from CAD/CAM applications.

Example: Consider the following database:
CAR(Serial-number, Owner, Make, Engine, Transmission, Body, Front-left-wheel Front-right-wheel, Rear-left-wheel, Rear-right-wheel, location)
where location is a cartesian coordinate in some 3-D space.
ENGINE(Serial-number, Speed, Acceleration, weight, location, drive-wheels)
TRANSMISSION(Serial-number, Gear-ratio, Weight, location)
Gear-ratio is the ratio of rotational speed of the engine with respect to that of the wheels.
BODY(Serial-number, Color, weight, location)
WHEEL(Serial-number, Model, location)
WHEEL-TYPE (Model, Size, weight)
SURFACE (Map, Friction-coef)

We rely on the reader's intuitive understanding of the data contained in this database. In fact, the relational system, by its lack of explicit representation of semantics, does exactly that: rely on the names of the attributes and of the relations and on the user's knowledge of the domain to make the right assumptions and the right inferences.

Using the relational calculus, it is possible to compute things such as the weight of a car (sum of the weights of its parts), its speed (as the engine speed times the gear ratio times the radius of the drive wheels), and so forth. One can also define views containing these derived attributes. We shall see a more transparent and more natural way of retrieving these attributes. However, consider the following updates:

1. Move car x from location A to location B.

2. Remove the body y of car x by moving it to location B.

3. Remove the front left wheel of car x by moving it to location B.

Using the relational calculus, the user would have to write some rather complex transactions using his knowledge of the domain (The layout of the different parts, e.g., the body rests on the four wheels, the remaining parts are supported by the body, etc.), of the laws of physics (the interaction between the different forces, resulting from the gravity, friction forces, externally exerted forces, etc.). Further, the user must be aware of all possible relationships between the objects, and of their possible implications (e.g. possible collisions when moving a car; the impact of the collision on the trajectory of both objects, etc.). In conclusion, manipulating this data base becomes rather complex due to the number of relationships involved —and not explicitly represented in the database. The user carries a heavy responsibility —that of maintaining the integrity of the database. We would like to relieve him from such a burden by providing him with atomic update operations, letting the system use the relevant relationships, and decide how to propagate the user's update across the different parts of the database.

2.2 Existing Database Models

Relational databases usually do not explicitly represent semantics of data as part of the data model. Integrity rules are occasionally used to represent invariant conditions. However,

- The expressive power of the integrity constraints and rules is typically limited (by efficiency requirements).
- The integrity rules are meant to be used as a *corrective* measure under exceptional conditions rather than as part of the normal update operations.
- The integrity conditions are usually expressed at a too low level. For example, something as general as the referential integrity, is coded individually for every relation rather than expressed only once at the database level.

Semantic data models, while incorporating common relationships more naturally, do not handle their implications and dynamics any better than the relational model.

Object-Oriented databases seem to be the natural model for handling the update problem. Object-oriented databases have been the subject of intensive research in the past few years [15, 27, 22, 26, 3]. While there is no general consensus on the precise meaning of object-orientation [13], its potential for modeling complex relationships is generally recognized. We briefly discuss some of the principles underlying these designs, and show their limitations.

Roughly speaking, OO databases represent entities by *classes*. Elements of these classes are called *instances*. The attributes of an entity are called *instance variables* (their values differ from one instance to another). An instance is not only a data store, but it also "contains" *methods* (procedures) used to manipulate its instance variables such as returning the value of an attribute or modifying its value. Methods are defined at the class level, and thus, are shared by all the instances of the same class. Retrievals and updates are no longer performed through a general purpose procedure that accesses an instance's attributes, but done by sending a *message* to that instance which applies its methods to "respond" to the message, either by returning the value of the attribute (in case of a retrieval), or by modifying its value (in case of an update).

Different OO database models have different modeling capabilities. King [14] distinguishes between *structure modeling* and *behavior modeling*. The structure modeling power of OODB derives from 1) the possibility for instance variables to be themselves complex objects with their own structure — rather than limiting them to simple data values, 2) the inheritance mechanism which allows to capture similarities between instances of the same class, and between instances of different classes [15].

The behavior modeling power of the OO paradigm derives mainly from 1) the encapsulation of data structures and procedures that operate on them into objects, and 2) the arbitrary complexity of an object's response to an incoming message, including message-passing with related objects. Consider the car database again. We could use an instance variable "weight" for the class of cars, without necessarily having that variable hold a value. A car would respond to the message "show-your-weight" by requesting the weights of its components (by sending them messages) and returning their sum, thus avoiding both redundancy and update complications; the value returned would remain up-to-date, should one component change its weight. Similarly, we could define the method "change-location-to" for CARs in a way such that it requests a car's components to change their locations accordingly. While both manipulations could be achieved in traditional databases by writing an application program, a database user does not have to use this program (unlike the case of an OO system where instances can only be accessed through the defined methods), and can circumvent the underlying constraints [15].

Nevertheless, we see two major problems with existing OO database models. First, existing object-oriented systems do not distinguish between the attributes of an object and its components, and represent both by instance variables. In the CAR example, the wheels, engine, body, and transmission are *components*, while the Owner, Make, Serial-Number and Location are *attributes*. Deleting the Owner instance has a different effect from deleting the body instance!. Similarly, deleting the car entails deleting its components, but does not delete the objects representing its owner, its make, or its color. Second, the methods attached to a class (entity) may depend on other classes. Thus, should new entities (or instances) come into play, these methods may have to be rewritten. In general, existing OO databases do not put any restrictions on the kind of behavior that must be embodied in class methods. Consider two cars A and B such that A is located in front of B. If the user wishes to move A, depending on the direction of the move, this may entail moving car B. Existing OO models do not say whether this behavior should be embodied in the "change-location" method attached to CAR, or in method associated with a relation called IN-FRONT-OF. Traditionally [21], this is done by coding the "change-location" method attached to CAR in a way such that it handles such situations. We argue that such a behavior should be embodied in the methods associated with a relation (class) IN-FRONT-OF, whose tuples (instances) are pairs of cars (A,B) such that A is in front of B. In our model, each time a car involved in such a relation is moved, it "notifies" the corresponding instance of BUMPER-TO-BUMPER which, in turn, asks the other car to move accordingly (if any).

In our model, we distinguish between the two kinds of behaviors, and argue that they should be treated differently: the *internal behavior*, which is a consequence of an object's structure, and thus, an inherent part of the object, and the *external behavior*, which is a consequence of external constraints with other objects. The internal behavior of CARs includes the requirement that a motion of a CAR be accompanied by an appropriate motion of its components— if the CAR is to stay in one piece. Such a behavior is intrinsic to the class of CARs, and is shared by all its instances. The external behavior of a CAR includes its reactions to updates occurring in objects other than its components. Such a behavior depends on the particular setting of the instance at hand, and is not shared by the instances of the same class. In the above example, the relation IN-FRONT-OF embodies one aspect of the external behavior of cars which is enforced *externally* to CARs, i.e., by methods other than the ones associated with CARs. These are the basic premises underlying our model. We discuss it in more details in the next section.

3 THE R^2 MODEL OF DATABASES

The R^2 model is driven by the following observations and goals

1. Update propagation is needed to enforce relationships between components after some external perturbation.
2. These relationships are often the result of structural relationships —internal and external.
3. We need a representation of these structural and behavioral relationships that ($\star$) highlights their interdependence ($\star$) provides logical independence by separating internal relationships (inherent to the object) from external relationships (incidental, subject to frequent modifications).

We first present the representation selected, and then illustrate its use for the different concepts and semantic constructs needed.

3.1 Relations: A Universal Representation

Mathematical relations have long been recognized as a convenient representation for constraints. Furthermore, using them in the context of database is particularly attractive for the uniformity that would provide with the relational model. The model of relations, as defined and used in the relational model, defines a relation by its schema and its instance. We augment this model by incorporating more semantic information. In addition to the schema and the set of instances, we also include: 1) all the conditions that must hold in the relation, 2) satisfiers, which are procedures to be executed in case some of these conditions are violated, 3) the set of actions (operations) that can be performed on this relation, and 4) the relationships between this relation and other relations. More precisely:

Relation $\equiv$

1. **relation schema** this is the same as the relational model relation schema.
2. **tuple-level condition**: An n-ary predicate expressing the condition that must be satisfied by any n-tuple belonging to this relation. Because of the time-varying nature of database relations, this condition —while *necessary*— is typically *not sufficient* to grant membership to tuples verifying it. Very often, these conditions are quite simple, and they involve only some of the attributes of a tuple.
3. **relation-level condition**: A predicate expressing all the conditions put globally on the relation. This includes *cardinality constraints* [20] and *functional dependencies* [2]. Functional dependency constraints are assertions of the type "x_i is a

function of x_{j_1} ,..., x_{j_k}". These assertion can be expressed by the predicate:
$(\forall(x_1,...,x_n),(x'_1,....,x'_n) \in R)$

$$[(x_{j_1} = x'_{j_1}) \wedge (x_{j_2} = x'_{j_2}) \wedge ... \wedge x_{j_k} = x'_{j_k}) \rightarrow (x_i = x'_i)]$$

4. **set of instances**: a set of data structures representing the tuples currently belonging to the relation. In addition to the n values composing the tuple, we choose to include two other properties, namely, the status and the type of the tuple. The status property indicates whether the tuple verifies all tuple-level conditions. The main motivation behind keeping tuples with negative status is the temporary nature of the status. When a tuple becomes negative, we may want to keep it in the database until we restore its status. For instance, if we disassemble a car in order to repair it, technically, it does not exist since all its parts are apart, but we do not want to loose track of it by removing it from the database. We keep it, with a negative status. The second property is the Type of the tuple. It takes values INCIDENTAL or ENFORCEABLE. This property differentiates between tuples that must remain in the relation —whose membership must be reinstated whenever it becomes negative— and tuples whose membership is incidental —they just happen to be part of the relation and can be deleted with no consequences. The type is dynamic, it is contingent upon the global state of the database. In summary,
INSTANCE ≡ ((Status ⟨ POSITIVE or NEGATIVE ⟩)
(Type ⟨ INCIDENTAL or ENFORCEABLE ⟩)
(N-Tuple ($X_1, X_2, \ldots, X_n$))).

5. **set actions**: The actions (or *methods*) needed to manage the set of instances. More detail is given under satisfier.

6. **satisfier**: The action (or set of actions) that needs to be carried out to enforce the underlying constraint on a given tuple. Because of the inter-relationship between the actions and the satisfier, we discuss them together. Set actions are used to manage the sets of instances. The most common actions are Add-Instance (i, Set), which attempts to add instance i to Set , where Set can be either the set of positive instances (SPI), or the set of negative instances (SNI), and Delete-Instance(i,Set), which removes i from Set. These actions are called upon when the status of an instance has (or may have) changed. Operationally, the objects involved in a relationship notify the corresponding relation object whenever their attributes are modified. Such modifications may change the status of the corresponding instance. Let i be an instance with n-tuple $(x_1,...,x_n)$ such that x_j, for some $1 \leq j \leq n$, has changed value. It is assumed by default that the status of i has changed consequently. Thus, Delete-Instance(i,Set) is called upon with Set = SPI, or SNI depending on the prior status of i. Next, the new status of i is determined by evaluating the tuple-level and the relation-level conditions. If i has become POSITIVE, then Add-Instance(i,SPI) is called upon. If i has become NEGATIVE, then the actions that follow depend of the type of i. If i is INCIDENTAL, then Add-Instance(i,SNI) is called upon. If i is ENFORCEABLE, an attempt is made at making it POSITIVE again.

7. **relations to other relations**: The set of set-relationships (such as inclusion) that exist between the relation at hand, and other relations. In practice, it is the

set of all other relations that contain one tuple relating this relation to some other relation(s). For instance, if the current relation —call it R_1 is included in some relation R_2, and relation R_1 implies another relation R_3, we include here the list

$$\{(INCLUSION, R_1, R_2), (IMPLICATION, R1, R_3)\}$$

where INCLUSION and IMPLICATION would be two relations on their own, represented using the model just described here. Because of the importance and generality of the IMPLICATION relation, we present it in more details.
Let $R_1 = (X_1, X_2, \ldots, X_k)$ and $R_2 = (Y_1, Y_2, \ldots, Y_m)$, we say that R_1 implies R_2 if:

$$\forall (x_1, x_2, \ldots, x_k) \in R_1 \rightarrow f_1(x_1, x_2, \ldots, x_k), \ldots, f_m(x_1, x_2, \ldots, x_k)) \in R_2$$

where $f_1,\ldots,f_m$ are arbitrary k-ary functions from $X_1 \times X_2 \times \ldots \times X_n$ to $Y_1, \ldots, Y_m$, respectively.
Consider the relations WHMW = (Wife, Husband, Mother-of-Wife) and HML = (Husband, Mother-in-Law). For all $(X, Y, Z) \in WHMW$, $(Y, Z) \in HML$. In this case WHMW *implies* HML in the sense defined above, where f_1(X,Y,Z) = X, and f_2(X,Y,Z) = Z. In other words, projection is one example of generalized implication. We could define a variety of other relationships based on the generalized implication relationship, such as generalized equivalence and generalized mutual exclusion [16]. If we choose to represent generalized implication by a relation object, we need to specify for each instance, the two relations involved, as well as the mapping functions. An instance of such a relation object might look like:
(Status POSITIVE)
(Type ENFORCEABLE)
(N-Tuple $(R_1, R_2, f_1, \ldots, f_m)$))
A POSITIVE status indicates that the implication condition of the relation holds for the pair (R_1, R_2). Because this tuple is enforceable, any update in the database that invalidates the implication must be propagated in a way that will enforce it. Whenever a change occurs in R_1 or R_2, the status of the tuple $(R_1, R_2, f_1, \ldots, f_m)$ must be checked, and reinstated to positive if necessary.

Maintaining relations of relations in an OO system has a number of advantages. First, it allows the designer/user to build a rich web of constraints from a combination of simple relations between objects and relations between relations. It also provides alternative ways for satisfying relationships whose satisfiers are not known or hard to compute, and provide a mechanism for "propagating" the enforceability of instances, relieving the designer of some of the guess work involved in deciding whether an instance should be made enforceable or incidental [16]. Some of these advantages will be discussed in more detail in later sections of this paper.

3.2 A Model of Objects

In section 3.1, we have presented a general-purpose formalism that can be used to describe specific aspects of objects. We concentrate here on the objects, and identify all aspects that need to be represented. Traditionally, class objects in object-oriented programming are described by four properties: 1) *superclasses*, 2) *subclasses*, 3) *methods*, and 4) *attributes*. Subclasses and superclasses organize object classes in *inheritance hierarchies*. As mentioned earlier, we find it useful to divide the dynamic constraints into *internal relations* and *external relations*. Internal relations express the constraints that hold between a compound object and its components. These constraints convey an object its form and behavior. As such, the internal relationships of an object constitute an integral part of an object's definition. On the contrary, external relations express constraints that bind an object to objects other than its components. Unlike internal relationships, external relationships do not contribute to, nor do they affect, the definition of an object. Further, as we later see, changes in one object propagate to related objects differently, depending on whether the relationship to those objects is internal or external.

Accordingly, we propose a model in which objects are described by the following properties:

1. *type relations*,

2. *(global) attributes*,

3. *internal relations*,

4. *actions*, and

5. *external relations*.

where we grouped subclasses and superclasses under "type relations". We leave now the car example, and use another example whose dynamic properties are much simpler. This will allow us to concentrate on the concepts, and to provide an intuitive understanding of the design choices made.

Consider a system of two vessels V_1 and V_2 connected through a pipe P, call this system CV. Assume that the vessels and pipe are filled with fluid, and that the whole set rests on a horizontal table. Such a device may be used to illustrate concepts related to pressure and thermal exchange. An experimenter may wish to perform actions on CV as a whole, such as moving CV, adding fluid to it, and heating the fluid in CV. The experimenter may also wish to perform actions on CV's components individually, such as heating the fluid in V_1, adding fluid to V_2, and so forth. These actions determine the appropriate level of granularity for an object-oriented design and simulation of CV, namely, CV and its components should be represented by an object each.

Global Variables: The state of CV can be described by a number of variables such as the volume of fluid it contains, the temperature of fluid in V_1, the volume of fluid in V_2, the specific heat of the pipe P [1] and so forth. Only few of these state variables qualify as "global attributes": the ones that do not refer explicitly to CV's components. For example, the volume of fluid in CV (call it VOF(CV)) is a global attribute of CV while the temperature of fluid in V_1 (call it TOF(V_1)) is not. The difference being that VOF(CV) makes no explicit reference to the components of CV. This restriction on attributes leads to a "localization" of state variables, facilitating the design of objects. It also has a number of other advantages, some of which are explained below.

[1]The specific heat Q of an object is defined as $C \equiv \frac{\Delta Q}{\Delta T}$ where Q is the amount of heat embodied in the object, and T its temperature. C is substance-specific and is proportional to the mass, or volume, provided a constant density.

Internal Relationships The particular arrangement of the vessels and the pipe distinguishes CV systems from arbitrarily assembled sets of two vessels and a pipe. It also dictates well-defined interactions between the vessels and the pipe. The description of the physical arrangement of the components of CV— called *structure relations* and the interactions between these components— called *behavior relations* constitute the *internal relations* of CV. The structure relations for CV may be called "Components" and "Connected-Thru", where (CV,V,V',P) ∈ "Components" means that V, V', and P are the components of CV, and (V,V',P) ∈ "Connected-Thru" means that the vessels V and V' are connected through the pipe P. Both relations will be represented by relation objects containing one instance to represent the structure of every CV. We could define a number of behavior relations for CV, depending on the user requirements. For illustration purposes, we limit our attention to the thermal properties of CV. First, we can define TOF(CV) synthetically as the weighted sum:

$$TOF(CV) = \frac{TOF(V_1)C(V_1) + TOF(P)C(P) + TOF(V_2)C(V_2)}{C(V_1) + C(P) + C(V_2)}$$

where C(X) is the specific heat of object X, and TOF(X) the average (across the volume) temperature of X. Also, heat conduction in the fluid dictates that, at equilibrium:

$$TOF(CV) = TOF(V_1) = TOF(P) = TOF(V_2)$$

The two equations define the tuple-level conditions of the behavior relations of CV. Both relationships will be represented by relation objects, containing one instance for every connected CV. We call the relation whose tuple-level condition is expressed by the last equation THERMAL-EQUILIBRIUM.

Actions A CV may perform a number of actions upon other objects' requests. We limit such actions to three categories: 1) display the value of a global attribute, 2) change (or set) the value of a global attribute, and 3) receive and send messages. We exclude the actions that are directed explicitly at one of the components of the object. CV may only respond to requests to change or display its own TOF, C, or VOF. It ignores requests to display TOF(V_1) for example. Such request is more appropriately addressed to V_1. Assume that TOF(CV) was initially T_0, and that the user asks CV to set its TOF to T_1. We want the end result to be TOF(CV) = TOF(V_1) = $TOF(P)$ = $TOF(V_2)$ = T_1. This can be done simply by:

1. changing TOF(CV) to T_1,
2. sending a message to THERMAL-EQUILIBRIUM bringing the change to its "attention", and
3. let THERMAL-EQUILIBRIUM, "realizing" that the instance involving CV and its components no longer satisfies its tuple-condition, "ask" the components to set their TOF to T_1.

Accordingly, THERMAL-EQUILIBRIUM's satisfier does the following:

- TOF(V_1) ← TOF(CV)
- TOF(P) ← TOF(CV)
- TOF(V_2) ← TOF(CV)

which corresponds to imposing a reference-only constraint upon CV. This is a general result: objects act as reference-only variables vis a vis their components in internal constraint satisfaction. The complete definition of the relation object THERMAL-EQUILIBRIUM is provided in Appendix A.

External Relations The external relations of CV represent the relation between CV and objects other than its components. One such relation expresses the fact that CV is supported by the table. Call the corresponding relation object SUPPORTED-BY. The external relations of CV will include a reference to an instance of SUPPORTED-BY with tuple, say, (CV,Table), meaning that CV is supported by the table.

A complete definition of CV is given in Appendix B.

We follow similar guidelines in designing V_1, P and V_2. We could use the same set of global attributes, namely, TOF, C, and VOF. Assuming that the designer does not wish to elicit further the structure of the components, none of the three objects will have internal relations. The relations that were internal to CV are external to its components, because from a component's perspective, these are relations to objects other than its own components. Should we use the same instances to represent CV's internal relations and the components' external relations? The answer is a somewhat counter-intuitive no, as explained below.

Assume that the user request a change in the temperature of V_1, from T_0 to T_1. After this action is carried out, and once the whole system reaches an equilibrium state, we expect the temperature of fluid to be the same across all three components, and to be somewhere between T_0 and T_1. Precisely, assuming heat conservation (i.e. no heat exchange with the environment of CV), the final temperature T_e is given by:

$$T_e = \frac{T_1C(V_1) + T_0C(P) + T_0C(V_2)}{C(V_1) + C(P) + C(V_2)}$$

or, more generally:

$$T_e = \frac{TOF(V_1)C(V_1) + TOF(P)C(P) + T(V_2)C(V_2)}{C(V_1) + C(P) + C(V_2)}$$

A satisfier for thermal equilibrium when V_1's (or any orther component's) temperature changes must do the following:

- Compute T_e as defined above
- Set TOF(V_1) to T_e
- Set TOF(P) to T_e
- Set TOF(V_2) to T_e
- Set TOF(CV) to T_e

This satisfier is different from that of THERMAL-EQUILIBRIUM, and there is no longer reference-only constraint on CV. Thus, we should create a second relation object, call it THERMAL-EQUILIBRIUM$_2$. THERMAL-EQUILIBRIUM and THERMAL-EQUILIBRIUM$_2$ are equivalent (they have the same instance sets) but differ by —at least— their satisfiers. Assuming the existence of a relation object EQUIVALENCE, we should include an instance of EQUIVALENCE in both THERMAL-EQUILIBRIUM and

THERMAL-EQUILIBRIUM$_2$'s "relations to other relations". Figure 5 shows schematically CV, its components, and the various relationships between them.

We should mention at this point a valuable design tool that we did not illustrate here: The use of the generalized implication to relate behavioral aspects to the structural aspects. In the CV example, thermal balance is implied by the connectivity relation between the components. With this information, the designer needs only to specify the structural relations, and still obtain the right behavior for CV, temperature-wise [16].

4 CONCLUSION

In this paper, we presented a model of databases that allows for both structural and behavioral modeling of database objects. Our model provides a unifying framework for the relational model, object-oriented models, and semantic models. Relations constitute a mature and well developed mathematical formalism for representing associations between data. This represents both the strength and weakness of the relational model: uniformity of representation, but also, no explicit distinctions between the semantics of the various relations. While we use relations as the sole mathematical formalism for representing associations, we make a clear and intuitive distinction between the different roles they play (e.g. attributes versus components versus relationships or constraints). In our model, the nature of these associations determines the kind of behavior of related data reacting to change. Existing object-oriented models do not make such distinctions.

In this paper, we focussed only on the modeling aspects of our model. We did not discuss operational issues such as indexing, nor did we address the problem of distinguishing between persistent objects and temporary objects, both because of space limitations, and because of the infancy of our work in this area. We have shown elsewhere alternative representations of sets (crucial for indexing) using our model [17]. We are currently exploring a number of issues both in the context of databases, and in the context of object-oriented programming in general. Suffice it to mention concurrency, combinations of relationships (to speed up constraint propagation in real-time systems) and a developing an application-independent modeling tool using our model [18].

References

[1] Bachman C., and M. Daya "The Role Concept in Database Models" Proceedings of VLDB. October, 1977.

[2] Borning, A. and R. Duisberg, "Constraint-Based Tools for Building User Interfaces", **ACM Transactions on Graphics**, 5:4, October, 1986.

[3] Bretl, R., Maier, D., Otis, A., Penney, J., Schubardt, B., Stein, J., Williams, E. H., and Williams, M., "The GemStone Data Management System," in *Object-Oriented Concepts, Databases, and Applications*, Ed. F. Lochovsky and W. Kim, Addison Wesley, 1989.

[4] Chen, P. "The Entity Relationship Model: Toward a Unified view of Data", **TODS**, 1:1, March, 1976.

[5] Codd, E. "A Relational Model for Large Shared Data Banks", **CACM**, 13:6, June 1970.

[6] Codd, F. "Relational Completeness of Database Sublanguages" **IBM Research**, RJ 987, Mach, 1972.

[7] Codd, E. "Extending The Database Relational Model to Capture More Meaning", **TODS**, 4:4, December, 1979.

[8] Diedrich, J. and Milton, J., "Objects, Messages, and Rules in Database Design," in *Object-Oriented Concepts, Databases, and Applications*, Ed. F. Lochovsky and W. Kim, Addison Wesley, 1989.

[9] Goldberg, A. and Robson, D. *Smalltalk, The Language and its Implementation.* Addison Wesley, 1983.

[10] Hammer, M. and McLeod D. "Database Description with SDM: A Semantic Data Model", **TODS**, 6:3, September 1980.

[11] Katz, R. *Information Management for Engineering Design*, Springer Verlag, 1985.

[12] Katz, R., E. Chang, and R. Bhatheja "Version Modeling Concepts for Computer Aided Design databases". Proceedings of the ACM SIGMOD International Conference on Management of Data. May, 1986.

[13] Hull, R. and R. King "Semantic Database Modeling: Survey, Applications, and Research Issues" **ACM Computing Surveys**. June 1988.

[14] King, R. "My Cat is Object-Oriented," in *Object-Oriented Concepts, Databases, and Applications*, Ed. F. Lochovsky and W. Kim, Addison Wesley, 1989.

[15] Maier, D., Stein, J., Otis, A., and Purdy, A. "Development of an Object Oriented DBMS", Proceedings of the ACM Conference on Object-Oriented Programming, Systems, Languages, and Applications, 1986.

[16] Mili, H. "Relationships as Semantic Constructs in Object Oriented Programming". Proceedings of the 10th Tunisian-French Seminar On Computer Science. May, 1989.

[17] Mili, H and J. Sibert "A Model of Objects Based on Relations," in **Journal of Systems and Software**, To appear, 1989.

[18] Mili, H. "Object Design Using Relations," Technical Report, Department of Maths and Computer Science, University of Quebec at Montreal, Montreal, Canada, September 1989.

[19] Nierstrasz , O. M. and Tsichritzis, D. C., "Integrated Office Systems," in *Object-Oriented Concepts, Databases, and Applications*, Ed. F. Lochovsky and W. Kim, Addison Wesley, 1989.

[20] Rumbaugh, J. "Relations as Semantic Constructs in an Object-Oriented Language", Proceedings of the OOPSLA, 1987.

[21] Schmucker, K.J. in *Object-Oriented Programming for the Macintosh*, Center for the Human Information Processing, Portland, Oregon, June, 1983.

[22] Skarra, A. H. and Zdonik, S.B., "Type Evolution in an Object-Oriented Database," in *Research Directions in Object-Oriented Programming*, Ed. Shriver, B., and Wegner, P., MIT Press, 1986.

[23] Smith, J. and Smith D. "Database Abstractions: Aggregation and Generalization", **TODS**, 2:2, June 1977.

[24] Stonebraker, M. "Document Processing in a Relational Database System". **ACM TOOIS**, April, 1983.

[25] Stonebraker, M., "Future Trends in Data Base Systems". Proceedings IEEE Data Engineering Conference. February, 1988.

[26] Weiser, S. P., and Lochovsky, F. H., "OZ+: An Object-Oriented Database System," in *Object-Oriented Concepts, Databases, and Applications*, Ed. F. Lochovsky and W. Kim, Addison Wesley, 1989.

[27] Zdonik, S. B. and Wegner, P., "Language and Methodology for Object-Oriented Database Environments," Proceedings of the 19th Hawaii International Conference on System Sciences, 1986.

Appendix A: Thermal-Equilibrium
Relation: Thermal Equilibruim$_2$
tuple-level condition:

$$P_{tof}(W,X,Y,Z) \equiv (TOF(W) = TOF(X) = TOF(Y) = TOF(Z))$$

set of instances

$$\{[positive, enforceable, (CV, V_1, V_2, P)]\}$$

satisfier

$$Te \leftarrow \frac{TOF(X)VOF(X)+TOF(Y)VOF(Y)+TOF(Z)VOF(Z)}{VOF(X)+VOF(Y)+VOF(Z)}$$

$TOF(X) \leftarrow Te$
$TOF(Y) \leftarrow Te$
$TOF(Z) \leftarrow Te$
$TOF(W) \leftarrow Te$

Appendix B: Definition of CV
Object CV
Global Attributes
TOF
VOF
LOF

Internal Structure
{(relation STRUCTURE)(N-Tuple (CV, V_1, V_2, P))}
{(relation THERMAL-EQUILIBRIUM)(N-Tuple (CV, V_1, V_2, P))}
Actions
Show-Attribute-Value(attribute)
Set-Attribute-Value(attribute, value)
External Relations
[(relation ON-TOP-OF)(N-tuple (CV, Table)]

COMMERCIAL DATABASE PERFORMANCE – DO WE KNOW WHERE WE ARE, MUCH LESS WHERE WE ARE GOING?

Ken J. McDonell
Pyramid Technology Corporation
Melbourne, Australia
kenj@yarra.oz.au

ABSTRACT

The hardware-vendor-independent class of commercial database systems is growing strongly in importance as end-user organizations embrace both open systems architectures (as typified by the UNIX* operating system) and portability of data resources and applications software across heterogeneous hardware platforms.

For this class of database management systems, performance is an important differentiator in the marketplace. However many of the techniques that have been employed in proprietary database systems are not technically feasible for software products that must be maintained over literally hundreds of different hardware and software platforms.

This paper explores the recent historical developments as they have influenced performance, and identifies a number of unresolved and pending issues. It is left as an exercise for the reader to draw conclusions about integration of research results into released products, and the extent to which current areas of research activity may address the outstanding performance issues for this class of commercial database management systems.

1. INTRODUCTION

We are interested in database management systems that are supported across a range of hardware and (operating system) software platforms. We shall further limit our investigations to systems that have some basic commitment to the relational data model.

Systems of this nature allow end-users to benefit from both selecting systems from a very wide price-performance spectrum (e.g. system value of $2,000 to $10,000,000), and having the option of migration to a larger machine or newer technology with

---

* UNIX is a trademark of AT&T

minimal functional risk to the installed applications software and the operational database.

Database vendors are keen to maximize their market share and market exposure, and so porting their products to new hardware-software platforms is an on-going necessity. Innovation and refinement to their database product is typically concentrated on the generic parts, to allow rapid implementation in released products across as many platforms as possible. However to maintain control over the process and cost of software maintenance, the DBMS architecture and implementation strategies are significantly constrained in comparison to a hardware-vendor's proprietary database management system.

Database products in the class of interest include, but is most definitely not limited to Informix[1], Ingres[2], Oracle[3], Sybase[4] and Unify[5].

These products are well-respected and the basis for implementation of some very large databases. They have done many things well, however the subject of interest in this paper is the current barriers to, and possible techniques to realize, even better performance from the DBMS software.

2. QUERY OPTIMIZATION

The benefits to be derived from even first-order statistical cost models of query optimization have been long known (Astrahan, Blasgen, Chamberlin, Eswaran, Gray, Griffiths, King, Lorie, McJones, Mehl, Putzolu, Traiger, Wade and Watson (1976); Yao and Jong (1978); Selinger, Astrahan, Chamberlin, Lorie and Price (1979); Astrahan, Kim and Schkolnick (1980)).

However many DBMS in the class of interest rely on *ad hoc* heuristics (e.g. pattern matching), or employ cost models that are only weakly correlated with buffer management strategies.

This produces several serious performance anomalies;

1. A sub-optimal access plan may be selected, often because predicate selectivity and operand cardinality are ill-considered.

2. Optimal access plans are apparently never considered, even for the simplest queries, in some DBMS products. The most glaring examples involve the refusal to employ relevant indices to evaluate aggregate functions such as MAX, MIN and COUNT.

---

1. INFORMIX is a registered trademark of Informix Software, Inc.
2. INGRES is a trademark of Relational Technology, Inc.
3. ORACLE is a registered trademark of Oracle Corporation.
4. SYBASE is a registered trademark of Sybase, Inc.
5. UNIFY DBMS is a trademark of Unify Corporation.

3. Minor re-arrangement of the surface syntax of an SQL query (without changing the semantics) can result in a radically different query evaluation plan (QEP) due to the behaviour of the "tie breaker" algorithm used in the pattern matching optimizers that *do not* include a cost model.

These factors often introduce differences of an order of magnitude, or more, in the performance of otherwise functionally equivalent applications and/or queries.

In systems where the QEP is not available in human-readable form, the application tuner is reliant on folk lore to coax optimal performance from the system. Even when a sub-optimal QEP can be identified, there may be no avenue by which the DBA can coerce the optimizer into choosing a better plan.

3. QUERY COMPILATION

The overheads associated with query parsing, access control checking, view translation, query optimization and QEP selection may account for as much as 50% of the processor time consumed by the DBMS.

The frequency with which this penalty must be incurred can be dramatically reduced by storing partially processed queries within the DBMS. Once the query has been processed, subsequent executions invoke the partially processed form, thereby avoiding the overheads, until some schema change invalidates the partial processing.

Even further reductions in query execution time and cost can be achieved by translating the QEP into machine code rather than an intermediate interpretive code, for example (Lorie and Wade, 1977) and (Chamberlin, Astrahan, King, Lorie, Mehl, Price, Schkolnick, Selinger, Slutz, Wade and Yost, 1981).

Support for stored procedures in the current DBMS products offers some assistance, but this is generally aimed at reducing the parse-time component and the volume and frequency of message exchanges between the application frontend and the backend DBMS server.

Stored procedures help, but their effectiveness is sensitive to the following factors.

1. The extent to which multi-query sequences can be *a priori* parameterized and "wrapped" into a stored procedure. The aggregate performance gains increase as more SQL interactions are included in a stored procedure, however application design and error handling combine to reduce the number of SQL interactions that can be successfully rolled into a single stored procedure.

2. The amount of information retained from query parsing, access control checking, view translation, optimization and QEP formulation, and saved with the stored procedure. The more information saved, the cheaper the stored procedure is to subsequently execute.

3. The extent to which parameterization may necessitate dynamic QEP re-evaluation and optimization at each execution of the stored procedure.

4. Relative frequency of true *ad hoc* enquiries, for which stored procedures are of no assistance.

Serious QEP preservation (storage, time-stamping and schema dependency analysis) is not common for the class of DBMS under consideration, and translation to efficient machine code access modules is unlikely to ever be featured, given the heterogeneous processor architectures on which these DBMS products must be supported.

4. SYNCHRONIZATION PRIMITIVES

DBMS implementations rely on low-level synchronization primitives to guard critical code sections against re-entrant or multiprocessor execution.

The objects being manipulated in these critical sections are typically the shared data structures that implement page buffer pools, transaction control blocks, resource tables (e.g. locks held) and transaction logging. Their role is to provide the stable base upon which the higher level application services of transaction management, concurrent access control and data sharing are implemented.

At the low-level, latching or locking is typically used. Efficient implementation of the associated synchronization primitives must reflect consideration of the following factors.

1. The duration for which a latch is held may vary from a few microseconds (a head of buffer queue latch) to tens of milliseconds (transaction log buffer).

2. The standard UNIX System V semaphore operations provide more than the required functionality, with a consequent bloated cost. This is a case where software portability imposes an execution-time penalty that is simply unacceptable.

3. "Busy waiting" burns processor cycles on otherwise unproductive work; driving the processor utilization up to 100% **and** reducing the system throughput in the pathological extreme.

4. Context switches that may lose hardware cache context are comparatively expensive.

5. Multiprocessor systems can only achieve scaleable performance if the synchronization primitives may be executed symmetrically on any processor.

6. Atomic instructions (e.g. bit set and test) in multiprocessor architectures are typically very expensive in their consumption of bus bandwidth.

7. Very fine resolution interval timers are not generally available in all systems, and sometimes access to them requires privileged instructions.

Most of the high-performance DBMS products require careful integration of the synchronization support into the host hardware and software platform, usually with the assistance of the platform vendor.

Common techniques involve adaptive algorithms that "back-off" into progressively less resource hungry modes the longer a request for a latch cannot be satisfied. Unfortunately these algorithms are often implemented in a manner that is neither parameterized or tuneable. Even were tuning an option, it would be difficult to optimize due to application sensitivity and instrumentation problems. The performance of the low-level synchronization mechanism cannot be readily instrumented because such instrumentation could easily perturb the dynamic behaviour of the synchronization mechanism itself.

5. BUFFER AND PHYSICAL I/O MANAGEMENT

Dramatic improvements in DBMS performance could be achieved if better use was made of the available memory allocated to the database page buffer pool (or buffer cache) and the available disk bandwidth.

Buffer colouring or priority labelling is relatively uncommon, with replacement algorithms typically based on simple least recently used (LRU) algorithms. This results in anomalies such as,

1. Index pages may be no more likely to be retained in the buffer cache than data pages.
2. Serially scanned data pages may not be marked available for immediate re-use.
3. Leaf index pages may be retained in preference to root index pages.

Buffer management schemes that evolved when 1 megabyte was a lot of memory, often do not scale well (i.e. the algorithms are linear, and in some cases quadratic!) as the buffer cache size approaches 100 megabytes. Data structures such as statically sized hash chain tables, linear linked lists, re-scanned free space bit maps, etc. are common.

At the physical device level, there is a general fixation on performing all data transfers in 2 Kbyte multiples. For today's disks and buffer cache sizes, this is often much too small. As a counter example, VSAM data sets underneath IBM's DB2 product employ a default 4 Kbyte physical block size. The choice of physical block size is usually not a tuneable option.

Several years ago, operating systems researchers (McKusick, Joy, Leffler and Fabry, 1983) discovered that file system throughput increased dramatically when,

1. the physical block size was substantially increased, and
2. data block and file system control information was physically placed on the disk in a manner that retained locality of reference with respect to the device's geometry and electromechanical operation.

The DBMS vendors have yet to embrace these principles. Of particular interest would be transfers involving bigger physical blocks, cylinder-level free space and control information, the notion of "clustering" being extended to maximize the locality of reference at the cylinder-level, and application of some parameterized spiral skewing of logical blocks to improve serial processing performance.

Related to buffer management is the simple-minded manner in which checkpoints are typically implemented by acquiring and holding a single mutually exclusive lock over all dirty pages in the buffer cache, thereby dramatically reducing the degree of concurrent transaction processing. Adaptive algorithms that lock the leading edge of a buffer cache "sweep", and re-order dirty pages currently in demand to be the next ones checkpointed would provide far higher degrees of concurrent transaction processing during checkpoint operations, without compromising data consistency or recoverability.

A common practice has been to move the database and logging storage outside the UNIX file system and onto the so-called "raw" disk devices. The advantages are,

1. in-memory buffer copying is avoided
2. input-output operations are synchronous (hence guaranteed writes)
3. avoidance of file system overheads, especially for large files that require indirect data block pointers in the UNIX file system, and
4. DBMS control over disk space management, allowing contiguous space allocation.

From a performance point of view, DBMS control of space management and input-output request scheduling (especially for synchronous operations) means that there is considerable potential for serial input-output (e.g. full table scans, bulk inserts, log writing, checkpoints) to be very inefficient due to inadequate use of concurrent pending requests, reluctance to initiate multiple block transfers, shallow read ahead and no "spiral skew" in physical block allocation. In pathological (but not uncommon) cases this may reduce the data bandwidth from a peak of around 2 Mbytes per second per spindle down to an effective aggregate rate of 120 Kbytes per second across all spindles.

6. TRANSACTION LOGGING

High performance in the transaction logging subsystem demands some special techniques, because in most cases, disk spindle bandwidth is the limiting resource.

Successful techniques will include some combination of,

1. Asynchronous and guaranteed log writes, so multiple commits can be processed concurrently. Multiple outstanding write requests at the physical device allows the mean service time to be reduced by request re-sequencing. The mutually exclusive section is reduced from the time for a physical synchronous write down to the time to allocate a log buffer; this allows greater concurrency between commit operations, and more potential overlap between processing and disk input-output.

2. "Piggy-back" or batched commits, in which log records for multiple committing transactions are written in a single write operation.

3. Multiplexed logs. Increases the parallelism in the logging subsystem by reducing the conflict for log buffers and enabling multiple pending log writes, but at the expense of a slightly more complicated recovery protocol.
4. Reducing the volume of logged data (e.g. tuple differences, rather than page images).

Further improvements will probably require some physical or logical spiral skewing of the block mapping on the log device to allow more than one write per disk rotation.

7. ACCESS METHODS

Many DBMS products provide little or no option for varying the physical file organization and access method that underlies the relation and index storage system.

The ubiquitous B-tree, so aptly named by Comer (1979), has become a panacea for all storage structure problems.

Unfortunately, for a large class of access patterns, the B-tree (or its ISAM ancestor) offers sub-optimal performance. There is a definite place for at least one of the adaptive hashing techniques, e.g. linear hashing (Larson, 1982), and good old fashioned serial organizations.

Not only is the B-tree sub-optimal in some cases, but it is the worst-possible in terms of lock conflicts for chronologically sequenced tables. When multiple transactions are trying to insert into the end of such a data structure, they must be in conflict logically (over the "leading edge" of the data structure) and physically (over the database page and buffer). The problem is so bad that bulk loading a single table typically runs fastest as a single-threaded operation, even on multiprocessor systems.

8. SEMANTIC INTEGRITY CONSTRAINTS

The general lack of DBMS support for semantic integrity constraint enforcement and trigger mechanisms has left the burden of responsibility on the application program. Aside from all the normal data integrity and software engineering arguments, this practice also has a serious performance impact.

To implement the constraint checks, the application must typically execute several SQL queries before the "real" transaction is executed. These additional queries are more expensive in terms of resource consumption than internal execution of the logically equivalent operations by the DBMS. Not only is additional query parsing and optimization required (as described in Sections 2 and 3 above), but additional message exchanges and context switches may be required between the frontend application and the backend DBMS (at least 2 context switches per SQL query).

9. TP1 CONSIDERED HARMFUL

The acceptance of TP1 (a mutation of the debit-credit benchmark first proposed by Anon. et al. (1985)) as a yardstick for comparing OLTP performance has been particularly unfortunate.

1. Functionally, the debit-credit transaction has, at best, weak correlation with the types of transactions found commonly in UNIX DBMS environments. Consequently, TP1 is a very poor predictive measure of DBMS performance in common operational environments.

2. Attempts to maximize TP1 throughput have yielded an amazing range of dubious practices that either pervert the intent of the benchmark specifications, or execute the tests in an environment that is operational nonsense (e.g. disable or cripple transaction logging so that database recovery can never be guaranteed), or use prototype hardware/software configurations that are not, and never will become, deliverable products.

3. The emphasis in performance tuning and optimization efforts within the DBMS vendor companies has been driven by the desire to maximize TP1 scores. The resultant improvements may offer little benefit to a broader class of application environments, and have been achieved at the cost of reduced efforts in other generally important areas that do not impact TP1 performance, e.g. query optimization, or improved buffer management algorithms.

Fortunately the efforts of the Transaction Processing Performance Council (TPC)[6] offers the promise of containing the unethical aspects of TP1 benchmarking, and providing a framework within which a wider class of applications and transaction types may achieve common acceptance as standard DBMS performance metrics.

Such a development would foster a more balanced distribution of R&D effort within the DBMS vendor organizations.

10. DBMS PERFORMANCE INSTRUMENTATION AND TUNING

DBMS products typically provide the DBA with a plethora of "tuning" options. There are several endemic problems here.

1. It is unclear, in general terms, how each option may influence performance, e.g. sensitivity to changes in the parameter or configuration value, symptoms that would indicate over-supply or chronic contention for a resource, and inter-relationship between tuning options.

2. Lack of suitable performance monitors that help diagnose what is going on internally within the DBMS code, much less suggest ways to improve the behaviour of that code.

3. Experience gained with tuning one particular DBMS product is likely to be of little use when trying to tune another product (may even be the next version of

6. Further information of the membership and activities of the TPC are available from the administrator, Mr. Omri Serlin, ITOM International Co., PO Box 1450, Los Altos, California 94022, (e-mail to {uunet,sun}!uworld!omris).

the product from the same vendor!).

Software instrumentation of the DBMS product to support the necessary performance monitoring is a difficult problem because,

1. For low-level operations (e.g. latching) the duration is short, but the frequency is high – instrumentation may well cost more in terms of resource consumption than the operation itself.

2. Real-time event durations may differ by **six** orders of magnitude (e.g. comparing the duration of a latch request to a disk read). This makes it difficult to choose appropriate counting techniques and sampling frequencies.

3. System behaviour is often schizophrenic, oscillating between processor bound and disk bandwidth bound. "Beat" frequencies between the two modes may also occur, with periods as short as 30 milliseconds. Even sampling the statistics as often as every few seconds may result in a characterization of the system in which **both** the processor and disk bandwidth is clearly under-utilized, and there is no apparent way to discover what is really happening, much less make it all go faster.

4. The necessary statistics may be spread across the UNIX kernel, the DBMS kernel, shared memory segments and the private address spaces of many processes.

In summary, a major barrier to improved DBMS performance is the frustration associated with trying to tune an installed system. The DBA is often confronted with a situation in which one cannot identify the performance bottleneck, or decide if the system is saturated as opposed to ill-tuned.

11. CONCLUSIONS

To achieve higher performance, especially in transaction processing environments, the DBMS products in the UNIX market place will have to address the following issues.

- Generalized query optimizers.
- Partial query processing and storage within the database.
- Adaptive and scaleable synchronization techniques.
- Restructuring the physical disk I/O strategies (for data storage and retrieval, as well as transaction logging) to increase concurrency subject to the physical and operational constraints of the devices.
- Buffer management strategies that will operate successfully and uniformly with time over very large buffer caches, and adapt to different patterns of buffer usage.
- Better instrumentation and performance monitors to assist with tuning.

For many of these areas, appropriate techniques are known but not yet incorporated into released products. In other areas, collaborative research and development between the DBMS vendors and the UNIX vendors is destined to provide a better match between the functionality required by the DBMS and that supported by the underlying operating system and hardware.

REFERENCES

Anon. et al. (1985): A Measure of Transaction Processing Power. *Datamation*, vol. 31, no. 7, Apr. 1, pp. 112-118.

Astrahan, M. M., Blasgen, M. W., Chamberlin, D. D., Eswaran, K. P., Gray, J. N., Griffiths, P. P., King, W. F., Lorie, R. A., McJones, P. R., Mehl, J. W., Putzolu, G. R., Traiger, I. L., Wade, B. W. and Watson, V. (1976): System R: Relational Approach to Database Management. *ACM Trans. on Database Sys.*, vol. 1, no. 2, Jun., pp. 97-137.

Astrahan, M. M., Kim, W. and Schkolnick, M. (1980): Evaluation of the System R Access Path Selection Mechanism. *Proc. IFIP Congress*, Melbourne, Australia, North-Holland, Amsterdam, Sep., pp. 487-491.

Chamberlin, D. D., Astrahan, M. M., King, W. F., Lorie, R. A., Mehl, J. W., Price, T. G., Schkolnick, M., Selinger, P. G., Slutz, D. R., Wade, B. W. and Yost, R. A. (1981): Support for Repetitive Transactions and Ad Hoc Queries in System R. *ACM Trans. on Database Sys.*, vol. 6, no. 1, Mar., pp. 70-94.

Comer, D. (1979): The Ubiquitous B-Tree. *ACM Comp. Surveys*, vol. 11, no. 2, pp. 121-137.

Larson, P. (1982): Performance analysis of linear hashing with partial expansions. *ACM Trans. on Database Sys.*, vol. 7, no. 4, pp. 566-587.

Lorie, R. A. and Wade, B. W. (1977): The Compilation of a Very High Level Data Language. Report RJ 2008, IBM Thomas J. Watson Research Center, Yorktown Heights, New York, May.

McKusick, K., Joy, W. N., Leffler, S. J. and Fabry, R. (1983): A Fast File System for UNIX. *UNIX Programmer's Manual, 4.2BSD Version*, vol. 2C, Jul.

Selinger, P. G., Astrahan, A. A., Chamberlin, D. D., Lorie, R. A. and Price, T. G. (1979): Access Path Selection in a Relational Database Management System. *Proc. ACM SIGMOD International Conf. on Management of Data*, Boston, Massachusetts, ACM, New York, May, pp. 23-34.

Yao, S. B. and Jong, D. D. (1978): Evaluation of Access Paths in a Relational Database System. Report Comp. Science Dept.-Tech. Rep. 280, Dept. of Comp. Science, Purdue Univ., West Lafayette, Indiana, Aug.

The Influence of Skew Distributions on Query Optimization

Chee Chin Low
Daryl J. D'Souza
Anthony Y. Montgomery

Department of Computer Science
Royal Melbourne Institute of Technology

email: {ccl, djds, aym}@goanna.cs.rmit.OZ.AU

Abstract

The query optimization subsystem is an indispensable component of a relational database management system. The query optimizer evaluates a range of access plans (strategies) that are often available to execute a given user query, and selects the optimal access plan. Such evaluation of access plans requires, amongst other factors, knowledge of attribute value frequency (of occurrence) distribution characteristics; to this end, the uniform distribution has been assumed traditionally. Previous work [2, 3, 8, 9] have shown that, at least when evaluating relational algebraic operators in isolation, the uniform assumption is inadequate. This is not surprising as non-key attribute values are usually non-uniformly distributed. Another important factor is the query access frequency [2, 4], which is ignored in most relational database query optimizers. This paper reports on the influence of attribute value and query access frequency distributions on cost estimation of a sequence of relational algebraic operators.
Keywords and Phrases: relational database, query optimization, skewed, non-uniform, query access plan.

1. INTRODUCTION

1.1. Background

Whilst the approaches to query optimisation vary greatly [5] a key determinant that cannot be disregarded in choosing an appropriate query strategy is knowledge about the distributions of attribute value frequency of occurrence, in the underlying database. Most query optimisers that take this into account employ the uniform distribution to model such frequencies. Previous work [2, 3, 9] which considered the effect of "skewness" in the distributions of attribute values has shown that, with respect to relational algebraic operations investigated in isolation, the uniform assumption leads to vastly differing estimations of the number of records selected, in comparison to a model which recognizes that data are skewed. Accurate prediction of the number of records selected leads towards the computation of a well-known parameter known as record selectivity [1, 12]. The record selectivity may be used to determine the number of secondary storage accesses; this result, in turn, assists towards choosing an optimal strategy to answer a query. Hence, a bad choice of data distribution model can lead to either over or underestimates of the cost of each relational algebraic operator being computed, thereby leading to poor choice of query evaluation strategy.

For attributes with a non-uniform frequency of occurrence range, query access frequency is another significant factor in selectivity and cost estimations [7].

Unlike earlier work on the effect of attribute value frequency distributions in cost estimation of individual relational algebraic operator in isolation, this paper reports on the effect of attribute value (and query access) frequency distributions in cost estimation of a sequence of relational algebraic operators (*restriction*, *join* and *projection*). This paper reports on the investigation [6] on the influence of attribute value and query access frequency distributions on a query optimizer, in selecting an access plan to evaluate a query, specifically on the following :

(1) A non-uniform based cost model, that takes into account attribute value and query access frequencies.
(2) The use of (1) to derive cost formulae for a known set of access plans within a specific query optimizer framework.
(3) The performance of the derived formulae in a controlled environment.
(4) A comparison of the non-uniform based formulae with corresponding uniform based formulae to test the hypothesis that "in the long term" a non-uniform based model is likely to better support a query optimizer in its

selection of access plans to evaluate a query.

1.2. Organization of Paper

This paper is organised as follows. Section 2 presents an overview of the skew distribution and its applicability to model attribute value and query access frequency distributions. Section 3 presents the query optimizer framework and the cost model used in the query optimizer. Section 4 describes the experiments performed, and presents a performance analysis of the experimental results. Finally, section 5 presents some concluding remarks and reports on ongoing work in this area.

2. MODELLING ATTRIBUTE VALUE AND QUERY ACCESS FREQUENCY DISTRIBUTIONS

In this section, we present the Zipfian distribution used to model the characteristics of attribute value frequency distributions as well as the query access frequency distributions.

2.1. Attribute Value Frequency Distribution

Most query optimizers employ the uniform distribution to model all their data distributions. In most practical situations it is not reasonable to assume that data are uniformly distributed. For instance, in a non-key attribute of a relation, the values are usually not evenly (uniformly) represented. A more appropriate model is one which reflects the uneven distribution of values within an attribute.

The ideal method to represent characteristics of attribute value frequency of occurrences is to store the frequencies of all values. The drawback of this method is the huge amount of storage required, with the current storage technology, this method is still not feasible.

Satoh [11] and Piatetsky-Shapiro [10] propose variations of the histogram structure to model the non-uniform distributions of attribute value frequency. These structures suffer from distribution distortion within a partition, because the distribution of attribute values within a partition is assumed to be uniform. These structures work well only with attributes of numeric type and Piatetsky-Shapiro's method is efficient only for range queries.

In the model reported in this paper, Zipf's distribution [14] is used. Consider a non-key attribute A. It is very likely that some values in A will be represented more often than others. If the attribute values of A are ranked from the most frequently occurring to the least frequently occurring, and a graph is plotted extending from the highest ranked value to the lowest ranked value, in general, a graph similar to Zipf's curve [14] is obtained, which is characterised by:

$$p_i = \frac{\alpha_d}{i^{S_d}} \tag{1}$$

$$f_i = N * p_i \tag{2}$$

where p_i is the probability of occurrence of the ith ranked value, f_i is the frequency of occurrence of the ith ranked value, N is the total number of records in the relation and the constant α_d, derived from the fact that the sum of all probabilities is unity, is given by :

$$\alpha_d = \frac{1}{\sum_{i=1}^{|D|} \frac{1}{i^{S_d}}} \tag{3}$$

where $|D|$ is the number of unique values in the domain of A.

The parameter S_d is called the *data skew factor*. It represents the skewness of a distribution. Techniques for computing S_d can be found in [3]. Note that $S_d = 0$ represents a uniform distribution, and $S_d = 1$ represents a Zipf distribution [14].

2.2. Query Access Distribution

Consider the queries directed at attribute A. If the frequency of query accesses (with respect to the afore-mentioned ranking of attribute values) are monitored, a definite behaviour would be expected to emerge in the long term; that is, certain attribute values would be accessed more frequently than others.

For the rest of this paper, only the following cases are considered :

(1) attribute value with the *highest* frequency of occurrence is most likely to be queried.

(2) attribute value with the *lowest* frequency of occurrence is most likely to be queried.

(3) all attribute values have *equal* probability of being queried.

These three cases can be modelled using the Zipfian distribution, with the skew factors greater than zero, less than zero and equal to zero, respectively. Let

$$g_i = \frac{\alpha_q}{i^{S_q}} \tag{4}$$

where g_i is the query access probability function with respect to the ith ranked attribute value. The constant α_q is derived as follows :

$$\alpha_q = \frac{1}{\sum_{i=1}^{|D|} \frac{1}{i^{S_q}}} \tag{5}$$

and S_q is the skew factor of the query access distribution, *query skew factor*.

3. A SKEW BASED ESTIMATION MODEL

3.1. Query Optimizer Framework

The framework of the query optimizer is based on the one used in [13], which optimizes simple (one and two-variable) queries only; a complex query is first decomposed into a sequence of simple subqueries. One of the advantages of optimizing simple subqueries only, is that only a small number of access plans have to be considered, thereby reducing the optimization overhead time.

Table 1 presents the basic operations supported by the system. Four categories, with a total of 17 access plans, are defined. Each category varies in the sequence

	Operations	
JI	Join Indexing	Scan the index of the join attribute to retrieve the record pointers of all the records in the associated relation.
JF	Join Filtering	Filter out records that are not part of the join.
RI	Restriction Indexing	Perform *restriction* by comparing the index values with the restriction predicate. The output of this operation is a set of record pointers pointing to records that satisfied the predicate.
RF	Restriction Filtering	Perform *restriction* by comparing the restriction predicate with actual records.
P	Projection	Project column(s) of values from a relation (or a set of records).
A	Access	Given a set of record pointers, retrieve the records referenced by the record pointers.
SS	Serial Scan	Physically scan a file to retrieve all its records.
S	Sort	Rearrange a set of records into a specific sequential order. A 3-way external merge-sort is used to sort records.
C	Concatenation	Amalgamation of two sets of records, with matching join attribute values.

Table 1: Basic Operations

of evaluation of the three basic relational algebraic operators, *restriction*, *join* and *projection*.

(1) Access ⟶restriction ⟶join

(i) SS ⟶RF ⟶S ⟶JF ⟶C ⟶P

(ii) SS ⟶RF ⟶S ⟶P ⟶JF ⟶C ⟶P

(iii) SS ⟶RF ⟶P ⟶S ⟶JF ⟶C ⟶P

(iv) SS ⟶P ⟶RF ⟶S ⟶JF ⟶C ⟶P

(2) Access ⟶join ⟶restriction

(i) SS ⟶S ⟶JF ⟶RF ⟶C ⟶P

(ii) SS ⟶S ⟶JF ⟶P ⟶RF ⟶C ⟶P

(iii) SS ⟶S ⟶P ⟶JF ⟶RF ⟶C ⟶P

(iv) SS $\longrightarrow$P $\longrightarrow$S $\longrightarrow$JF $\longrightarrow$RF $\longrightarrow$C $\longrightarrow$P

(3) Join $\longrightarrow$access $\longrightarrow$restriction

(i) JI $\longrightarrow$JF $\longrightarrow$A $\longrightarrow$RF $\longrightarrow$C $\longrightarrow$P

(ii) JI $\longrightarrow$JF $\longrightarrow$A $\longrightarrow$P $\longrightarrow$RF $\longrightarrow$C $\longrightarrow$P

(iii) JI $\longrightarrow$JF $\longrightarrow$A $\longrightarrow$C $\longrightarrow$RF $\longrightarrow$P

(iv) JI $\longrightarrow$A $\longrightarrow$JF $\longrightarrow$RF $\longrightarrow$C $\longrightarrow$P

(4) Restriction $\longrightarrow$access $\longrightarrow$join

(i) RI $\longrightarrow$A $\longrightarrow$RF $\longrightarrow$S $\longrightarrow$JF $\longrightarrow$C $\longrightarrow$P

(ii) RI $\longrightarrow$A $\longrightarrow$RF $\longrightarrow$S $\longrightarrow$P $\longrightarrow$JF $\longrightarrow$C $\longrightarrow$P

(iii) RI $\longrightarrow$A $\longrightarrow$RF $\longrightarrow$P $\longrightarrow$S $\longrightarrow$JF $\longrightarrow$C $\longrightarrow$P

(iv) RI $\longrightarrow$A $\longrightarrow$P $\longrightarrow$RF $\longrightarrow$S $\longrightarrow$JF $\longrightarrow$C $\longrightarrow$P

(v) RI $\longrightarrow$A $\longrightarrow$S $\longrightarrow$JF $\longrightarrow$RF $\longrightarrow$C $\longrightarrow$P

Within each category, the access plans vary mainly in the application of additional projection operations. The potential advantage in having additional projection operations is that they reduce the record size and also the number of records (by removing duplicate records) for subsequent processing.

For a two-variable query, the query optimizer selects two access plans to evaluate the query; one plan for each of the two relations in the query.

Example

Relations :

supplier (supp_no, supp_name, city)

part (part_no, part_name)

sp (supp_no, part_no, qty)

Attributes supplier.supp_no and sp.part_no are indexed.

Query :

Print the name of all suppliers in Melbourne who supplied part number p001.

Solution :

view1 = select *sp* (part_no = 'p001')

view2 = select *supplier* (city = 'Melbourne')

view3 = join *view1* (supp_no) *view2*

view4 = project *view3* (supp_name)

One of the options of evaluating the query above is to combine plans 3.*iv* (for relation supplier) and 4.*v* (for relation sp).

$$\begin{array}{l} \text{(Relation } \textit{supplier}\text{) JI} \longrightarrow \text{A} \longrightarrow \text{JF} \longrightarrow \text{RF} \searrow \\ \qquad\qquad\qquad\qquad\qquad \updownarrow \qquad\qquad\qquad \text{C} \longrightarrow \text{P} \\ \text{(Relation } \textit{sp}\text{) RI} \longrightarrow \text{A} \longrightarrow \text{S} \longrightarrow \text{JF} \longrightarrow \text{RF} \nearrow \end{array}$$

The combined plans for the two relations of a query are selected as follows:

(1) Find applicable access plans for the first relation.

(2) Estimate the costs and find the access plan with the minimum cost for the first relation.

(3) Find applicable access plans for the second relation.

(4) Estimate the costs and find the access plan with the minimum cost for the second relation.

(5) Combine the two selected plans to evaluate the query.

3.2. Cost Model

See [6] for derivations of the formulae below.

Nomenclature

R	:	relation R
A	:	attribute A
N	:	number of records in relation
$\|D\|$	:	number of (unique) values in domain D
I_A	:	number of unique values in attribute A
$RecSize$	:	record size (bytes)
$PageSize$	:	size of a secondary storage page (bytes)
$PtrSize$	:	size of a record pointer (bytes)
$IndexHeight(A)$	:	number of levels in the index of attribute A
$LeafNode(A)$	:	number of leaf nodes in the index of attribute A
$Pages(R)$	:	number of pages used to store relation R

Selectivities

- Restriction Selectivity

$$Sel_{Restr}(A) = \sum_{i=1}^{|D|} \frac{\alpha_d}{i^{S_d}} \times \frac{\alpha_q}{i^{S_q}}$$

- Join Selectivity

$$Sel_{Join}(R_1, R_2) = \sum_{i=1}^{min(|D_1|,|D_2|)} \left(\frac{\alpha_{d_{R1}}}{i^{S_{d_{R1}}}} \times \frac{\alpha_{d_{R2}}}{i^{S_{d_{R2}}}} \right)$$

- Projection Selectivity

$$Sel_{Proj}(R[A_1, A_2, A_3, \ldots, A_n])$$
$$= \begin{cases} \frac{\sum_{i_1=1}^{|D_{A_1}|} \sum_{i_2=1}^{|D_{A_2}|} \cdots \sum_{i_n=1}^{|D_{A_n}|} \left(1-(1-(P(A_1,i_1)P(A_2,i_2) \ldots P(A_n,i_n)))^N\right)}{N} & \text{if unique records only} \\ 1 & \text{otherwise} \end{cases}$$

where $P(A,i)$ is the probability of attribute A containing the ith ranked value, $P(A,i) = \frac{\alpha_d}{i^{S_d}}$. where $P(A,i)$ is the probability of the relation containing the ith ranked value of attribute A, $P(A,i) = \frac{\alpha_d}{i^{s_d}}$.

Costs

The cost formulae below only estimate the number of page accesses (read and write) incurred when processing the operations.

- Access

  Let n be the number of records to retrieve.

$$Cost_A^{RI}(R,n) = \begin{cases} Pages(R) \times \left(1 - \left(1 - \frac{1}{Pages(R)}\right)^n\right) & \text{if not clustered} \\ \frac{n \times RecSize(R)}{PageSize} & \text{if clustered} \end{cases}$$

  for accessing records via a restriction indexing process, and

$$Cost_A^{JI}(R,A) = \begin{cases} \sum_{i=1}^{I_A} Pages(R) \times \left(1 - \left(1 - \frac{1}{Pages(R)}\right)^{N_R \times \frac{\alpha_d}{i^{s_d}}}\right) & \text{if not clustered} \\ \frac{N_R \times RecSize(R)}{PageSize} & \text{if clustered} \end{cases}$$

  for accessing records via a join indexing process.

- Join Indexing

$$Cost_{JI}(A) = IndexHeight(A) + LeafNode(A) + \sum_{i=1}^{|D|} \left[\frac{\frac{N \times \alpha_d}{i^{s_d}} \times PtrSize}{PageSize}\right]^+$$

- Restriction Indexing

$$Cost_{RI}(P', N) = v \times \left(IndexHeight(A) + \left[\frac{Sel_{Restr}(A) \times N \times PtrSize}{PageSize}\right]^+\right)$$

  where v is the number of queried values.

The symbol $[...]^+$ represents round-up. For example $[10.01]^+ = 10$.

- Serial Scan

$$Cost_{SS}(R) = Pages(R) = \left\lceil \frac{RecSize \times N}{PageSize} \right\rceil^{+}$$

- Sort

$$Cost_S(n) = 2 \times \left(\frac{n \times RecSize}{PageSize} \right) \times \left(\left(log_m \left(\frac{n \times RecSize}{PageSize} \right) \right) - 1 \right)$$

where n is the number of records to be sorted.

The cost of the remaining operations (*concatenation*, *join filtering*, *restriction filtering* and *projection*) is equal to zero, since the inputs to these operations are obtained from other processes, and their outputs are passed on to other processes.

4. PERFORMANCE EVALUATION

4.1. Experiment Design

The experiments were performed in a controlled environment, where attribute and query values were generated with a known skew. A series of relations were used, with

(1) $|D|$ ranging from 20 to 10000 values
(2) S_d ranging from 0 to 10
(3) S_q ranging from -10 to 10
(4) and N equal to 15000 records

For each set of parameter values, a series of 1000 two-variable queries (which involved *restriction*, *join* and *projection*) were evaluated. The 1000 queries were the same, except with different queried values, where the queried values have a known distribution. The performance of the skew-based model was then compared against the performance of the uniform-based model described in [6].

4.2. Results and Analysis

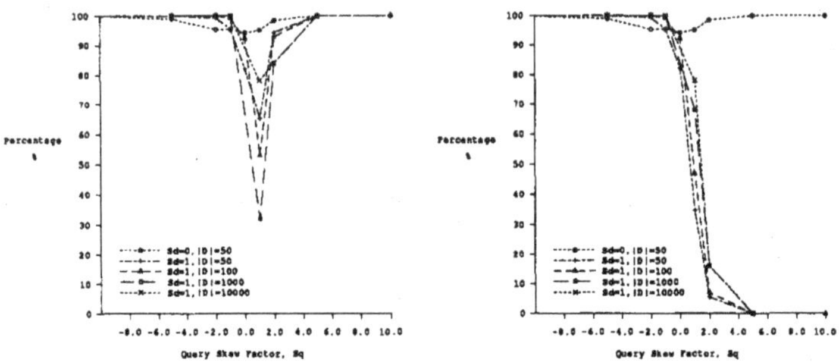

(a) Skew-Based (b) Uniform-Based

Figure 1: Percentage of selecting the (actual) minimum cost access plan versus query skew factor

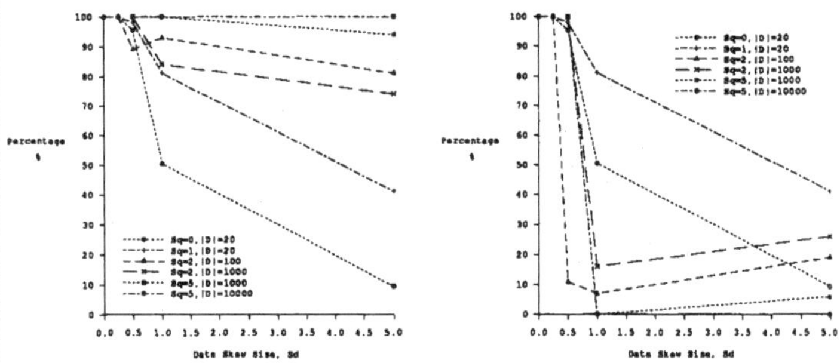

(a) Skew-Based (b) Uniform-Based

Figure 2: Percentage of selecting the (actual) minimum cost access plan versus data skew factor

Figures 1 and 2 present the results of the experiment described in section 4.1. Figures 1 (a) and (b) present the percentage of queries for which each models (skew and uniform) selects a minimum cost access plan to evaluate a query, as the value of the query skew factor varies from -10 to 10. Figure 2 presents the similar results for varying data skew factor.

For skewed attribute values ($S_d > 0$), the percentages of choosing the minimum cost access plans is low for both the skew and uniform-based models, when the query skew factor is small ($-2 \leq S_q \leq 2$). This is because the expected frequency of an attribute value estimated by both models is independent of the queried value. For a low query skew, a significant amount of queries are directed at attribute values with frequencies of occurrence that are either higher or lower than the expected frequency. As the skewness of the query access distribution increases* ($S_q > 2$), the skew-based model chooses the minimum cost access plan for more than 90% of the queries, whilst the uniform-based model chooses the minimum cost access plan for less than 20% of the queries when $S_q > 2$ and chooses the wrong (more expensive) access plan for all queries when $S_q \geq 5$.

For uniform attribute values ($S_d = 0$), both the skew and uniform-based model choose the minimum cost access plans for more than 95% of the queries; when $S_d = 0$, all attribute values have the same frequencies of occurrence in a relation.

For small query skew ($S_q = 0$ or $S_q = 1$), the percentage of selecting the minimum cost access plans for the skew-based model is very low especially for highly skewed attribute values, but it has the same performance as the uniform-based model (see figure 2). The performance of the uniform-based model decreases rapidly when the data skew increases, especially when the query skew is high ($S_q \geq 2$). When the query skew is very high ($S_q = 5$), the skew-based model chooses minimum cost access plan for more than 95% of the queries for all S_d values, whilst the uniform-based model chooses a more expensive access plan for all queries (when attribute values are skewed $S_d > 0$).

*or decreases when $S_q < -2$

5. CONCLUSION

The foregoing results clearly present the skew-based model as an improvement over uniform-based model, in terms of selecting the minimum cost access plan to evaluate a query. The results were associated with attribute values which were skewed and where the query skew was high ($S_q > 2$ or $S_q < -2$). In cases where the performance of the skew-based model was poor (small query skew factor, $-2 \leq S_q \leq 2$), the same performance, as the uniform-based model was realised.

This paper has shown that, although the skew-based model does not choose the minimum cost access plan for every query, in general, it does select the minimum cost access plan to evaluate a query, more often than the uniform-based model.

At the time of writing this paper, more intensive experiments were being conducted which will be reported in the future.

References

[1] BLASGEN, M. W., AND ESWAREN, K. On the evaluation of queries in a relational data base system. Tech. Rep. RJ1745, IBM Research, San Jose, California, 1976.

[2] CHRISTODOULAKIS, S. Implication of certain assumptions in database performance evaluation. *ACM Transaction on Database System 9*, 2 (1984), 163–186.

[3] D'SOUZA, D. Evaluation of the join relational algebraic operation. Master's thesis, Monash University, Melbourne, 1982.

[4] FALOUTSOS, C., AND CHRISTODOULAKIS, S. Design of a signature file method that accounts for non-uniform occurrence and query frequencies. In *Proc. of the 11th. VLDB Conf.* (Stockholm, 1985), pp. 165–170.

[5] JARKE, M., AND KOCH, J. Query optimization in database system. *Computing Survey 16*, 2 (1984), 111–152.

[6] Low, C. C. Query optimization taking attribute value and query access frequencies into consideration. Tech. Rep. in preparation, Dept. of Comp. Sc., Royal Melbourne Institute of Technology, Melbourne.

[7] Low, C. C., D'Souza, D., and Montgomery, A. Estimating selectivities: Taking data and query access distributions into consideration. Tech. Rep. 88/3, Dept. of Comp. Sc., Royal Melbourne Institute of Technology, Melbourne, 1988.

[8] Lynch, C. Selectivity estimation and query optimization in large databases with highly skewed distributions of column values. In *Proc. of the 14th. VLDB Conf.* (Los Angeles, California, 1988), pp. 240–251.

[9] Montgomery, A., D'Souza, D., and Lee, S. Cost of relational algebraic operations on skewed data estimates and experiments. In *IFIP - Info. Processing* (1983), pp. 235–241.

[10] Piatetsky-Shapiro, G., and Connell, C. Accurate estimation of the number of tuples satisfying a condition. In *Proc. ACM-Sigmod: International Conference on the Management of Data* (1984), ACM, pp. 256–276.

[11] Satoh, K., Tsuchida, M., Nakamura, F., and Oomachi, K. Local and global query optimization mechanisms for relational databases. In *Proc. of the 11th. VLDB Conf.* (Stockholm, 1985), pp. 405–417.

[12] Selinger, P. G., Astrahan, M. M., Chamberlain, D. D., Lorie, R. A., and Price, T. G. Access path selection in a relational database management system. In *Proc. ACM-Sigmod: International Conference on the Management of Data* (1979), ACM, pp. 23–34.

[13] Yao, S. Optimization of query evaluation algorithm. *ACM Transaction on Database System 4*, 2 (1979), 133–155.

[14] Zipf, G. K. *Human behaviour and the principle of least effort.* Addison-Wesley, Cambridge, Mass., 1949.

AUDIT EXPERT AND STATISTICAL DATABASE SECURITY

Mirka Miller

Department of Mathematics, Statistics and Computing Science

University of New England, ARMIDALE, e-mail: mirka@neumann.une.oz

and

Jennifer Seberry

Department of Computer Science

University College, ADFA, CANBERRA, e-mail: jennie@csadfa.cs.adfa.oz

ABSTRACT

A statistical database is a database in which only queries of statistical type are allowed, such as SUM, COUNT, MAX, MIN, MEAN. The security problem for a statistical database is to find suitable control mechanisms so that while statistical information is provided, no sequence of queries is sufficient to infer the values of protected fields of individual records. If such an inference is possible we say that the database has been compromised. Various types of compromise have been defined, including positive, negative and relative compromise. We attempt to classify the types of compromise considered to date.

In this paper we consider the Audit Expert proposed by Chin and Ozsoyoglu for the prevention of absolute compromise due to weighted SUM queries and we suggest some possible improvements to the algorithm which result in space saving.

Secondly, we give an extension of the Audit Expert mechanism incorporating the prevention of relative compromise using SUM type of queries. The paper concludes with some open problems in the area of security of statistical databases.

CR categories: H.3.3 (Query Formulation - Information Search and Retrieval), H.3.5 (Data Bank Sharing - Information Storage and Retrieval)

Key words: data security, database inference, statistical databases, compromise of statistical databases, relative compromise, auditing, Audit Expert

1. INTRODUCTION

A database D is a finite set of N records (or tuples) in which each record has a finite number of fields (or attributes). For the purpose of this study we shall assume that one of these fields or attributes, say X, is to be kept secret for all records i in the database. Furthermore, we assume that the elements $x_i \in X$ are real numbers.

A statistical database is a database in which only statistical type queries are allowed. The purpose of a statistical database is to supply statistical information about subsets of the database while at the same time preventing the disclosure of confidential information (the values of attribute X) of individual records.

A statistical database can be classified according to its size, whether it is static or dynamic, on-line or off-line.

Various mechanisms for the prevention of disclosure of confidential information have been proposed, but none of these mechanisms are suitable for all types of databases. The mechanisms can be grouped into two broad categories.

One category of control mechanisms employs noise addition (e.g., perturbation of data or responses). The second category uses controls which restrict the responses to queries to only those queries which will not lead to compromise. Noise addition can be used effectively for the protection of large databases, static or dynamic, on-line or off-line. However, most of the noise addition methods are not applicable to small databases.

In this paper we shall consider the case of a small statistical database (say up to about 1000 records at present). There are many situations when a statistical database is of necessity small, for example, a database of records of people with a rare disease, or an employee database of a small company. In such a case it is only possible to use a query restriction type of control mechanism for the prevention of compromise. For most of this paper we shall assume that the database is on-line and static although we will discuss briefly the dynamic case in Section 4. In the next Section we present a short overview of database compromise and the possible query restriction controls. One of these controls, the Audit Expert proposed by Chin and Ozsoyoglu[3] seems particularly promising for small databases. We shall describe the Audit Expert in Section 3 and make some observations for its possible improvement.

Sometimes, there are situations when exact information is protected but relative information may be accessible[19],[20], resulting in a 'relative compromise'. We describe this type of compromise in Section 4 and show how the Audit Expert could be modified to incorporate the prevention of relative compromise.

The paper concludes with a list of open problems in the area of security of statistical databases.

2. DATABASE COMPROMISE

A legitimate user of a statistical database has available

(a) working knowledge

(b) responses to statistical queries

(c) supplementary knowledge

(a) Working knowledge is knowledge about the attributes in the database and their domains (legal values). Such a knowledge is typically obtained by querying the data dictionary of the database system although it could alternatively be supplied in the form of a list of attribute names (or a subset of it, if appropriate) together with a corresponding list of legal values (or a subset thereof).

(b) In a statistical database the only responses given by the system concerning the actual data records are the responses to statistical types of queries, such as COUNT, SUM, MEAN, MIN, MAX.

A statistical query $q(S;X)$ (or $q(S)$ if q=COUNT) operates on the values of the attribute X (or on the whole records in case of COUNT) of a subset S of the database. The subset S is called the query set and it is selected by a characteristic formula. A characteristic formula is, informally, any logical formula over the values of the attributes using the logical operators OR, AND and NOT.

For example, using our sample database EMP of Table 1, in which we will use Salary as the confidential attribute X,

MAX(Age> 20 AND Sex=M; Salary)

is a query with the query set identified by the characteristic formula

Age> 20 AND Sex=M

The response to a query is some value (40000 in the above example) or * (undefined or unanswerable).

For example, the query MIN(City=Sydney AND Status=S; Salary)

would be answered by * (that is, the system would give no answer or possibly an error message) since the query set selected by the characteristic formula

City=Sydney AND Status=S is empty.

Name	*City*	*Sex*	*Status*	*Age*	*Child*	*Start*	*Salary*
White	Darwin	F	S	41	1	05.04.89	48700
White	Brisbane	M	M	19	4	10.07.88	16400
Mlynar	Adelaide	F	W	61	7	04.08.65	30000
Brown	Sydney	F	M	36	2	15.02.82	30000
Baker	Sydney	F	M	25	0	01.01.78	40000
Baker	Brisbane	F	D	25	1	12.02.85	17000
Peters	Melbourne	M	S	29	2	10.02.89	40000
Brown	Sydney	M	D	37	3	25.03.89	25000
Black	Melbourne	M	D	50	0	10.10.88	17000
Ling	Hobart	M	M	60	0	05.05.89	15000
Ling	Perth	M	S	42	2	14.02.70	16500
White	Brisbane	F	S	50	3	30.03.73	25500
Brown	Canberra	F	S	35	1	30.03.73	25000
Brown	Perth	F	W	44	2	01.01.89	22400

Table 1. Sample database EMP

For a more detailed explanation of the terms used here refer to Denning[10], Chapter 6.

For simplicity we identify both a characteristic formula and its corresponding query set by the same symbol; and we shall write $q(S)$ instead of $q(S;X)$ when X is understood. Similarly we shall use $q(S)$ to mean both a query and the response to the query when convenient.

Working knowledge and responses to statistical queries are obviously necessary for the statistical use of a database.

(c) The user's supplementary knowledge consists of any other knowledge concerning the individual records or groups of records in the database, that is, any knowledge which is not part of or directly derived from (a) and/or (b).

A more detailed study of supplementary knowledge and its classification is deferred to a future paper. For the purpose of the present study we shall assume that the user has a detailed knowledge of the unprotected fields of a sufficiently large number of the individuals in the database.

More precisely, we assume that the user knows a sufficient number of combinations of attribute values to identify a large enough subset of individual records in the database.

Moreover, we assume that the user knows the X-values of some t individuals (possibly including the user's own) prior to his use of the database.

Such knowledge does not constitute database compromise as it has nothing to do with the statistical use of the database. A database compromise will occur if the user can infer the X-value of some additional individual using his working knowledge, supplementary knowledge and the responses to some statistical queries.

In the absence of any restrictions on the queries a statistical database can be compromised simply by making the query SUM(S) where S is a characteristic formula that uniquely identifies a single individual.

For example, in our sample database the response to the query SUM(Age> 60) is 30000. Since there is exactly one individual in the database whose age is more than 60 years, 30000 is the salary of that person. If this information is not part of the user's initial knowledge then the database has been compromised.

Alternatively, we could deduce the value of SUM(S) from

SUM(S) = SUM (D) - SUM ($D - S$).

It is therefore obvious that to protect the field X we need to place some restrictions on the allowed queries. To prevent the above compromise we restrict the query set size $k = |S|$ (=COUNT(S)) to be within the range $[2, N-2]$, and taking into account possible initial knowledge of say $n-2$ individual X-values, we further restrict k to

$$n \leq k \leq N - n \qquad (*)$$

Since this restriction is necessary (although not sufficient) to prevent compromise we shall assume it from now on.

The best known and most powerful technique for subverting the restriction (*) is using the so called trackers[25],[24],[14],[11]. A tracker is a characteristic formula which can be used to pad a query that would otherwise be rejected because of its size, to make it answerable. The answer to the original query is then obtained by subtracting the effect of the tracker (or trackers) from the response to the padded query.

It was shown[11],[24] that finding trackers is easy. The tracker compromise techniques rest on :

(a) the ability to ask queries whose query sets overlap

(b) the ability to ask queries with variable size of query sets (within the general constraint (*))

(c) the ability to ask the number of queries needed to make the inferences.

(a) We say that the overlap of a set of queries is λ if any two queries of the set have at most λ individuals in common and some two queries have exactly λ individuals in common. If we restrict the overlap to $\lambda = 0$ then compromise using trackers is not possible, but such a database would not be very useful.

On the other hand, it has been shown[27],[4],[6],[9],[27],[18],[1] that other types of compromise are possible for any $\lambda \geq 1$ (by exploiting the overlap for MIN or MAX queries with cleverly chosen query sets; or by solving a system of linear equations for SUM queries).

Admittedly, most of these studies used key-specified queries but the same techniques may be applicable to queries specified by characteristic formula, especially in the case of a small database, assuming that the user has a sufficient amount of knowledge about the characteristics of various individuals in the database.

(b) Some of the studies mentioned above also considered queries with only constant query set size and found that compromise is still possible. Moreover, to allow only queries with fixed query set size would be too restrictive.

(c) Still another approach is to restrict the number of queries allowed, depending on the number of individuals involved in the queries. This seems to be the most promising control mechanism of the query restriction type. Chin and Ozsoyoglu[3] proposed a feasible method for implementing such a control mechanism, the Audit Expert, for the prevention of positive compromise using weighted SUM type of queries.

In the next Section we shall describe the Audit Expert and make some suggestions for its improvement.

3. AUDIT EXPERT

Threat monitoring as a mechanism for the protection of individual records in a statistical database has been suggested by various authors[17],[23]. Originally it was proposed that the system should keep record of all the statistical queries asked by a user in the form of logs. These logs would then be checked manually for any suspicious set of queries.

While this approach may be useful as a psychological deterrent and as possible evidence for legal proceedings in the case of a breach of security, it is not practical to implement.

It would be far better to delegate the task of checking to the system itself. The system could check each new query against the information it has about all the previous queries. On the basis of this information the system would then decide whether or not the present query is 'safe' and consequently whether or not it should be answered.

The Audit Expert exploits the fact that it is not necessary to store the information about all queries asked.

Compromise due to weighted SUM queries has been studied by Schwartz, Denning and Denning[26],[27]. A weighted SUM query can be thought of as a linear equation,

$$a_1x_1 + a_2x_2 + \ldots + a_Nx_N = q$$

where a_i is the weight given to record i; for example, $a_i = 0$ if the record i is not in the query set; x_i is the X-value of the individual i and q is the response to the query.

A set of weighted SUM queries can be then thought of as a system of linear equations,

$$AX = Q$$

where A is the query matrix, X is the column vector of the unknown values of attribute X, and Q is the column vector of the responses, or results of the queries. Since there is a direct correspondence between a SUM query and a row vector of a query matrix we shall say that two queries are linearly independent if the corresponding row vectors of the query matrix are linearly independent.

It is likely that not all the queries asked of the system will be linearly independent. For example, the query

SUM(Sex=M)

is linearly dependent on the queries

SUM(Sex=M AND Age$>$ 20) and SUM(Sex=M AND Age$\leq$ 20).

Note that in all the examples in this paper we restrict the weights to 0 and 1. The problem of using the Audit Expert for SUM queries is more difficult than using it for weighted SUMs. Since the SUM query is a more common query than weighted SUM we will devote our attention primarily to this problem.

The Audit Expert stores only a set of linearly independent queries. If there are k linearly independent queries then the Audit Expert stores a corresponding $k \times N$ query matrix B_k.

Of course, to prevent compromise we must have $k \leq N - 1$, otherwise the user could solve the system of equations which would result in the complete compromise of the database.

Furthermore, there is no need to store the query response vector Q as it is the composition of query sets that is the key to compromise. Chin and Ozsoyoglu[3] showed that it is possible to store the query matrix B_k in the form

$$B_k = (I_k | B_k^{'})$$

where I_k is the $k \times k$ identity matrix and $B_k^{'}$ is a $k \times (N - k)$ matrix. Thus the matrix B_k is in a normalized form and the row vectors of B_k form a basis of the space of all the queries that have been answered or whose responses could be derived from the answered queries.

For simplicity, we shall assume the user has no preknowledge of the X-value of any individual record. The use of Audit Expert with supplementary knowledge is considered in Remark 2.

Then we have

Theorem 1 (Chin and Ozsoyoglu[3]). A statistical database is compromised if and only if there is a row vector in the query matrix B_k which contains exactly one nonzero element.

Let us suppose that B_k does not contain such a row. Then a new query $q(S)$ is checked for compromise as follows.

If S is a linear combination of the row vectors of B_k then the query is 'safe' and the system is informed to answer the query. Otherwise, S is temporarily added to B_k to form a new query matrix which is then normalized, resulting in a new query matrix B_{k+1}. If the new matrix contains a row with exactly one nonzero element then the system is informed not to answer the latest query. Otherwise the query is answered and B_{k+1} is retained as the new normalized query matrix.

Example 1. After making the queries

q_1 : SUM(Child< 3)

q_2 : SUM(Sex=F AND Age< 40)

q_3 : SUM(City=Darwin OR City=Sydney)

the normalized query matrix B_3 could be

$$\begin{array}{r} \text{record} \\ B_3 = \end{array} \begin{array}{c} \begin{array}{cccccccccccccc} 1 & 4 & 6 & 2 & 3 & 5 & 7 & 8 & 9 & 10 & 11 & 12 & 13 & 14 \end{array} \\ \begin{pmatrix} 1 & 0 & 0 & 0 & 0 & 0 & 1 & 1 & 1 & 1 & 1 & 0 & 0 & 1 \\ 0 & 1 & 0 & 0 & 0 & 1 & -1 & 0 & -1 & -1 & -1 & 0 & 0 & -1 \\ 0 & 0 & 1 & 0 & 0 & 0 & 1 & 0 & 1 & 1 & 1 & 0 & 1 & 1 \end{pmatrix} \end{array}$$

Now, if the next query is

q_4 : SUM(Child$<$ 3 OR (Sex=F AND Age$<$ 40))

then the query is answered and there is no change to the query matrix.

If the new query is

q_5 : SUM(City=Sydney)

then the query will not be answered as the normalization of the new (temporary) query matrix results in a unit vector.

Lastly, if the next query is

q_6 : SUM(NOT Status=D)

then the query will be answered and added to the query matrix. After normalization the new query matrix might be for example

$$\begin{array}{rcccccccccccccc} \text{record} & 1 & 4 & 6 & 8 & 2 & 3 & 5 & 7 & 9 & 10 & 11 & 12 & 13 & 14 \end{array}$$

$$B_4 = \begin{pmatrix} 1 & 0 & 0 & 0 & 0 & 0 & 0 & 2 & 1 & 2 & 2 & 0 & 1 & 2 \\ 0 & 1 & 0 & 0 & 0 & 0 & 1 & -1 & -1 & -1 & -1 & 0 & 0 & -1 \\ 0 & 0 & 1 & 0 & 0 & 0 & 0 & 1 & 1 & 1 & 1 & 0 & 1 & 1 \\ 0 & 0 & 0 & 1 & 0 & 0 & 0 & -1 & 0 & -1 & -1 & 0 & -1 & -1 \end{pmatrix}$$

Since storing the query matrix takes up to $N^2 - N$ storage spaces, the Audit Expert is not applicable to large databases.

3.1 Improved Audit Expert

We would like to point out that in order to carry out the normalization process, it will be necessary to store not only the query matrix but also labels of the columns (labels or keys of the records in the database) as it may be necessary to permute the columns during normalization. This was indeed the case in the example above.

If the labels of columns are kept then it is not necessary to store the identity matrix I_k. It will be sufficient to store the matrix $B_k^{'}$. This will take $k \times (N - k)$ space plus N for the labels and will be maximum ($\frac{N^2}{4}$, respectively $\frac{N^2-1}{4}$) when the number of answered linearly independent queries is $k = \frac{N}{2}$ if N even, respectively $k = \frac{N+1}{2}$ or $k = \frac{N-1}{2}$ if N is odd. This could be a significant space saving in the case of a small database.

Remark 1. To reduce the size of the matrix B_k' further, in case statistics are to be done only for a portion of the database, we could use the view mechanism if available. Alternatively, it may be advantageous to store in B_k' only columns for the records involved in the queries.

Ultimately there may be up to $N-1$ answered linearly independent queries, in which case B_{N-1}' will be a column vector so that only $N-1$ elements will need to be stored plus the N labels. This fact could be exploited to make Audit Expert applicable to larger databases as a static type of control by designing B_{N-1} beforehand (or as a partially dynamic control by designing B_{N-m} for some suitable $m < \frac{N}{2}$).

Let us assume that ultimately we have the normalized query matrix

$$B_{N-1} = (I_{N-1} | B_{N-1}')$$

where the transpose of B_{N-1}' is $(b_1, b_2, \ldots b_{N-1})$.

Then all the queries involving the 'weighted' individuals

$$\lambda_1 y_1, \lambda_2 y_2, \ldots, \lambda_{N-1} y_{N-1}, \lambda_N y_N$$

where $\lambda_N = b_1\lambda_1 + b_2\lambda_2 + \ldots + b_{N-1}\lambda_{N-1}$, and $y_1, y_2, \ldots, y_N$ are the X-values of the individuals corresponding to columns $1, 2, \ldots, N$ in the matrix B_{N-1}, will be answerable.

Thus in the case of weighted SUM queries there will be infinitely many answerable queries. However, the same is not true of SUM queries.

If the weights can be only 0 or 1 then the only answerable queries will be those with $\lambda_i \in \{0, 1\}$. In particular, we must have $\lambda_N = b_1\lambda_1 + b_2\lambda_2 + \ldots + b_{N-1}\lambda_{N-1}$, and $\lambda_N \in \{0, 1\}$.

Thus the number of answerable queries will depend on the history of the answered SUM queries. This can be seem in the following example.

Example 2.

(a) Suppose that 6 SUM queries about 7 individuals have been asked with the following query sets $\{1,7\}$, $\{2,7\}$, $\{3,7\}$, $\{4,7\}$, $\{5,7\}$, $\{6,7\}$.

Using Audit Expert, these queries will be all answered and the query matrix will be

$$B_6 = \begin{pmatrix} 1 & 0 & 0 & 0 & 0 & 0 & 1 \\ 0 & 1 & 0 & 0 & 0 & 0 & 1 \\ 0 & 0 & 1 & 0 & 0 & 0 & 1 \\ 0 & 0 & 0 & 1 & 0 & 0 & 1 \\ 0 & 0 & 0 & 0 & 1 & 0 & 1 \\ 0 & 0 & 0 & 0 & 0 & 1 & 1 \end{pmatrix}$$

(b) Suppose that the 6 SUM queries concerned the query sets $\{1,7\}$, $\{2,7\}$, $\{1,2,3,7\}$, $\{1,4,6,7\}$, $\{1,5,6,7\}$, $\{6,7\}$.

These queries will be all answerable using Audit Expert and the query matrix will be

$$B_6 = \begin{pmatrix} 1 & 0 & 0 & 0 & 0 & 0 & 1 \\ 0 & 1 & 0 & 0 & 0 & 0 & 1 \\ 0 & 0 & 1 & 0 & 0 & 0 & -1 \\ 0 & 0 & 0 & 1 & 0 & 0 & -1 \\ 0 & 0 & 0 & 0 & 1 & 0 & -1 \\ 0 & 0 & 0 & 0 & 0 & 1 & 1 \end{pmatrix}$$

In case (a) there are only 6 answerable queries; these are exactly the 6 queries which resulted in the query matrix. On the other hand, in case (b) there are 34(!) answerable queries. These are the queries corresponding to the query sets $\{1,7\}$, $\{2,7\}$, $\{6,7\}$, $\{1,3\}$, $\{1,4\}$, $\{1,5\}$, $\{2,3\}$, $\{2,4\}$, $\{2,5\}$, $\{3,7\}$, $\{4,7\}$, $\{5,7\}$, $\{1,2,3,7\}$, $\{1,2,4,7\}$, $\{1,2,5,7\}$, $\{1,3,6,7\}$, $\{1,4,6,7\}$, $\{1,5,6,7\}$, $\{2,3,6,7\}$, $\{2,4,6,7\}$, $\{2,5,6,7\}$, $\{1,2,3,4\}$, $\{1,2,3,5\}$, $\{1,2,4,5\}$, $\{1,3,4,7\}$, $\{1,3,5,6\}$,

$\{1,4,5,6\}$, $\{2,3,4,6\}$, $\{2,3,5,6\}$, $\{2,4,5,6\}$, $\{1,2,3,4,7\}$, $\{1,2,3,5,7\}$, $\{1,2,4,5,7\}$, $\{1,2,3,4,5,6\}$.

In both cases the security is the same while the usability (the ratio of the number of answerable queries to the total number of possible queries) differs considerably. This opens up the question of a possible sabotage by a malevolent user (perhaps one who is frustrated at not being able to compromise the database). Another point is that the Audit Expert may be better suited to be used as a static type of control by predesigning the query matrix to ensure maximum possible usability of the database.

Remark 2. We have assumed that the user has no supplementary knowledge of the X-value of any of the individual records. However, if the user's preknowledge of say t X-values is known to the system (for example, the user's own record), Chin and Ozsoyoglu[3] showed that it can be easily incorporated into the Audit Expert simply by leaving out or ignoring the corresponding t columns in the query matrix B_k.

4. RELATIVE COMPROMISE AND AUDIT EXPERT

The compromise of a database using only SUM queries always involves the construction of some l linearly independent queries concerning l individuals. Such a set of queries can be expressed as a system of l linearly independent equations in l unknowns. Solving these equations leads to a complete compromise of the l individuals. To prevent this compromise the Audit Expert restricts responses to queries so that in any system of equations derived from the queries there would always be at least one more unknown than the number of equations. However, this restriction does not prevent another type of compromise, the "relative compromise".

Informally, a subset S ($|S| > 1$) of a database is *relatively compromised* if the relative order of magnitude of the individuals in the subset is known.

The simplest example of relative compromise occurs if we ask two SUM queries each concerning k individuals and having overlap $k-1$, for example

$$x_1 + x_3 + \ldots + x_k + x_{k+1} = q_1$$

$$x_2 + x_3 + \ldots + x_k + x_{k+1} = q_2$$

Then we can calculate the difference $x_1 - x_2 = q_1 - q_2$ and we have

$$x_1 < x_2 \text{ if } q_1 - q_2 < 0$$

$$x_1 > x_2 \text{ if } q_1 - q_2 > 0$$

$$x_1 = x_2 \text{ if } q_1 = q_2 > 0$$

The above relative compromise relies on large overlap of query sets. However, Miller and Seberry[20] showed that relative compromise can occur for any overlap $\lambda \geq 1$ by using the incidence matrix of a block design[29] for the query matrix.

Theorem 2. Let S be a subset of a database, $|S| = m + 1$. If the block design $(m+1, k, \lambda)$ exists then a subset of S can be relatively compromised using m SUM queries with overlap λ and query set size k.

Proof. See Miller and Seberry[20].

Example 3. Suppose we were allowed to make the following 5 SUM queries about 7 individuals.

(i) SUM(Sex=M AND Started>01.02.1989)

(ii) SUM(Age>20 AND Age<30)

(iii)SUM(Status=D)

(iv)SUM(City=Sydney)

(v) SUM(Child=0)

These queries correspond to the following set of 5 (linearly independent) equations in 7 unknowns.

$$y_1 + y_3 + y_7 = 80000$$

$$y_1 + y_2 + y_4 = 97000$$

$$y_2 + y_3 + y_5 = 59000$$

$$y_3 + y_4 + y_6 = 95000$$

$$y_4 + y_5 + y_7 = 72000$$

The query matrix of these 5 queries corresponds to the first 5 rows of the 7×7 incidence matrix D of the $(7,3,1)$ block design. Suppose we asked the queries corresponding to the last two rows of the matrix D and the system refused to answer those queries.

That is, we have

$$y_1 + y_5 + y_6 = C_1$$

$$y_2 + y_6 + y_7 = C_2$$

where C_1 and C_2 are unknown.

The corresponding queries to the last 2 equations could be for example

(vi)SUM((Sex=M AND (Age=29 OR (Status=D AND Child=0))) OR
(City=Sydney AND Age=36))

(vi) SUM((City=Sydney AND Age=36) OR (Age=60) OR (Sex=F AND Status+D)).

(Sex=F AND Status=D)) Then the system of equations can be written as

$$DY = Q$$

where

$Y^T = (y_1, y_2, y_3, y_4, y_5, y_6, y_7)$, $Q^T = (80000, 97000, 59000, 95000, 72000, C_1, C_2)$

and

$$D = \begin{pmatrix} 1 & 0 & 1 & 0 & 0 & 0 & 1 \\ 1 & 1 & 0 & 1 & 0 & 0 & 0 \\ 0 & 1 & 1 & 0 & 1 & 0 & 0 \\ 0 & 0 & 1 & 1 & 0 & 1 & 0 \\ 0 & 0 & 0 & 1 & 1 & 0 & 1 \\ 1 & 0 & 0 & 0 & 1 & 1 & 0 \\ 0 & 1 & 0 & 0 & 0 & 1 & 1 \end{pmatrix}$$

The inverse of D is

$$D^{-1} = \frac{1}{6}\begin{pmatrix} 2 & 2 & -1 & -1 & -1 & 2 & -1 \\ -1 & 2 & 2 & -1 & -1 & -1 & 2 \\ 2 & -1 & 2 & 2 & -1 & -1 & -1 \\ -1 & 2 & -1 & 2 & 2 & -1 & -1 \\ -1 & -1 & 2 & -1 & 2 & 2 & -1 \\ -1 & -1 & -1 & 2 & -1 & 2 & 2 \\ 2 & -1 & -1 & -1 & 2 & -1 & 2 \end{pmatrix}$$

$$Y = D^{-1}Q = \frac{1}{6}\begin{pmatrix} 128000 + 2C_1 - C_2 \\ 65000 - C_1 + 2C_2 \\ 299000 - C_1 - C_2 \\ 389000 - C_1 - C_2 \\ -10000 + 2C_1 - C_2 \\ -118000 + 2C_1 + 2C_2 \\ 53000 - C_1 + 2C_2 \end{pmatrix}$$

Thus we can calculate the values of $y_1, y_2, y_3, y_4, y_5, y_6$ and y_7 in terms of C_1 and C_2.

Since in some cases the unknowns C_1 and C_2 occur with the same coefficients we can find the differences

$$y_1 - y_5 = 138000$$

$$y_2 - y_7 = 12000$$

$$y_3 - y_4 = -90000$$

which lead to relative compromise.

In general, using the incidence matrix of a block design $(m+1, k, \lambda)$ for a query matrix we can guarantee getting some relative compromise whenever $m+1-r$ corresponding queries about $m+1$ individuals are answered, provided that $m+1 >$

2^r.

Before we consider the problem of preventing relative compromise by using the Audit Expert we shall digress and attempt to define more rigorously the types of database compromise studied to date.

4.1 Towards a Classification of Database Compromise

Let us suppose that the user has at his disposal supplementary knowledge with regard to the protected attribute X. Such knowledge may take various forms. For example, the user may know the X-value of some particular individual i, or he may know some bounds for the X-value for some individual, or he may know the relative order of magnitude of the X-values for a pair of idividuals.

Alternatively, the user may have a 'negative' knowledge in the sense that he knows that some particular value is not the X-value of a particular individual, or that some interval does not include the X-value.

We shall classify the user's knowledge with respect to the protected field X as follows.

Definition 1. A user has an *absolute knowledge*, AK, if he knows whether or not some particular value is the X-value of some particular individual in the database.

Absolute knowledge can be strong (positive), denoted AK^+, or weak (negative), AK^-. For example, if the user knows that the salary of Brown living in Canberra is 25000, then this is a strong absolute knowledge; while the knowledge that Peters' salary is not 50000 constitutes a weak absolute knowledge.

Definition 2. A user has an *approximate knowledge*, or near knowledge at ε-level, denoted NK_ε, if he knows whether or not some particular interval $[v-\varepsilon, v+\varepsilon]$ contains the X-value of some particular individual in the database.

Approximate knowledge can be strong (positive), NK^+, or weak (negative), NK^-. For example, a user knows that Peters' salary is between 30000 and 50000, then he has a strong approximate knowledge; while the knowledge that Peters' salary is not in the range [25000,35000] constitutes a weak approximate knowledge.

Definition 3. A user has a *relative knowledge*, RK, if he knows the relative order of magnitude of the X-values for a pair of individuals in a database.

If the user knows moreover the precise difference between the two X-values then we say he has a strong relative knowledge, RK^+; otherwise, if the user knows only the order, the relative knowledge is called weak and denoted by RK^-. For example, if the user knows that Black's salary is 23000 less than Peters' salary then the user has a strong relative knowledge; while if he knows that Peters' salary is greater than Black's (without knowing how much greater) then the user has a weak relative knowledge.

We shall use the above definitions to distinguish between corresponding types of database compromise.

Let us denote by $|AK^+|_i, |AK^-|_i, |NK^+|_i, |NK^-|_i, |RK^+|_i$ and $|RK^-|_i$ the number of individuals for which the user has strong absolute, weak absolute, strong approximate, weak approximate, strong relative and weak relative knowledge respectively, after receiving the responses to i statistical queries.

Definition 4. A database is *strongly absolutely compromised* if $|AK^+|_i > |AK^+|_0$ for some $i > 0$; it is *weakly absolutely compromised* if $|AK^-|_i > |AK^-|_0$ for some $i > 0$.

Definition 5. A database is *strongly approximately compromised* at ε-level if $|NK_\varepsilon^+|_i > |NK_\varepsilon^+|_0$ for some $i > 0$; a database is *weakly approximately compromised* at ε-level if $|NK_\varepsilon^-|_i > |NK_\varepsilon^-|_0$ for some $i > 0$.

The question of approximate compromise will be discussed in another paper. For the present paper we assume $|NK_\varepsilon|_0 = 0$. Note that ε is a measure of the accuracy of the knowledge of individual X-values as well as a measure of the security of the system.

Definition 6. A database is *strongly relatively compromised* if $|RK^+|_i > |RK^+|_0$ for some $i > 0$; it is *weakly relatively compromised* if $|RK^-|_i > |RK^-|_0$ for some $i > 0$.

Note that the strong types of compromise are the more dangerous ones, while the weak types of compromise are likely to be much harder (if not impossible) to prevent. To our best knowledge no study has been done about the latter type. The Audit Expert has been used for the prevention of strong absolute compromise. We shall next show how the Audit Expert could be modified to include also the prevention of strong relative compromise.

4.2 Extended Audit Expert

To extend the algorithm for the Audit Expert to incorporate the prevention of relative compromise as well as positive compromise we shall make use of the following theorem.

Theorem 3. A set of linearly independent queries is strongly relatively compromised if and only if one of the following conditions holds in the corresponding normalized query matrix B_k

(i) there is a row i with exactly two nonzero elements $B_{ii} = 1$, $B_{ij} = -1$ for some $j > k$

(ii) there are rows i and j, $i \neq j$, such that $B'_{il} = B'_{jl}$ for all l.

Proof. Let B_k be the query matrix as in the Audit Expert.

If the condition (i) holds for some row i then $x_i - x_j$ can be calculated from the responses to the queries; while if the condition (ii) holds then $x_i - x_j$ can be obtained by subtracting the jth row of B_k from the ith row. In either case the set of queries is strongly relatively compromised.

On the other hand, if a set of linearly independent queries is strongly relatively compromised then $x_m - x_n = d$, that is, d can be deduced from the queries for some m and n. If both m and n are labels within the first k columns of B_k then the corresponding rows must have the same elements in B_k' (condition (ii)). Otherwise there must be a row in B_k which contains exactly two nonzero elements 1 and -1 in the columns labeled m and n (in either order). Since we assume that $x_m - x_n$ is deducible from the k queries, at least one of the labels m and n must be a label of one of the first k columns of B_k.∎

We shall use Theorem 3 to modify the Audit Expert to prevent relative compromise as well as positive compromise.

In fact, the only step which needs to be modified is checking for compromise in case the query set S of a new query is not a linear combination of the rows of the normalized query matrix B_k. In such a case we check not only for a positive compromise (a unit row in the new normalized matrix B_{k+1}) but also for the two conditions of Theorem 3.

Example 4. Using the first three queries of Example 1 (which are free from either positive or negative compromise), we have

$$\begin{array}{rcccccccccccccc} \text{record} & 1 & 4 & 6 & 2 & 3 & 5 & 7 & 8 & 9 & 10 & 11 & 12 & 13 & 14 \end{array}$$

$$B_3 = \begin{pmatrix} 1 & 0 & 0 & 0 & 0 & 0 & 1 & 1 & 1 & 1 & 1 & 0 & 0 & 1 \\ 0 & 1 & 0 & 0 & 0 & 1 & -1 & 0 & -1 & -1 & -1 & 0 & 0 & -1 \\ 0 & 0 & 1 & 0 & 0 & 0 & 1 & 0 & 1 & 1 & 1 & 0 & 1 & 1 \end{pmatrix}$$

If a new query is

SUM((NOT City=Brisbane) OR Age=50) AND (NOT Child>5)

then this query is linearly independent of the previous queries so it is temporarily added to B_3 and normalized, resulting in the new query matrix

$$\begin{array}{c} \text{record} \\ \\ B_4 = \\ \\ \end{array} \begin{array}{c} \begin{array}{cccccccccccccc} 1 & 4 & 6 & 12 & 2 & 3 & 5 & 7 & 8 & 9 & 10 & 11 & 13 & 14 \end{array} \\ \begin{pmatrix} 1 & 0 & 0 & 0 & 0 & 0 & 0 & 1 & 1 & 1 & 1 & 1 & 0 & 1 \\ 0 & 1 & 0 & 0 & 0 & 0 & 1 & -1 & 0 & -1 & -1 & -1 & 0 & -1 \\ 0 & 0 & 1 & 0 & 0 & 0 & 0 & 1 & 0 & 1 & 1 & 1 & 1 & 1 \\ 0 & 0 & 0 & 1 & 0 & 0 & 0 & 1 & 0 & 1 & 1 & 1 & 1 & 1 \end{pmatrix} \end{array}$$

Since rows 3 and 4 in B_4' are the same, the query is not answered and the query matrix B_3 is retained as the query matrix.

On the other hand, if the next query is

SUM(Status=D)

then the new query is answered and the new normalized query matrix is

$$\begin{array}{c} \text{record} \\ \\ B_4 = \\ \\ \end{array} \begin{array}{c} \begin{array}{cccccccccccccc} 1 & 4 & 6 & 7 & 2 & 3 & 5 & 8 & 9 & 10 & 11 & 12 & 13 & 14 \end{array} \\ \begin{pmatrix} 1 & 0 & 0 & 0 & 0 & 0 & 0 & 0 & 0 & 1 & 1 & 0 & 0 & 1 \\ 0 & 1 & 0 & 0 & 0 & 0 & 1 & 1 & 0 & -1 & -1 & 0 & 0 & -1 \\ 0 & 0 & 1 & 0 & 0 & 0 & 0 & -1 & 0 & 1 & 1 & 0 & 1 & 1 \\ 0 & 0 & 0 & 1 & 0 & 0 & 0 & 1 & 1 & 0 & 0 & 0 & 0 & 0 \end{pmatrix} \end{array}$$

Remark 3. The Extended Audit Expert can be used also for the prevention of strong relative compromise for weighted SUM queries.

Remark 4. We have considered using the Audit Expert for small static databases. It would be possible to modify the Audit Expert for use in a dynamic statistical database[3]. However, obtaining statistics from a small dynamic database may not be very meaningful.

Consider for example that the query

MEAN(Sex=M AND Started>01.02.89) (=27333)

was made, then the record Peters was subsequently deleted. If we next ask the query

MAX(Sex=M AND Started>01.02.89) (=25000)

then the results of the two queries will be inconsistent.

5. CONCLUSION

The Audit Expert proposed by Chin and Ozsoyoglu[3] provides a high degree of security (the only possible insecurity of the system would be due to supplementary knowledge) and a reasonable level of usability for weighted SUM queries.

In this paper we consider the Audit Expert for the prevention of compromise using SUM queries. We suggest some possible improvements to the Audit Expert and an extension of the Audit Expert to incorporate also the prevention of relative compromise of a statistical database.

We shall conclude this paper by listing some open problems.

1. The Audit Expert would be more useful if it could be extended to other types of statistical queries, such as MAX, MIN, MEAN and COUNT.

2. Using Audit Expert guarantees perfect security only if the user has no preknowledge of the X-values of individual records. If the user's preknowledge is known, it can be easily incorporated into the Audit Expert. However, if the preknowledge is unknown there is no way of dealing with it at present.

3. In view of the above, more study of supplementary knowledge needs to be done, in particular to classify supplementary knowledge and to deal with it in a systematic way.

4. In case of static use of Audit Expert for protection against compromise more analysis needs to be done to find suitable designs of the query matrix which ensure maximum usability for both the Improved and the Extended Audit Expert.

5. Usability of the database using Audit Expert for weighted SUMs is not effected by including the prevention of relative compromise. The same cannot be said for SUM queries. More study needs to be done on the usability in such a case.

ACKNOWLEDGEMENT

We would like to thank Dr. Ivan Fris for many helpful discussions.

REFERENCES

[1] CHIN, F., Security problems on inference control for SUM, MAX, and MIN queries, *Journal of the Association for Computing Machinery*, 33, No.3, pp.451-464 (1986)

[2] CHIN, F.Y. and OZSOYOGLU, G., Statistical database design, *ACM Transactions on Database Systems*, 6, No.1, pp.113-139 (1981)

[3] CHIN, F.Y. and OZSOYOGLU, G., Auditing and inference control in statistical databases, *IEEE Transactions on Software Engineering*, $SE-8$, No.6, pp.574-582 (1982)

[4] CHIN, F.Y., Security in statistical databases for queries with small counts, *ACM Transactions on Database Systems*, 3, No.1, pp.92-104 (1978)

[5] CHIN, F.Y., KOSSOWSKI, P. and LOH, S.C., Efficient inference control for range SUM queries, *Theoretical Computer Science*, 32, pp.77-86 (1984)

[6] DAVIDA, G.I., LINTON, D.J., SZELAG, C.R. and WELLS, D.L., Database security, *IEEE Transactions on Software Engineering*, $SE-4$, No.6, pp.531-533 (1978)

[7] DAVIDA, G.I., WELLS, D.L. and KAM, J.B., Security and privacy, *Proceedings of COMPSAC 78 Computer Software and Applications Conference*, Chicago IL, 13-16 Nov 1978, pp.194-203 (1978)

[8] DE JONGE, W., Compromising statistical databases responding to queries about means, Jan 1981, *ACM TODS*, 8, No.1, pp.60-80 (1983)

[9] DEMILLO, R.A., DOBKIN, D. and LIPTON, R.J., Even data bases that lie

can be compromised, *IEEE Transactions on Software Engineering*, SE – 4, No.1, pp.73-75 (1978)

[10] DENNING, D.E.R., *Cryptography and Data Security*, Addison-Wesley, Sydney (1982)

[11] DENNING, D.E. and SCHLORER, J., A fast procedure for finding a tracker in a statistical database, *ACM Transactions on Database Systems*, 5, No.1, pp.88-102 (1980)

[12] DENNING, D.E. and SCHLORER, J., Inference controls for statistical databases, *Computer*, pp.69-82 (1983)

[13] DENNING, D.E., Secure Statistical databases with random sample queries, *ACM Transactions on Database Systems*, 5, No.3, pp.291-315 (1980)

[14] DENNING, D.E., DENNING, P.J. and SCHWARTZ, M.D., The tracker : A threat to statistical database security, *ACM Transactions on Database Systems*, 4, No.1, pp.76-96 (1979)

[15] DOBKIN, D., JONES, A.K. and LIPTON, R.J., Secure databases : Protection against user influence, *ACM Transactions on Database Systems*, 4, No.1, pp.97-105 (1979)

[16] FERNANDEZ, E.B., SUMMERS, R.C. and WOOD, C., *Database Security and Integrity*, Addison-Wesley (1981)

[17] HOFFMAN, L.J. and MILLER, W.F., Getting a personal dosier from a statistical data bank, *Datamation*, pp.74-750 (1970)

[18] MICHALEWICZ, Z., Compromisability of a statistical database, *Inform. Systems*, 6, No.4, pp.301-304 (1981)

[19] MICHALEWICZ, Z., A coin-weighing problem and its connection with the security of a statistical database, *Fundamenta Informaticae* X, pp.81-92 (1987)

[20] MILLER, M. and SEBERRY, J., Relative compromise of statistical databases, *Australian Computer Journal*, 21, No.2, pp.56-61 (1989)

[21] OZSOYOGLU, G. and CHIN, F.Y., Enhancing the security of statistical databases with a question-answering system and a kernel design, *IEEE Transactions on Software Engineering*, $SE-8$, No.3, pp.223-234 (1982)

[22] SCHLORER, J. and DENNING, D.E., Protecting query based statistical output in multipurpose database systems, *Security, IFIP/Sec'83*, V.A. Fak(ed.), North-Holland, pp.37-46 (1983)

[23] SCHLORER, J., Confidentiality of statistical records: A threat-monitoring scheme for on line dialogue, *Methods of Information in Medicine*, 15, No.1, pp.36-42 (1976)

[24] SCHLORER, J., Disclosure from statistical databases: Quantitative aspects of trackers, *ACM Transactions on Database Systems*, 5, No.4, pp.467-492 (1980)

[25] SCHLORER, J., Identification and retrieval of personal records from a statistical data bank, *Methods of Information in Medicine*, 14, No.1, pp.7-13 (1975)

[26] SCHWARTZ, M.D., DENNING, D.E. and DENNING, P.J., Securing data bases under linear queries, *Information Processing 77*, B. Gilchrist(ed.), IFIP, North-Holland, pp.395-398 (1977)

[27] SCHWARTZ, M.D., DENNING, D.E. and DENNING, P.J., Linear queries in statistical databases, *ACM Transactions on Database Systems*, 4, No.2, pp.156-167 (1979)

[28] SEBERRY, J. and PIEPRZYK, J., *Cryptography : An Introduction to Computer Security*, Prentice-Hall, Sydney (1988)

[29] STREET, A.P. and WALLIS, W.D., *Combinatorial Theory : An Introduction*, Charles Babbage (1977)

Implementation of a Multilevel Encryption Scheme for Database Security

T. Hardjono, M. Jennings and C. J. Lokan

Department of Computer Science
University College
University of New South Wales
Australian Defence Force Academy
Canberra, ACT 2600, AUSTRALIA
email: thomas@cs.adfa.oz, cjl@cs.adfa.oz

Abstract

This paper describes the implementation of an encryption scheme based on modulo exponentiation to secure database systems. Users are divided into three groups with different security clearances. The "read-down" and "write-up" rule is observed, where users can only read data of the same or lower security level, and can only write to data areas of the same or higher security level. Each user is required to enter a key which determines the security clearance of the user. The scheme was developed on the $UNIFY^{TM}$ database management system under the $Unix^{TM}$ operating system. Various implementation decisions are discussed, together with an explanation of the representation of security information used in the implementation.

Keywords: Data encryption, Security, Database systems.

CR Categories: E.3, H.2.0, H.3

INTRODUCTION

This paper describes the implementation of a multilevel encryption scheme for database system security. This scheme was proposed by Hardjono and Seberry 1). It permits authorized users to read data with only their own or lower security classification, and prevents unauthorized users from accessing any information in the database.

The encryption scheme was implemented in the C programming language on the UNIFY [1] Database Management System (DBMS), version 3.2, running on the Unix [2] operating system. UNIFY is a full relational database system, with a menu driven user interface.

[1] $UNIFY^{TM}$ is a registered trademark of Unify Corp.

[2] $Unix^{TM}$ is a registered trademark of AT&T Bell Laboratories.

The main menu provides the user with several options, including creating and modifying a database, report generation, database reconfiguration, and backups.

A database in UNIFY can be accessed via the SQL language or via the UNIFY interface called ENTER. The ENTER interface consists of "templates" or "forms" of screen fields which are filled-in by the user, and record searching is based on the completed screen fields. This method of presenting queries to UNIFY is called *Query By Forms.* The advantages of SQL over ENTER lie in its ability to perform partial-match and range queries. However, since partial-match and range queries cannot be done with encrypted data, it was decided that a software tool similar to ENTER was all that was required to manage an encrypted database.

Throughout this paper the term "user" refers to the general user who does not have any knowledge of the internal workings and implementation of UNIFY and the security software. The term "developer", "super user" or "database administrator" refers to persons who manage the database management system and the security software. The implementation concentrated on the multilevel encryption scheme, and no attempt was made to create a completely secure database management system running on the Unix operating system.

BACKGROUND

This section gives a brief background to the multilevel encryption scheme proposed by Hardjono and Seberry [1]. The scheme is based on exponentiation modulus similar to that of the Rivest-Shamir-Adleman (RSA) [2] and the Diffie-Hellman (DH) [3] cryptosystems. In this discussion we assume three security levels, namely the A-level, B-level and C-level. The A-level is assumed to be the highest and C-level the lowest.

Given a message M, encryption key K_e and decryption key K_d, encryption and decryption are as follows:

$$C = E_{K_e}(M) \equiv M^{K_e} \bmod N \tag{1}$$

$$M = D_{K_d}(C) \equiv (M^{K_e})^{K_d} \bmod N \tag{2}$$

where C in this case is the resulting cryptogram. Here K_e and K_d are chosen such that:

$$K_e.K_d \equiv 1 \bmod \phi(N) \tag{3}$$

Here $\phi(N)$ is the Euler Totient Function. In the RSA cryptosystem $\phi(N) = lcm(p-1, q-1)$ and $N = p.q$ (both p and q primes).

In the proposed scheme the keys K_e and K_d are derived from

$$D(N) = (c.\phi(N)) + 1 \tag{4}$$

where c is an integer greater than zero. Any two factors of $D(N)$ whose product equals $D(N)$ can be used as K_e and K_d.

The scheme gets its multilevel property from the fact that given a pair of keys (K_e, K_d) generated using $D(N)$ for a suitable N and c, these keys can encrypt and decrypt data which was already encrypted using some of the other keys generated from the same $D(N)$. Let $D(N)$ have the divisors $(d_1, d_2, \ldots, d_n)$ in an increasing order and that the product of each pair

$$(d_1, d_n), (d_2, d_{n-1}), \ldots, (d_k, d_{n-k+1})$$

equals $D(N)$. To each of the security levels A-level, B-level and C-level we assign a pair of these divisors. If we encrypt data using d_{n-j} and $d_{j+1} \mid d_k$ (the symbol "|" means "divides") then we can decrypt it using d_k because $d_k = \alpha.d_{j+1}$ for some integer $\alpha > 0$ and positive $j < n$. Thus we have:

$$d_{n-j}.d_k \equiv d_{n-j}.(\alpha.d_{j+1}) \equiv \alpha \bmod \phi(N) \tag{5}$$

and

$$K_{decrypt} = d_k/\alpha = d_{j+1} \tag{6}$$

where $K_{decrypt}$ is the actual key used by the security software.

From the above discussion it is clear that a given key determines the "transformation" to be applied to itself in order to produce a decryption key for data of a given security level. Certain transformations, such as the division by α which gives a result less than 1, are defined as being equivalent to having an "insufficient privilege" and thus rejected. Consider the set (d_1, d_n), (d_2, d_{n-1}) and (d_3, d_{n-2}) where $d_1 \mid d_3$, $d_1 \mid d_2$ and $d_2 \mid d_3$. We encrypt all A-level data using d_{n-2}, all B-level data d_{n-1} and all C-level data using d_n. In this configuration all A-clearance user designated as having key d_3 can not only decrypt A-level data, but also B-level and C-level data. B-clearance users can decrypt B-level and C-level data, while C-clearance users can only decrypt C-level data. In following discussions the pairs of encryption and decryption keys will be denoted by (K_{e_A}, K_{d_A}) for A-level, (K_{e_B}, K_{d_B}) for B-level and (K_{e_C}, K_{d_C}) for C-level.

In this implementation we have chosen a prime N (unlike the RSA cryptosystem). The lowest level decryption key K_{d_C} is chosen from the factors of $D(N)$ such that it is relatively prime to $D(N)$. The other keys are are chosen using a suitable α and β such that $K_{d_C}.\alpha = K_{d_B}$ and $K_{d_B}.\beta = K_{d_A}$ where both K_{d_A} and K_{d_B} are also factors of $D(N)$ and coprime to $\phi(N)$.

The user keys are issued by concatenating the user-ID to one of the three decryption keys K_{d_A}, K_{d_B} or K_{d_C} and then encrypting this result with a separate master encryption key and modulus N. Since each user has a unique secret user-ID held by the super user, each user will have a unique user decryption key. When a user first logs on to the database system for a session, his or her key is decrypted using a secret (master) decryption key, resulting in the original concatenation of the user-ID with one of K_{d_A}, K_{d_B} or K_{d_C}. This concatenation is kept in main memory for determining the user's access restrictions until the end of the session.

TESTBED FOR THE IMPLEMENTATION

To test the implementation of the encryption system, a database was created containing information from a telephone directory. This database was chosen for the following reasons:

- Telephone information has several levels of security. The lowest security level would correspond to an ordinary, listed number. The next level would correspond to an unlisted number belonging to an ordinary member of the public. Higher levels of security would be possessed by "important" parties, such as government members.
- Test data was readily available in the form of the computer science departmental telephone directory. The departmental telephone directory has some duplication of names and numbers (for instance, two people with the same surname, or a number of people sharing the same phone). Therefore we could easily test search routines that result in multiple successful matches.

A user accessing the database can attach levels of security to each of the database fields, and thus the database can become a testbed for the encryption scheme. He or she can only modify fields with security level equal to or less than his or her security clearance.

The telephone directory database consists of one record-type with the following fields:

- *Account Number*: this is the common account number found on telephone bills. It is a 15 character field.
- *Surname*: this is a 30 character field.
- *Initials*: this field contains a person's initials and additional titles, and it is 30 characters long.
- *Status*: the occupational status of the person is stored in this field, which is 45 characters long.
- *Phone Number*: this is a 15 character field, which only contains digits (without any of the dashes or brackets which are commonly used by different people in writing phone numbers).

Note that all the fields are declared to be of type *string* or *char*. There are three reasons for only using characters to store the field data. First, the type *numeric* in UNIFY has a maximum length of only 9 decimal digits. This is clearly insufficient to hold cryptograms of up to 100 decimal digits. Second, the arbitrary precision mathematical routines used in the encryption module accept and return numbers in the form of character strings. Since not all commercial database management systems allow fields to contain arbitrary bit strings or *raw bits*, keeping fields in the general form of type *string* conforms with the third motivation, which is that of portability of the encryption module. The only disadvantage in this implementation in using character representation of numbers is that users can enter non-numeric values into the *Phone Number* and *Account Number* fields. As will be discussed later, this problem was overcome by using input checking routines for each field updated or created by a user.

In the current implementation the modulus N is 32 decimal digits long, and the length of each field must be a multiple of fifteen characters. Before encryption, each field entry is broken down into fifteen character segments and each segment is converted into a 30-digit number, each character represented by a two digit number. The 30-digit number results from concatenating the fifteen 2-digit numbers. When this 30-digit number is raised to a power modulo N it may result in a number cryptogram of up to 32 digits. Similar to the conversion before encryption, the resulting cryptogram is converted back to strings of up to 16 characters which are then placed in the database as type *string*. This conversion and upper limit of fifteen-character segments is necessary to ensure that the message M is always less than the modulus N. The characters used to represent numbers are a subset of the ASCII character set: specifically, the ASCII octal \001 to \005 and \040 to \176. For example, the letter A (or \101) takes the 38th position in the list of representative characters, hence it is represented as the 2-digit number 38. In this configuration the word 'PHONE' is represented as '5345525142'.

One of the main problems faced with this character representation is that UNIFY expects screen input via ENTER to have the same length as the predefined field storage space. In this case, we require the message M to be less than the modulus N, hence the user input for a 16 character field space must be limited to only 15 characters. As will be discussed later, to overcome this problem an independent routine was written which would accept $n-1$ characters for a predefined n character space, employing the same low level functions as the library input routines. This approach provided the most direct and fastest solution to the problem.

SECURITY INFORMATION

In the implementation of the secure database system, a certain amount of security information is maintained for each record in the database. Since encryption is performed on a field basis, each field must have attached to it information concerning its security level. Other information is also useful, namely the user who last updated the field and the time of last update. This information is particularly useful to perform audit trails on the database records, and to be used in checksums to detect illegal manipulation by malicious users [4]. The security information must be kept separate from the database.

Two data structures in the C programming language have been chosen to hold the necessary security information and they are implemented in the form of a linked list. The first data structure is associated with the fields of a given record and contains three components, namely the user-ID and security level of the user who last updated the field, the date of last modification and the time of the last update of the field. The second data structure is associated with the records of the database. It contains two pointers for the purpose of the linked list, an integer for the logical record number (maintained by UNIFY) and an array of pointers to the first data structure. The length of the array equals the number of fields in the record.

The security information for each field of every record in the database is stored in a file in encrypted format. The encryption follows the same method of exponentiation modulus as before, with a different set of encryption parameters to that of the actual data in the records. During storage, the security information contained in the two data structures are concatenated and then encrypted. Specifically, the user-ID, date, time, logical record number and the field number are concatenated to form an integer of up to 20 digits (the length of the concatenation depends on the user-ID, record number and field number). This 20-digit number is then encrypted and stored in a separate file.

It is here that the assumption about the availability of a secure storage becomes important. It is very difficult or impossible to maintain security without having some kind of secure storage to hold the cryptographic information (such as keys) and the field security information. Although this information may be kept in secondary storage in an encrypted form, nothing prevents a malicious user from arbitrarily modifying the cryptograms, rendering them useless. In this implementation we also assume that a periodic backup is made of the database file (and other associated files) and of the cryptographic and record security information.

CUSTOMISING UNIFY

In implementing of the multilevel encryption scheme on the UNIFY database management system, three approaches were taken in turn in the effort to customize UNIFY with respect to our needs. In all cases the UNIFY low level routines provided what we think is a reasonable set of options, namely the ability to create new records, to modify and delete records and to perform searching through the database.

One aspect of searching in encrypted records that must be stressed is that only exact matches can be sought in the database. Since encryption "destroys" the information contained within a field, the organization of records by the database management system is based on cryptograms, not on plaintext field entries. Hence, if the user wants to find a record with Account Number M, the value M is encrypted into cryptogram C and the cryptogram is used as the search field into the database. Related to this aspect is the unavailability in most commercial database management systems (including UNIFY) of functions that allow access to blocks (or pages) of data which contain records. Had such functions existed, encryption of records could be postponed until a record is to be written to a block.

Alternatively, each encrypted record in the database could be fetched, decrypted and then compared to the requirements and conditions of the user query. This would certainly allow partial-match and range queries to be performed. However, retrieving every record in order to satisfy one query will probably result in too many mismatches. Hence it is not a viable method for encrypted databases. We consider the solution of encrypting the screen field entries in queries as better than decrypting all the records of the database.

The first approach taken in customizing UNIFY was simply to use ENTER as it was. ENTER already had a number of *screen functions* which are associated with the individual screen fields in *Query By Forms*. The encryption module was then attached to these screen functions and was invoked whenever a field entry passed through the screen functions. However, after a short time the limitations of this approach became evident, particularly in the case of the multilevel nature of the encryption scheme. The ENTER screen functions would only allow one retrieval for each field value. This means that if a user had security clearance for two (or more) levels, he or she needed to perform the search manually twice.

The screen functions did not allow a search field value to be encrypted, searched, re-encrypted and then searched again. Another related difficulty was the fact that the screen functions were invoked by ENTER only when new records were added to the database. These functions were not invoked in the case of browsing and deletion of records.

The second approach was to attach independent routines to ENTER. A separate C program was written to perform record searching, using the low level record access routines of UNIFY. Hence when a user runs ENTER he or she is placed into the independent search routine instead of ENTER, and ENTER itself is only used as a passage into the separate routines. Depending on the modes of usage, the user will either run the customized ENTER or the independent search routines, with no difference apparent to the user. This set-up solved the problems in the first approach. Users with access to more than one security level could perform one search that covered all the security levels available to him or her.

One of the major disadvantages of this configuration was that a user was still able to access the database file using another execution of UNIFY and modify the encrypted data. Even though he or she could not understand the encrypted records, the user could still delete or modify the characters within the fields of the records. In this implementation this problem has not been addressed since the cause of the problem lies partly in the operating system. The design of UNIFY on Unix allows several users to have independent processes running an instance of UNIFY, each accessing a single common database file. If this problem is to be solved, then all users on the computer system must use the current implementation of the encryption scheme on UNIFY. Otherwise, different users can run different customized UNIFY programs on the common database file, hence having access to the *Delete* and *Modify* commands.

The third and final approach in this implementation was to incorporate into UNIFY an independent C program to perform all our needs, by way of "registering" it with the UNIFY main menu. In a sense this effort was a continuation of the second approach of using an independent search routine. This program had a user interface which was very similar to that of ENTER and all its functions were written to simulate the options available in ENTER. Complete independence was not possible since the program still employed the low level screen initialization and database routines of UNIFY. This configuration is shown in Figure 1. In this configuration access to the encrypted database is through the separate program, which is invoked via the UNIFY main menu. The program consists of a number of smaller routines, two among which perform browsing and searching of records in the database. Such programs can be attached to the main menu by compiling it and "loading" it with ENTER. The resulting ENTER executable is placed in the same *bin* directory as the database file. On running UNIFY, this executable is invoked instead of the normal UNIFY executables.

In moving from the first approach to the second and finally to the third approach little modification was necessary to the code. The main reason for this ease in moving from screen functions to a separate program lie in the fact that the C code of the program made much use of the UNIFY low level routines, in particular those that involve record accesses into the database. It is here that we have learnt an important lesson in the customization of UNIFY. Having completed the foundations of the customization in the form of a program which uses the low level routines, the task of attaching an interface to the program or

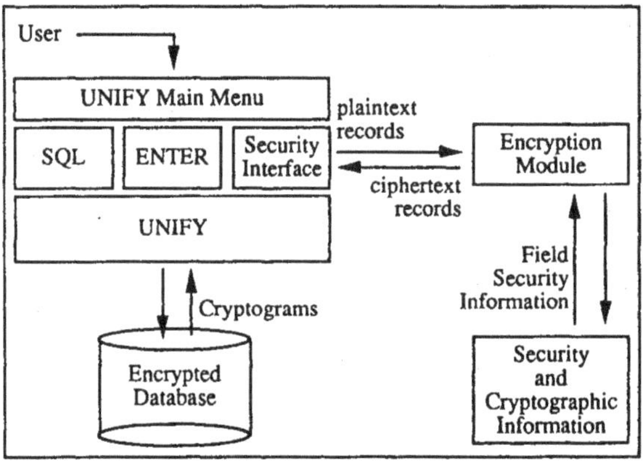

Figure 1: UNIFY configuration with the encryption scheme

attaching the program to the screen functions did not present any difficulties. Although the screen functions had some limitations, the use of these "hooks" into the low level routines allowed the shift from one approach to the next with considerable ease.

PERFORMANCE AND SECURITY

One of the most important aspects of cryptographic algorithms is their speed and ease of implementation, both in software and in hardware. Although some research has been done in the effort to benchmark the speed of exponentiation modulus (such as the RSA cryptosystem) in hardware, little work has been done in benchmarking the software implementations. One reason for this lack of interest is simply that a software implementation is not nearly as fast as hardware implementations.

In the current implementation of the multilevel encryption scheme we have employed software to perform exponentiation modulus, using a small library of arbitrary precision mathematics routines[3]. This library contains the exponentiation modulus procedure which takes input in terms of strings (hence the choice of the *char* type for all the fields in the records).

In general the speed of exponentiation modulus depends on the size of its parameters, namely the encryption key, the message M and the modulus N. In this implementation the length of each of the parameters are less than 32 decimal digits. With this choice for

[3]The mathematics routine employed in this implementation was derived from a collection of routines written by Mark S. Manasse (Digital Equipment Corporation, Palo Alto) and Arjen K. Lenstra (University of Chicago). The routines were written for use in a world-wide attempt to factor 100-digit numbers. For more details see Ruthen [5].

```
[phnbk]                         UNIFY Release 3.2              7 FEB 1989 - 11:22
[I]NQUIRE                       Phone Book Maintenance


Account Number: Ar2zc]1<~8<BcPf2
Surname       : A>fs%L<RN`xQ_Oql;tAFOv{Odx9B'p<
Initials      : j7!WXlc7*}LhSxkzl;tAFOv{Odx9B'p<
Status        : L&'Na&Z2bwYDc{rgl;tAFOv{Odx9B'p<l;tAFOv{Odx9B'p<
Phone Number  : CgNFo\g,McV!R v"












[N]EXT, [P]REVIOUS, [S]TOP
searched:     15 selected:     15 current:     1
```

Figure 2: An example of the encrypted fields of the record

the size of the parameters, the speed of exponentiation is reasonably fast, enough for the user not to notice the difference when using *Query By Forms* in UNIFY. Again, the speed depends on the overall load by other users on the operating system at any given time.

In terms of security we consider 30 to 32 digits for the modulus N as being sufficient since the modulus is kept secret. Attacks on the RSA cryptosystems have been based mainly on factoring the modulus N. In our case the modulus N and all other parameters are kept secret, hence the opponent cannot even attempt to solve the factorization and discrete logarithm problems. The opponent can only perform a ciphertext-only attack, by looking at the cryptograms in the database, an example of which is shown in Figure 2. Furthermore, we envisage that the cryptographic information for each user should be placed in a "tamper-proof" device such as a smartcard. Such devices should also be used by a super-user or database administrator who holds master keys for initialization of the database system every day. This avoids the need to store the cryptographic information in the computer system.

CONCLUSION AND COMMENTS

This paper has discussed the implementation of a multilevel encryption scheme on the UNIFY database management system. The multilevel encryption scheme allows the designation of keys to a number of security clearances, where each key determines the "transformation" applied to the key in order to derive the actual record decryption key. In this implementation the length of the modulus N is 32 decimal digits, which is considered secure enough provided the modulus remains secret. The speed of the record retrieval has had little effect on the normal speed of query answering via the *Query By Forms* method. In this case it is important to realize that the speed of record retrievals depend on the load of the overall operating system at the time of the query, due to the software implementation of the arbitrary precision mathematical routines employed in the encryption module. Hence a hardware implementation of the encryption module will provide faster access to the encrypted records of the database.

During the implementation three approaches to the problem of attaching the encryption scheme to the UNIFY database management system were taken. The implementation started with the use of the ENTER screen functions and culminated in the use of separate record searching and encryption routines which were "registered" with the UNIFY main menu. Throughout the implementation one prevailing problem was the availability of the database files to unauthorized users via different executions of the UNIFY database program under the Unix operating system. This problem can be solved by installing UNIFY with the multilevel encryption scheme as the default database system for every user. It must be understood, however, that no matter how secure a database management system is configured, such security will be of no use if the underlying operating system is unsecure. With this in mind, one suitable solution to this overall problem is to use a separate database machine running a database security kernel, allowing more control over security by the database controllers and administrators.

Acknowledgements

We would like to thank Prof. J. Seberry and Dr. J. Pieprzyk for comments and suggestions concerning the implementation. This work was supported by a University College Special Research Grant.

References

[1] Hardjono, T. and Seberry, J., "A Multilevel Encryption Scheme for Database Security", Proceedings of the 12th Australian Computer Science Conference, 209–218 (1989).

[2] Rivest, R. L., Shamir, A. and Adleman, L., "A method for obtaining digital signatures and public-key cryptosystems", Communications of the ACM, 21, 120–128, (1978).

[3] Diffie, W. and Hellman, M., "New directions in cryptography", IEEE Transactions on Information Theory, IT-22, 397–427 (1976).

[4] Denning, D. E., "Cryptographic checksums for multilevel database security", Proceedings of the 1984 IEEE Symposium on Security and Privacy, 52–61 (1984).

[5] Ruthen, R., "Factoring googols", Scientific American, 259, 12–13 (1988).

Proof of a Concurrency Control Algorithm Using a Possibilities Mapping

J. K. Lee and A. Fekete
Basser Department of Computer Science,
University of Sydney

Abstract: This paper explores concurrency control in nested transaction systems. An algorithm is presented based on Moss's read-update locking, and verified by providing a possibilities map to a similar but more abstract algorithm previously proved correct.

1 Introduction

Several systems for distributed programming (for example, Argus [5] and Camelot [7]) are based on the notion of nested transactions, which allow the programmer to write distributed applications which contain internal concurrency and localized recovery from failure without needing to deal explicitly with synchronizing access to shared data or rolling back failed activity. Of course, relieving the application programmer of these worries is only possible because the system itself provides the locking and logging necessary to avoid inconsistencies appearing in the shared data. Considerable research effort is currently being given to analysing and verifying the algorithms that can be used to provide the concurrency control and recovery needed in a nested transaction system (see among others [2], [1], [3], [4].) So far, this research has concentrated on verifying very abstract and non-deterministic algorithms, in the belief that these reveal the essential features of the algorithms actually used, and allow proofs of correctness to concentrate on the key features. It is claimed in [2] that more traditional algorithms (with less abstract data structures, less freedom in control flow, and less activity in each atomic action) can often be easily understood as "implementations" (in a technical sense) of the abstract algorithms presented in that paper, and the correctness of the traditional algorithms therefor follows from the correctness proof of [2]. In this paper we substantiate that claim in one case.

We present a formal model for Moss's algorithm for read-update locking. This algorithm was given in [6] and is used in the Argus system as the default algorithm for concurrency control. In [2] this algorithm was modeled by a "Moss object" M_X, in which acquiring a lock and computing the return value for an access to an object were all done in a single action (called REQUEST_COMMIT), that is in one indivisible step of the system. Now in order to have a real system do things in a (seemingly) indivisible step, a critical section is needed, and sensible design calls for such a critical section to be as short as possible. Indeed, in the Argus system itself, a lock is obtained first and the return value computed later, in a separate step. Here we model Moss' algorithm by a "Kyu object" with separate actions called OBTAIN_LOCK and REQUEST_COMMIT. We prove that a Kyu object is an implementation of the corresponding Moss object, using a possibilities mapping as defined in [2]. From Theorem 71 of [2] it follows that K_X is dynamic atomic.

This paper uses (without comment) many concepts and formal definitions from commutativity-based locking for nested transactions as presented in [2], and familiarity with that paper is assumed.

Section 2 contains the generic object automaton K_x used to model Moss's algorithm, and also gives several invariants. Section 3 then contains the proof that K_X is dynamic atomic.

2 Kyu Objects

For each object name X, we describe a generic object automaton K_X (a "Kyu object") that models Moss's algorithm with obtaining a lock separated from computing a return value. The automaton K_X maintains a collection of "versions" of the corresponding serial object S_X, and manages "read locks" and "update locks". The construction of K_X is based on a classification of all the accesses to X as either *read accesses* or *update accesses*. We assume that this classification satisfies the property that every operation (T,v) of a read access T is transparent (as defined in [2].)

K_X has the usual external actions of a generic object automaton for X. Also it has internal actions, OBTAIN_LOCK(T) for each T an access to X. A state k of K_X has components k. created, k. commit-requested, k. update-lockholders, k. read-lockholders, k. version-holders, all sets of transactions, and k. map, which is a function from k. version-holders to states of the serial object automaton S_X. We say that a transaction in update-lockholders *holds an update-lock*, and similarly that a transaction in read-lockholders *holds a read-lock*. The start states of K_X are those in which version-holders = update-lockholders = $\{T_0\}$ and map(T_0) is a start state of the serial object S_X, and the other components are empty. Here is the transition relation for K_X:

CREATE(T)

Effect:

- k. created(T) = k'. created(T) $\cup$ {T}

OBTAIN_LOCK(T) T an update access to X

Precondition:

- k'. update-lockholders $\cup$ k'. read-lockholders $\subseteq$ ancestors(T)

Effect:

- k. update-lockholders = k'. update-lockholders $\cup$ {T}

OBTAIN_LOCK(T) T a read access to X

Precondtiions:

- k'. update-lockholders $\subseteq$ ancestors(T)

Effect:

- k. read.lockholders = k'. read-lockholders $\cup$ {T}

REQUEST_COMMIT(T,v) T a read access to X

Precondition:

- T $\in$ k'. created - k'. commit-requested
- T $\in$ k'. read-lockholders
- There is a state n of S_X such that (k'. map(least(k'. version-holders)),perform(T,v),n) is a move of S_X.

Effect:

- k. commit-requested = k'. commit-requested $\cup$ {T}

REQUEST_COMMIT(T,v) T an update access to X

Precondition:

- T $\in$ k'. created - k'. commit-requested
- T $\in$ k'. update-lockholders
- There is a state n of S_X such that (k'. map(least(k'. version-holders)), perform(T,v),n) is a move of S_X

Effect:

- k. commit-requested = k'. commit-requested $\cup$ {T}
- k. version-holders = k'. version-holders $\cup$ {T}
- k. map(T) = n
- k. map(U) = k'. map(U) for all U $\in$ k. version-holders - {T}

INFORM_COMMIT_AT(X)OF(T)

Effect:

- If T $\in$ k'. update-lockholders, then
  k. update-lockholders = (k'. update-lockholders - {T}) $\cup$ {parent(T)}
- If T $\in$ k'. version-holders, then
  k. version-holders = (k'. version-holders - {T}) $\cup$ {parent(T)},
  k. map(parent(T)) = k'. map(T) and
  k. map(U) = k'. map(U) for U $\in$ k. version-holders - {parent(U)}
- If T $\in$ k'. read-lockholders, then
  k. read-lockholders = (k'. read-lockholders -T) $\cup$ {parent(T)}

INFORM_ABORT_AT(X)OF(T)

Effect:

- k. update-lockholders = k'. update-lockholders - descendants(T)
- k. read-lockholders = k'. read-lockholders - descendants(T)
- k. version-holders = k'. version-holders - descendants(T)
- k. map(U) = k'. map(U) for U $\notin$ descendants(T)

Thus, when an access transaction is created, it is simply added to the set created. When K_X is informed of a commit, it passes any locks held by the committing transaction to its parent, and also any version held (in map) for the transaction is transferred to the committing transaction's parent. When K_X is informed of an abort, it discards all locks and versions held by descendants of the aborted transaction. A lock can be obtained for an access when every conflicting lock is held by an ancestor of the transaction seeking a lock. A response containing return value v to an access T can be returned only it the access has been created but not responded to, T holds an appropriate lock, and the response is appropriate, based on the version currently held by the least transaction in the set version-holders. When this response is given, T is added to commit-requested. Also, if T is an update access, a new version is created for it.

We next prove two fundamental invariants of the state of K_X, which can be proved by the usual techniques (using induction on the length of the schedule leading to the state k).

Lemma 1 *Let k be a reachable state of K_X. Suppose T ∈ k. update-lockholders and T' ∈ k. read-lockholders ∪ k. update-lockholders. Then either T is an ancestor of T' or else T' is an ancestor of T.*

Lemma 2 *Let k be a reachable state of K_X. Then k. version-holders ⊆ k. update-lockholders.*

3 Correctness Proof

We show that K_X is dy1amic atomic. This follows from Theorem 71 of [2], once we show that K_X implements M_X, which we do by producing a possibilities mapping from K_X to M_X.

Lemma 3 *K_X implements M_X.*

Proof: Let f map a state k of K_X to the set of states m of M_X that satisfy the following conditions.

1. k. created = m. created
2. k. commit-requested = m. commit-requested
3. m. read-lockholders is a subset of k. read-lockholder
4. m. update-lockholders = k. version-holders
5. m. map(T) = k. map(T) for T ∈ m. version-holders

We claim that f is a possibility map.

To demonstrate the claim, it is easy to see that $m_0 \in$ f(k_0), where k_0 and m_0 are start states of K_X and M_X, repectively. In addition, we must show that if k' and m' are reachable states of K_X and M_X respectively such that m' ∈ f(k'), and (k',π,k) is a step of K_X, then there is an extended step (m',γ,m) of M_X such that m ∈ f(k). If π is an action of M_X, we will produce m such that (m',π,m) is a step of M_X and m ∈ f(k). Otherwise we will show that m' ∈ f(k) (that is, γ will be empty.)

We proceed by cases.

1. π = CREATE(T), T an access to X.

   Since π is an input of M_X, it is enabled in state m'. Choose m so that (m',π,m) is a step of M_X. We must show that m $\in$ f(k). The effects of π as an action of K_X and M_X imply that k. created = k'. created $\cup$ {T} and m. created = m'. created $\cup$ {T}. Since m' $\in$ f(k'), we have k'. created = m'. created, so that k. created = m. created, thus showing the first condition in the definition of f. The other conditions hold in k and m because they hold in k' and m' and none of the relevant components are modified by π.

2. π = OBTAIN_LOCK(U), U a read access to X.

   Since π is not an action of M_X, we will take m = m' and show m $\in$ f(k).

   Of course m. read-lockholders = m'. read-lockholders. The effects of π as an action of K_X imply that k. read-lockholders is equal to k'. read-lockholders $\cup$ {U}. Since m' $\in$ f(k'), m'. read-lockholders is a subset of k'. read-lockholders. Therefore, m. read-lockholders is a subset of k. read-lockholders. Thus condition three holds, and the other conditions hold in k and m because they hold in k' and m' and none of relevant components are altered.

3. π = OBTAIN_LOCK(U), U an update access to X.

   Since π is not an action of M_X, we will take m = m' and show m $\in$ f(k). Thus m. update-lockholders = m'. update-lockholders.

   The effects of π as an action of K_X imply that k. version-holders is equal to k'. version-holders. Since m' $\in$ f(k'), m'. update-lockholders is equal to k'. version-holders. Therefore, m. update-lockholders is equal to k. version-holders.

   Thus the fourth condition holds, and the others hold in k and m because they hold in k' and m' and none of relevant components are modified by π.

4. π = INFORM_COMMIT AT(X)OF(U).

   Since π is an input of M_X, it is enabled in state m'. Choose m such that (m',π,m) is a step of M_X. We must show m $\in$ f(k).

   The first and second conditions hold in k and m because they hold in k' and m' and none of the relevant components are modified by π.

   Now to consider the third condition.

   a. U $\in$ m'. read-lockholders.

   The effects of π as an action of M_X imply that m. read-lockholders is equal to m'. read-lockholders - {U} $\cup$ {parent(U)}. Since m' $\in$ f(k'), then m'. read-lockholders is a subset of k'. read-lockholders, and so U $\in$ k'. read-lockholders. Thus the effects of π as an action of K_X show that k. read-lockholders = k'. read-lockholders - {U} $\cup$ {parent(U)}, thus m. read-lockholders is a subset of k. read-lockholders.

   b. U $\notin$ m'. read-lockholders.

   Then m. read-lockholders is equal to m'. read-lockholders.

   b-1. U $\in$ k'. read-lockholders.

   Then k. read-lockholders = k'. read-lockholders - {U} $\cup$ {parent(U)} by the effects of π as an action of K_X. Since m' $\in$ f(k'), k'. read-lockholders contains m'. read-lockholders and further, since U $\notin$ m'. read-lockholders we have m'. read-lockholders $\subseteq$ k'. read-lockholders - {U}. Therefore, we can deduce that m. read-lockholders is a subset of k. read-lockholders.

b-2. U $\notin$ k'. read-lockholders.
Then k. read-lockholders = k'. read-lockholders. Since m' $\in$ f(k'), k'. read-lockholders contains a m'. read-lockholders. Therefore, m. read-lockholders is a subset of k. read-lockholders.

These show the third condition.

We now will consider the fourth condition.

a. U $\in$ m'. update-lockholders.
The effects of π as an action of M_X imply that m. update-lockholders = m'. update-lockholders - {U} $\cup$ {parent(U)}. Since m' $\in$ f(k'), U $\in$ k'. version-holders. Therefore,the effects of π as an action of K_X imply that k. version-holders = {k'. version-holders - {U} $\cup$ {parent(U)}. Since m' $\in$ f(k'), then m'. update-lockholders = k'. version-holders. Therefore, m. update-lockholders = k. version-holders.

b. U $\notin$ m'. update-lockholders.
The effects of π as an action of M_X and K_X imply that m. update-lockholders = m'. update-lockholders and k. version-holders = k'. version-holders. Since m' $\in$ f(k'), then m. update-lockholders = k. version-holders.

These demonstrate the fourth condition.

We now will now consider the fifth condition. So take T $\in$ m. update-lockholders.

a. T = U
This is impossible, as the effects of π as an action of M_X show that U $\notin$ m. update-lockholders.

b. T = parent(U)

b-1. U $\in$ k'. version-holders
The effects of π as an action of M_X and K_X imply that m. map(parent(U)) = m'. map(U) and k. map(parent(U)) = k'. map(U). Since m' $\in$ f(k') and U $\in$ m'. update-lockholders, m'. map(U) = k'. map(U). Then m. map(parent(U)) = k. map(parent(U)).

b-2. U $\notin$ k'. version-holders
Since m' $\in$ f(k'), then U $\notin$ m'. update-lockholders. So, we have that m. map(parent(U)) = m'. map(parent(U)), m. map(U) = m'. map(U), k. map(U) = k'. map(U) and k. map(parent(U)) = k'. map(parent(U)). Since m' $\in$ f(k') and U $\notin$ m'. update-lockholders, then we have that m. map(U) = k. map(U) and m. map(parent(U)) = k. map(parent(U)).

c. T is neither U nor parent(U)
Since the effects of π as an action of M_X imply that m. update-lockholders = m'. update-lockholders - {U} $\cup$ {parent(U)} or m. update-lockholders = m'. update-lockholders [if U $\notin$ m'. update-lockholders], then T $\in$ m'. update-lockholders.

The effects of π as an action of K_X mean that k. update-lockholders = k'. update-lockholders - {U} ∪ {parent(U)}.

The effects of π as an action of M_X and K_X imply that m. map(T) = m'. map(T) and k. map(T) = k'. map(T).

Since m' ∈ f(k') and T ∈ m'. update-lockholders, m'. map(T) = k'. map(T). Then k. map(T) = m. map(T).

So these demonstrate the fifth condition as required.

5. π = REQUEST_COMMIT(U,u), U a read access to X.

We first show that π is enabled as an action of M_X in state m'. That is, we must show that U ∈ m'. created - m'. commit-requested, m'. update-lockholders ⊆ ancestors(U), and that there is a state n of S_X such that (m'. map(least(m'. update-lockholders)), perform(U,u),n) is a move of S_X. Since m' ∈ f(k'), m'. created = k'. created and m'. commit-requested = k'. commit-requested. Since π is enabled in as an action of K_X in state k', we have that U ∈ k'. created - k'. commit-requested. Therefore, U ∈ m'. created - m'. commit-requested.

Since m' ∈ f(k'), m'. update-lockholders = k'. version-holders, and by Lemma 2 thus is a subset of k'. update-lockholders. Since π is enabled in as an action of K_X in state k', we have that U ∈ k'. read-lockholders and so by Lemma 1, k'. update-lockholders ⊆ ancestors(U). Therefore, m'. update-lockholders ⊆ ancestors(U). Since m' ∈ f(k'), m'. update-lockholders = k'. version-holders. Since π is enabled in as an action of K_X in state k', we have the fact that there is a state k of S_X such that (k'. map(least(k'. version-holders)), perform(U,u),n) is a move of S_X. Therefore, we also have the fact that there is a state m of S_X such that (m'. map(least(m'. update-lockholders)), perform(U,u),n) is a move of S_X.

Thus, π is enabled as an action of M_X in state m'.

Choose m such that (m',π,m) is a step of M_X. We will show that m ∈ f(k).

The effects of π imply that k. created = k'. created, m. created = m'. created, k. commit-requested = k'. request-commit ∪ {U} and m. commit-requested = m'. commit-requested ∪ {U}.

Since m' ∈ f(k'), we have m'. created = k'. created and m'. commit-requested = k'. commit-requested. Thus, k. created = m. created and k. commit-requested = m. commit-requested, so the first and second conditions hold.

The effects of π as an action of K_X imply that k. read-lockholders = k'. read-lockholders. By the preconditions of π, U ∈ k'. read-lockholders and the effects of π as an action of M_X imply that m. read-lockholders = m'. read-lockholders ∪ {U}. Since m' ∈ f(k'),m'. read-lockholders ⊆ k'. read-lockholders, and since U ∈ k'. read-lockholders, m'. read-lockholders ∪ {U} ⊆ k'. read-lockholders. Then m. read-lockholders is a subset of k. read-lockholders, so the third condition holds.

It is easy to see that the fourth and fifth conditions hold in m and k, because each holds in k' and m' and none of relevant component is modified.

6. π = REQUEST_COMMIT(U,u), U an update access to X.

We first show that π is enabled as an action of M_X in state m'. The proofs that U ∈ m'. created - m'. commit-requested and that there is a state n of S_X such that (m'. map(least(m'. update-lockholders)), n) is a move of S_X, are identical to the corresponding proofs for the read case. In particular, we can take n to be the state of S_X that is assigned as k. map(U).

Since m' $\in$ f(k'), m'. update-lockholders is a subset of k'. update-lockholders and m'. read-lockholders is a subset of k'. read-lockholders. Since π is enabled as an action of K_X in state k', we have that U $\in$ k'. update-lockholders. By Lemma 1 k'. update-lockholders $\cup$ k'. read-lockholders $\subseteq$ ancestors(U). Therefore, m'. update-lockholders $\cup$ m'. read-lockholders $\subseteq$ ancestors(U).

Choose m such that (m',π,m) is a step of M_X and m. map(U) = k. map(U). As noted above, this is possible. We show that m $\in$ f(k). The first and second conditions follow as for the read case. The third condition holds in k and m because it holds in k' and m' and the relevant components are not modified.

We now consider the fourth condition. The effects of π as an action of K_X and M_X imply that k. version-holders = k'. version-holders $\cup$ {U} and m. update-lockholders = m'. update-lockholders $\cup$ {U}. Since m' $\in$ f(k'), then m'. update-lockholders = k'. version-holders. Therefore, m. update-lockholders = k. version-holders. So, the fourth condition holds.

Finally, we show the fifth condition. Fix any transaction name T such that T is in m. update-lockholders.

If T $\neq$ U, then by the effects of π as an action of M_X we have T $\in$ m'. update-lockholders, and since m' $\in$ f(k') we have m'. map(T) = k'. map(T). By the effects of π also m. map(T) = m'. map(T) and k'. map(T) = k. map(T). Thus m. map(T) = k. map(T).

On the other hand if U = T, m was chosen so m. map(T) = k. map(T). Thus the fifth condition holds.

7. π = INFORM_ABORT_AT(X)OF(U)

   Since π is an input of M_X, it is enabled in state m'. Choose m such that (m',π,m) is a step of M_X. We show m $\in$ f(k).

   The first and second conditions hold in k and m because they hold in k' and m' and none of the relevant components are modified by π.

   The effects of π as an action of M_X and K_X imply that m. read-lockholders = m'. read-lockholders - descendants(U) and k. read-lockholders = k'. read-lockholders - descendants(U). Since m' $\in$ f(k'), m'. read-lockholders is a subset of k'. read-lockholders. So, m. read-lockholders is a subset of k. read-lockholders.

   Thus the third condition holds. The proof of the fouth condition is similar.

   Now we consider the fifth condition. Suppose T $\in$ m. update-lockholders. We must have that T is not a descendant of U. By the effects of π as an action of M_X we deduce that T $\in$ m'. update-lockholders, so (since m' $\in$ f(k')) we have m'. map(T) = k'. map(T). The effects of π (together with T not being a descendant of U) imply that m. map(T) = m'. map(T), and that k. map(T) = k'. map(T). Thus m. map(T) = k. map(T), and so the fifth condition holds as required.

4 Acknowledgements

The first author wishes to thank his employers, E. H. O'Brien and more recently IBM Australia, for their understanding while he has pursued his studies.

References

[1] Aspnes, J. and Fekete, A. and Lynch, N. and Merritt, M. and Weihl, W.
A Theory of Timestamp-Based Concurrency Control for Nested Transactions.
In *Proceedings of 14th International Conference on Very Large Data Bases.* August 1988.

[2] Fekete, A. and Lynch, N. and Merritt, M. and Weihl, W.
Commutativity-Based Locking for Nested Transactions
Technical Memo MIT/LCS/TM-370, Laboratory for Computer Science, Massachusetts Institute Technology, August 1988. Also, to appear in JCSS.

[3] Goldman, K. and Lynch, N.
Nested Transactions and Quorum Consensus.
In *Proceedings of 6th ACM Symposium on Principles of Distributed Computing.* August 1987.

[4] Herlihy, M. and Lynch, N. and Merritt, M. and Weihl, W.
On the Correctness of Orphan Elimination Algorithms.
In *Proceedings of 17th IEEE Symposium on Fault-Tolerant Computing.* March 1987.

[5] Liskov, B.
Distributed Computing in Argus.
Communications of the ACM 31(3):300–312. March 1988.

[6] Moss, J.E.B.
Nested Transaction: An Approach to Reliable Distributed Computing.
PhD thesis, Massachusetts Institute Technology, 1981.
Technical Report MIT/LCS/TR-260, Laboratory for Computer Science, Massachusetts Institute Technology, April 1981.

[7] Spector, A. *et al.*
Camelot: A Distributed Transaction facility for Mach and the Internet. Technical Report CMU-CS-87-129, Department of Computer Science, Carnegie-Mellon University. 1987.

Multi DataBase Enquiry Service
MDB-ES

Ahmad A. Barfoursh ahmad@uk.ac.bristol.compsci
G. N. Lance lance@uk.ac.bristol.compsci
M. H. Rogers mike@uk.ac.bristol.compsci

Department of Computer Science,
University of Bristol,
Bristol BS8 1TR.
England

Abstract

There is a requirement to extract data from distributed databases and then to edit the results in such a way that the enquirer can easily understand the results. The system described in this paper shows how this can be achieved and uses as an example existing distributed library databases. The procedure uses the Joint Academic Network **JANET** to access 26 academic libraries located throughout the U.K.. The questions are posed in a user friendly way and these are interpreted to suit each database using its protocol before they are forwarded to the database. The final results are also presented in a user friendly fashion. The system is written in such a way that it can easily be expanded to cope with additional databases which use new protocols. The model described is sufficiently general to be applied to any kind of database, it is not restricted to bibliographic databases.

1 INTRODUCTION

Since the application of computers to administrative information processing began in 1954 computers have become a key instrument in the development of organisation and formal information processing [1]. The use of information systems and particularly Computer-Based Information Systems should improve decision making, problem solving, planning, controlling and increase organisational effectiveness [1, 2].

The rapid development of information technology has helped to establish firmly the general attitude that information systems are a powerful instrument for organisational activities. This idea has been found to have difficulties in many empirical information systems [3, 4]. The success of an information system is highly dependent upon the information which can be presented to the user. The Information System *(IS)*, itself is a set of organised procedures together with data which provides an output called *Information*. In this context *Information* can be defined as processed data which is useful in a particular subject and will reduce the uncertainty attached to a future state of events.

The Database is an essential part of any Information System and current *ISs* are highly dependent on data stored in databases and easy access to them is crucial for an effective *IS*. The special requirements of the user often cannot be met by reference to just one database. In a multi database environment it should be possible to access data in more than one database by a single query [5]. Also, it should be possible to recognise data with the same semantics but different syntax.

Improved networking capabilities allow access to several databases; in particular to databases that provide large amounts of information about similar topics. Many organisations have a pressing need to access all their data rapidly and reliably. This need is very difficult to satisfy when the data that are important to the organisation are stored in many, independent databases. Formulating and implementing queries that require data from more than one database requires knowing where all the data are stored, mastering all the necessary interfaces and correctly combining partial results from individual queries into a single answer. As an example of the kind of application where the MDB-ES is useful consider a researcher who is looking for a particular reference in several remote library databases. Databases were developed independently for local use and they may or may not contain the same information about similar topics.

To answer a certain query the user must:

1. Access different databases by knowing their addresses in a communication network.

2. Know the location of the necessary data and the query languages used by the various DBMSs.

3. Change the query format to suit the database to be accessed.

4. Arrange for the partial results to be accumulated at one place.

5. Arrange for storage of the received in a new database, for future use.

As we can see, without an integrated interface, this procedure is time consuming and error prone. In MDB-ES we will try to answer this kind of multi-database query quickly and correctly. Before local databases can be accessed through MDB-ES, the local host system must be connected to a communications network which will normally be geographically distributed. MDB-ES does not provide the capability either to update the data in any local database or to perform other DBMSs activities except to read distributed, heterogeneous databases and subsequently combine the

results into a single Knowledge-Base.
This paper is divided into 5 sections. In the Section 2 we describe the aims of the system, Section 3 gives an overview about the architecture of the MDB-ES, (we also describe some details about the system characteristics in this section), Section 4 examines the system in a Multi-Library application and Section 5 concludes the paper.

2 AIMS OF THE Multi DataBase Enquiry Service

The task is to design, implement and evaluate a MDB-ES, based on a local workstation accessing a number of databases at remote locations via a wide area network. The main facilities to be provided by the system are:

1. In response to a request for a particular query, the system will automatically set up a series of dialogues with remote databases, using the appropriate protocols for accessing the system.

2. The response from each will be combined into a single knowledge base which, after consistency checking, will be available for local use[6].

In addition to these two major goals the system should be able to support the following subgoals [7].

1. The system must be easy to use and operate, it must be user friendly.
   ISs tend to fail if a variety of access rules have to be used. Furthermore, it should be possible to allow a wide variety of users to access the system in a standard manner and at the same time. Improving the system should not normally affect the user interface.

2. The system must be convenient to use.
   If the user is to retain interest in its operations, then it must perform queries quickly and efficiently, it must answer a high proportion of the user's questions without requiring him/her to make more queries.

3. The system must be easy to extend.
   In particular, a facility enabling one to add databases or new networks is essential.

4. The system should be executed in parallel when the hardware allows.
   To save time, the system should be able to access and execute the different databases in parallel and edit the output on arrival in whatever order the responses arrive.

5. The system must be easy to maintain.
   Problems and difficulties which occur in the system should be corrected in minimum time and for this the system should be easily modified.

3 ARCHITECTURE OF MDB-ES

The model for a Multi DataBase Enquiry Service has two major parts which are related to two external environments: User and Network.

1. A *Real Kernel*, is the main part of the system which controls all system activities. The Real Kernel is connected to the user and contains all information necessary for this connection, it also contains structured information about the databases.
   The system will start from the Real Kernel and will also end in this part.

2. The *Pseudo Kernel* is the second part of the system which contains preparation tasks and allows connection to the network. Acquisition and processing of information will take place in this part of the system and the processed information is then passed to the Real Kernel.

The following is a detailed description of the components of this model.

3.1 Real Kernel

The Real Kernel consists of three components: the Message Base, the Meta DataBase and the Knowledge Presentation subsystem.
The main task for this part of the system is to control the whole system cycle. This part of the system also has responsibility for accepting user queries and communicating with the Pseudo Kernel. Figure 3.1.a gives an overview of the Real Kernel.

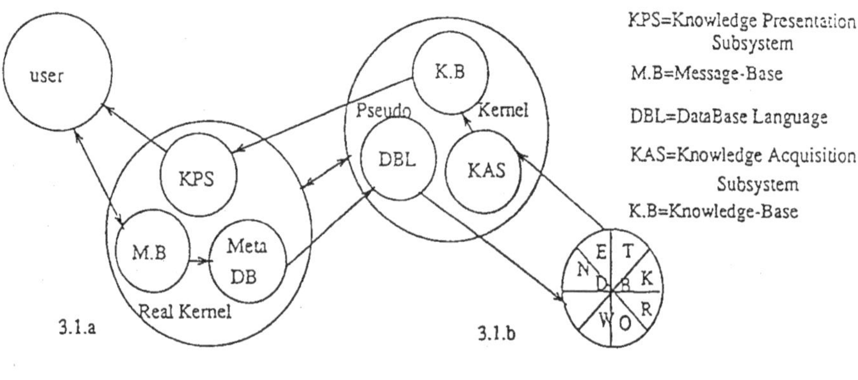

Figure 3.1-Architecture of the MDB-ES.

3.1.1 Message Base

Since the system is designed to be used by people not specifically trained in database languages, the front end must recognise a wide variety of user requests. Nevertheless we would like it to be as economical as possible, so for successful communication with the user and for the transfer of the request to the system, we suggest Message Base contains both facts and relationships in some kind of representation stored in a data structure. All relevant facts about the real world domain must be stored in this database.

Presentation of the communication could be in either Natural Language*(NL)* or it could be in menu driven form. For *NL* Pereira and Warren present a Definite Clause Grammar*(DCG)* [8], which is easy to extend and modify. For the menu driven approach it is necessary to look at a communication method and a search method in each database and to prepare a standard menu suitable for all databases. The main task of this part of the system is to transfer a user query from the system and pass it to the next stage.

3.1.2 Meta DataBase

The Meta DataBase contains the information about other databases and their relationships with the system (Message Base). Before the creation of a Meta DataBase can take place, there are three basic facilities that must be provided. First there needs to be some way to formulate the characteristics of each database to indicate how each performs a search. Second, some mechanism needs to be found that permits the system to communicate with the databases of the network. Third, each database needs to be specified in the Meta DataBase.

These three facilities can be provided by studying the databases of the network and inserting the information obtained into the Meta DataBase. The main task of the Meta DataBase is to provide enough information for interpreting the system language to individual databases in the network. This interpretation will be handled by interface software under the control of the real kernel.

3.1.3 Knowledge Presentation Subsystem

The final step in processing an enquiry in MDB-ES is to display the results in an acceptable form to the user, and this is done via the Knowledge Presentation Subsystem *(KPS)*. Presenting knowledge in the MDB-ES means choosing a set of conventions for answering queries and relations between available information. Users should believe that the information presented to them meets their information requirements.

The question of how to present information (output) to the user was and still is one of the major questions in the MDB-ES. Several options are available in this subject [9, 10] and we are not developing a new presentation model for this purpose at this stage.

We consider a user-friendly interface, mainly using standard output, together with some necessary and desirable features for such a system.

3.2 Pseudo Kernel

The Pseudo Kernel provides support for presenting user queries to databases in the network. The Real and Pseudo Kernels of the system are tightly connected and we can consider them as master and slave. Any data received by the Real Kernel (Master) is passed to the Pseudo Kernel (Slave) as an *Input*, these transactions are done by software interface and any data obtained from the Pseudo Kernel will be passed to the Real Kernel as an *Output*.
The Pseudo Kernel is supported by a pseudo terminal. The pseudo terminal is created in the Unix environment and consists of two devices which are known as a *Master* and *Slave*; full details of pseudo terminals (PTY) can be found in the Berkeley Unix manual version 4.3. The Pseudo Kernel is administered by the Real Kernel and will be opened and closed by interfaces in the Real Kernel.
The Pseudo Kernel components are: Database language, Knowledge acquisition subsystem and Knowledge Base subsystem. Figure 3.1.b gives an overview of the Pseudo Kernel.

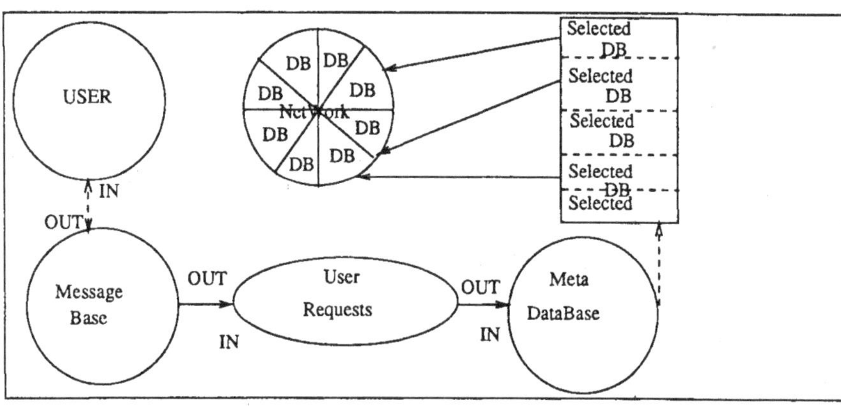

Figure 3.2-MDB-ES Communication overview

3.2.1 Database language

Each database in the network has the right to choose its own storage and methods for data and transaction management. Individual nodes (databases) are free to have their own schema, query languages, concurrency control techniques and crash

recovery. The advantage of such facilities is to provide ways for data sharing without impinging on the autonomy of individual databases. In the Database language, each node's (Database) language is translated and stored in the Database, this information should be able to do transactions among the host language in the system. Information obtained from the Meta DataBase is input for generating new information for processing the query in the network.
Figure 3.2 shows the communication between the Database language and the Meta DataBase on one hand and the network on the other.

3.2.2 Knowledge acquisition subsystem

Knowledge acquisition is an important task in building systems[11, 12] and current methods for transferring knowledge into a knowledge base are time consuming, expensive and inconsistent with the system development process[13]. In MDB-ES we consider an automated knowledge acquisition method and it is based on experiences in this field which have used knowledge acquisition software [14]. This software may allow the user to add new knowledge to the knowledge base and it should also be able to obtain, evaluate and prepare knowledge from the network's databases to add to the knowledge base.

3.2.3 Knowledge Base Subsystem

Significant improvements in the productivity of information systems require the treatment of information as knowledge. Knowledge identifies the general concepts of information, whereas data is information about specific instances. In general, the assignment of data and knowledge is situation dependent; items which appear as data at a higher level in the enterprise may appear to be knowledge to a person involved at a lower level. Both Artificial Intelligence*(AI)* and database researchers have accepted the importance of developing systems with access to large information bases[15]. In *AI* such information bases are called *Knowledge Bases*, on the grounds that they contain information about something; whereas in databases these information bases are called *Databases* [16] and are viewed mostly as large complex data structures that allow efficient storage and retrieval. One of the main contributions of *KBS* technology to DBMS will be better semantic models and a clear understanding of what knowledge is presented. For specifying a *KBS* we must provide two things [17] :
1. A specification of the system's underlying knowledge base and
2. A specification of the task to be performed by the system.
The Knowledge base subsystem in MDB-ES should at least be capable of fulfilling the following criteria from Moor [18].

1. "Say that something has a certain property without saying what thing has that property.". In the context of this paper:

(e.g. There is a Prolog book in a library, without saying which library.)

$$(\exists x)BOOK(prolog, x).$$

2. "Say that every thing in a certain class has a certain property without saying what every thing in that class is."
(e.g. All books have authors without listing all the books.)

$$(\forall x)BOOK(x) \supset AUTHOR(x).$$

3. "Say that at least one of two statements is true without saying which is true." (e.g. The Prolog books are available in Bristol or Bath library, without specifying which of these libraries actually has these books).

$$\mathrm{BOOK(prolog,bristol)} \vee BOOK(prolog, bath).$$

4. "Explicitly say that something is false."
(e.g. There are no Information Systems books in the Bristol library.)

$$\sim (\exists X)\ \mathrm{BOOK(information,X)}.$$

5. "Either settle or leave open to doubt whether two non-identical expressions name the same object."
(e.g. Author(Nilsson) and Artificial Intelligence book) that may or may not denote the same individual, if they do , we can explicitly say so:
Author(Nilsson) = Artificial Intelligence. If there is doubt about this naming the same individual, we omit the above equality, this omission does not preclude their naming the same individual, it simply leaves the knowledge base undefined about this possibility.

All data exploited from the databases in this network should be stored in such a knowledge base in our system and satisfy the above specification.
The main *KBS* tasks in the MDB-ES are : Consistency checking and Question-Answering. These two tasks make the information ready for presenting to the user, this event will happen after transferring them to the Knowledge Presentation Subsystem *(KPS)* in the Real Kernel.
The Pseudo Kernel will be closed after the *KBS* tasks are finished, but the knowledge base will be available for local use as well as use as a part of the system.

4 IMPLEMENTATION

The MDB-ES system described in the previous section is currently in the implementation and development phase. Our ultimate goal in this work is to build a full implementation of a MDB-ES. This implementation is based on Information Retrieval *(IR)*. Information Retrieval is one of the particular examples of information systems which is traditionally involved in library organisation and is defined as a method and procedure for recovering specific information from stored data [19, 20]. *IR* is a good test bed for theories of human -computer interaction because it is general and covers a diverse population and range of needs [21]. Ideally, one should be able to develop some general models of user behaviour in the retrieval process. We observed several *IR* systems and studied the causes of their failure. In many cases users do not understand much of the output received, there is duplication of output and we saw many complaints about information overhead. Massive output of data are provided by the system and some users may feel that computer-based *IR* are not worth the time or cost to develop and that organisations would be better off without it. However, the problems will be increased when we use several databases via networks.

Feasibility studies were started in the University of Bristol main library and the Bristol City main library, where they are using automatic *IR*; but for discovering all problems in the *IR* system the main research tool was the Joint Academic NETwork(**JANET**).

The hardware used for the implementation is the *SUN-3* workstation model 50M. under the *UNIX* [22] operating system and the programming language used for implementation is Edinburgh PROLOG version 1.5 (NewNip) [23] and it must be with -U argument in order to reserve some space for C functions to interface with PROLOG and in our experiment -U500 was sufficient. We developed a system "MUlti Library Enquiry Service" *(MULES)* based on the model discussed in section 3 and using the environment described above [24]. *MULES* can access 26 libraries which are in file *Library* in **JANET**. The file *Library* in **JANET** is being widely used by many academic organisations in the U.K and each library in this file has its own characteristics [25],query language, schema, concurrency control technique and crash recovery procedure; they also choose their own storage mechanism for data transaction management.

4.1 MULES; Overview

The prototype *MULES* has been developed based on each database characteristic and the MDB-ES model. The system for implementation is split into two major parts: Preparation and Processing.

Before a query can be processed in the MDB-ES there are two basic facilities that must be provided:

(i) Normalised search facilities in particular and formulated characteristics of each database in general (creating Message base and Meta database).

(ii) A dialogue file for each database which will make possible communication between the network databases and the system (Database Language).

The processing of queries based on the described preparation is split into the following steps:

(i) Selection of databases for a specify query.

(ii) Remote communication capability with selected databases in the network.

(iii) Production of NL text file results.

(iv) Conversion of the NL text file into prolog facts (accessing and manipulating data, Knowledge acquisition subsystem).

(v) Choice of proper facts for merging into a common database (Knowledge-Base Subsystem).

(vi) Reformat data, converting PROLOG facts into NL text (Knowledge presentation subsystem).

In the following sub-sections, each step will be described in detail. Detailed descriptions are concerned with techniques which have been used, data structures, inputs and outputs.

4.1.1 Normalisation

Since in this implementation we are using different databases; there needs to be some way to normalise the methods whereby each database is searching to answer a query.

The purpose of the *Normalisation* is to design Message-base and Meta-database. When we design databases we are interested in properties of data that are *true for all time*, not with properties that merely happen to apply in some specific instant. For example, *title* search is true for all libraries, by contrast, *author listing* is possible only in some libraries.

In this normalisation method, based on Codd's normalisation theory [26, 16], we minimise data duplication and maximise data accessibility; by reviewing all available data (all the databases in the network) we remove repeating groups and create a new relation / entity for such groups, each record contains a primary key and produces a one to many relationship. The Message-Base also contains all other user friendly messages and help descriptions for easy use of the system.

Each record (Library) in the Meta-database is represented by the predicates defined as :

$$\begin{array}{l}\mathrm{lib}(< name >,< [addr] >,< [lm] >,< s >,< key >)\\ \quad \mathrm{l}([< key >,< sm >,< lm >])\end{array}$$

where:

$< name >$ is a constant that uniquely identifies the library name.

$< [addr] >$ is a list of terms representing the library's address code for communication with the network and related password and any other necessary terms for connection to the library service.

$< [lm] >$ is a list of terms representing all facilities available in particular libraries based on the MDB-ES Main-menu.

$< s >$ is a constant that identifies the supplier which supports the library system.

$< key >$ is a constant that identifies the library in the MDB-ES and is used as a primary key, this key number is assigned by a system designer.

The relational predicate l defines the relationship between the particular library's menu and the system's Main-menu. The relation predicate l is presented as a list with the following definitions :

$< key >$ is a primary key .

$< sm >$ is a term representing a specific search facility based on the Main-menu.

$< lm >$ is a term representing a specific search facility based on the library's menu.

Interpreting a particular search facility in a library to the system search facility will be based on these l records.

4.1.2 Dialogue Facts

Each database in the network has its own Data Base Language *(DBL)*. For our purposes, the important thing about all such languages is that they should be accessible from the *Host language* .
Dialogue facts are part of the database language which make it possible for host languages to communicate with databases. For example, for connecting to a particular library system (GEAC at the Edinburgh library) the user must use the following 9 commands.

1.	spad 000016000006	* Connect to the Edinburgh library system*
2.	7	* Indicating terminal model*
3.	1	* Indicating type of enquiry*
4.	3	* Indicating type of search in this case 3 for *title**
5.	*title*	* Title of the search*
6.	D	*To display record(s)*
7.	C-P	* Break connection*
8.	a	* Back to PAD*
9.	clear	* Exit from GEAC*

In response to a particular query the MDB-ES should be able to go through this process automatically and also be able to have access to different remote databases and execute the appropriate protocols for each system.
For these purposes sequences of commands in each database were converted to the host language and introduced as Dialogue Facts to interface to the database language.

4.1.3 Database (Source) Selection

The questions which we are concerned with at this stage are:
- Is the query which the user makes relevant to the MDB-ES?
- Where should the system look for the answer?

This section describes and specifies the algorithm and includes a detailed explanation of input and output data structures.

Input data structures

The Input data are the user queries, the system's Main-menu in the Message-Base and library facilities from the Meta-Database. The structure of these data has already been discussed in section 4.1.1.
At the end of this stage we will have answers to two main questions which we addressed at the beginning of this section. According to them, if the first query is a member of the system's Main-menu then we surely will have at least one database(Source) from the Meta-database.

$$\text{if } q \in Main - menu \text{ then}$$
$$\exists DB \in Meta - database$$

The selected databases will be stored in the system *Auxiliary file*, (using "Assert" the built-in function in PROLOG), these data transformations will be without any change in the data structures. We have already discussed the Meta-DataBase structure, valid user's queries will also be stored in the same way as a user entry.

Algorithm

```
    Read query(Q1) from user
  LOOP
    Check query(Q1) with the Main-menu
   IF it is in the Main-menu THEN
     Assert query(Q1)
     Display relevant message
     Read second query(Q2)
     Assert second query(Q2)
   ELSE Display error message
  LOOP
    Check query(Q1) with the Meta-Database
    Find databases(Source)
    Assert databases(Source) records
```

4.1.4 Remote Communication

The architecture of the MDB-ES is shown in Figure 3.1. How the communication between user and network will be established is the main question in this section.

Pseudo Terminal:
Remote Communication will take place in the *Pseudo Terminal* which is a pair of devices supported by a *Pseudo Terminal driver (PTY)*. The two devices comprising a Pseudo Terminal are known as a master and a slave. The slave device, which is known as a "general terminal interface *(TTY)*", for conversational computing. The master and the slave sides of the *PTY* are tightly connected. Any data written on the master device is given to the slave device as input and any data written on the slave terminal can be read by the master device.

4.1.5 Result Collection

In response to a request for a particular query, the system will automatically access all the appropriate protocols(dialogue files) and communicate with each database. The responses in each case will be collected from the remote site by the C functions which interface with PROLOG. They are assembled as separate new auxiliary files, as a result, at the end of the communication session we will have as many auxiliary files as selected databases.
Each auxiliary file formed by this step contains the full response of the system, they are not suitable for the user and need to be filtered and edited before presenting to the user.

5 CONCLUSION

The model described in this paper is an attempt to solve one of the *ISs* problems which is related to different components of any *ISs* type, we have attempted to demonstrated how a model based on heterogeneous distributed data can be used in *IR* which is one of the *ISs* type in order to make it more effective.
The MDB-ES was designed to be a general, easily extendible system for user satisfaction. The project began with a study of the information systems and the causes for their failure. One of the *ISs* type should been chosen, *IR* is selected because of its availability and related facilities tools. As a result of a feasibility study we recognised several major causes for *ISs* failure and based on this result the design process really began.
The first step in this stage was a literature search and background reading for finding out *where the ISs is now* and *where the ISs will be in the future*, future *ISs* should be able to solve *ISs* problems.
The next step was to define the goals of the MDB-ES, the method presently used in library services is carefully studied and general requirement for any *ISs* type is

considered. Then the design of the MDB-ES began from the general ideas which developed after the implementation started. We are currently in the development phase, a prototype system has been tested. This is able to collect results from the remote databases but we have not yet fully implemented the part of the system which will reformat and edit the results for presentation to the enquirer.

ACKNOWLEDGEMENTS.

This study is being supported in part by the Iran Ministry of higher education. The authors would like to thank Neil Davies for his help in communication and implementation of C functions interface to Prolog and M.J.Paget for his help during the feasibility study in the University of Bristol's main library.

References

[1] Davis, G.B.; Olson, M. *'Management Information Systems: Conceptual foundations, structure,and development, Second Edition'*. Mcgraw-Hill, New York, 1985.

[2] Therauf, Robert J. . *'Effective Management Information Systems'*. Charles E. Merrill co., 1984.

[3] Lucas, Jr. Henry C. . *'Why Information Systems Faill?'*. Columbia University Press, 1975.

[4] Lyytinen, Kalle. 'Different Perspectives on Information Systems: Problems and Solutions'. *ACM Computing Surveys*, 19(1):5–46, March 1988.

[5] Landers, T.; Rosenberg, R.L. *'An Overview of MULTIBASE'*. Technical Report CCA-87-03, Computer Corporation of America, 1987.

[6] Barfoursh, Ahmad A.;Rogers, M. H. 'A Knowledge Acquisition Method for Information Systems: A Multi-DataBase Apprproach'. *presented on the Post-graduate AI Workshop 1990,University of Warwick, January, 1990*, 1990.

[7] Brooks, C.H.P.; Grouse, P.J.; RossJeffery, D.; Lawrence, M.J. . *'Information Systems Design'*. Prentice-Hall of Australia, 1982.

[8] Pereira, Fernando C. N.; Warren, David H. D. 'Definite Clause Grammers For Language Analysis–A Survey of the Formalism and a Comparison with Augmented Transition NetWorks'. *Artificial Intelligence*, 13(3):231–278, 1980.

[9] Buchanan, B.G.; Shortliffe, Edward H. *'Rule-Based Expert Systems'*. Addision-Wesley, 1985.

[10] Ives, B.; Olson, M.; Baroudi, J. 'The Measurement of User Information Satisfaction. *Communication of the ACM*, 26(10):758–793, October 1983.

[11] Kidd, Alison L., editor. *'Knowledge Acquisition For Expert Systems'*. Plenum Press, New-York, 1987.

[12] Michie, Donald, editor. *'Introduction Reading In EXPERT SYSTEMS'*. Gordon and Breach Science Pub., 1982.

[13] Grabowski, Martha. 'Knowledge Acquisition Methodologies: Survey and Empirical Assessment'. In *Proceedings of the Ninth International Conference on Information Systems Minneapolis,Minnesota*, pages 47–54, 1988.

[14] Kitakami, H.; Kunifuji, S.; Miyachi, T.; Furukawa, K. *'A Methodology for Implementation of A Knowledge Acquisition System'*. ICOT Technical Report: TR-037, Institue for New Generation Computer Technology, 1983.

[15] DeGross, Janice I.; Olson, M., editor. *'The Ninth International Conference on Information Systems'*, SIM, ACM, TIMS, Minneapolis, Minnesota, December 1988.

[16] Date, C.J. *'An Introduction to Database Systems, Volume II'*. Addison-Wesley, 1983.

[17] Peiter, Raymond. 'Foundation For Knowledge-Based Systems'. In H.J. Kugler, editor, *Information Processing*, pages 663–668, Elsevier science, North-Holland, 1986.

[18] Moor, R. *'Reasoning about knowledge and action'*. Technical note 191, AI, 25, 75-94, SRI International, Menlo Park, CA., 1980.

[19] Salton, Gerard. *'Automatic Information Organization and Retrieval'*. McGraw-Hill, 1968.

[20] Salton, Gerard; McGill, Michael J. . *'Introduction to Modern Information Retrieval'*. McGraw-Hill, 1983.

[21] Fox, Edward A. 'Research and Development of Information Retrieval Models and Their Application'. *Information Processing & Management*, 25(1):1–5, 1989.

[22] Kernighan, Brian W.; Pike, Rob. *'The UNIX Programing Environment'*. Prentic-Hall,Inc., 1984.

[23] Bowen, D.L.; Byrd, L.; et al.. *'Edinburgh PROLOG (The New Implementation) User Manual'*. 1987.

[24] Barfoursh, A. A.; Lance, G. N.; Rogers, M. H. *'A Model for Effective Computerised Information Systems: Multi DataBase Enquiry Service'*. Computer Science dep. Technical Report:TR-10, University of Bristol, 1989.

[25] Leeves, Juliet. *'A Buyers's Guide'*. Gower, 1987.

[26] Date, C.J. *'An Introduction to Database Systems, Volume I'*. Addison-Wesley, 1986.

Participants

David Able
CSIRO
Division of Information Technology
GPO Box 664
Canberra ACT 2601
Australia

Chris Avram
Department of Computer Technology
Chisholm Institute of Technology
PO Box 197
Caulfield, VIC 3145
Australia
*(avram@cit5.cit.oz)**

Issac Balbin
Department of Computer Science
RMIT
124 La Trobe Street
Melbourne, VIC 3001
Australia
(issac@goanna.cs.rmit.oz)

Jim Bell
Department of Computer Science
James Cook University
Townsville, QLD 4811
Australia
(jim@sheila.oz.au)

Peter Bernus
Department of Computer Science
The University of Queensland
St Lucia, QLD 4067
Australia
(bernus@batserver.cs.uq.oz)

Greg Butler
Deptartment of Computer Science
Syndeny University
Sydeny, NSW 2006
Australia
(greg@cluster.cs.su.oz)

John Cardiff
Department of Computer Science
University of Queensland
St Lucia, QLD 4067
Australia
(john@uqcspe.cs.uq.oz)

Ying K Chan
Department of Computer Science
University of NSW
PO Box 1
Kensington, NSW 2033
Australia

* The e-mail address of the participant, if known, is given in italics within brackets.

Bob Colomb
CSIRO
Division of Information Technology
Box 1599
North Ryde, NSW 2133
Australia
(colomb@ditsyda)

Peter Colville
Department of Computer Science
Ballarat CAE
PO Box 663
Ballarat, VIC 3350
Australia

Daryl D'Souza
Department of Computer Science
RMIT
124 La Trobe Street
Melbourne, VIC 3001
Australia
(djds@goanna.cs.rmit.oz)

John Daly
Department of Computer Technology
Chisholm Institute of Technology
PO Box 197
Caulfield, VIC 3145
Australia
(daly@cit5.cit.oz)

H. Everitt
Telecom Australia Research Labs
PO Box 249
Clayton, VIC 3168
Australia

Dan Eves
Department of Computer Technology
Chisholm Institute of Technology
PO Box 197
Caulfield, VIC 3145
Australia

Alan Fekete
University of Sydney
Sydeny, NSW 2006
Australia
(fekete@cluster.cs.su.oz)

Iain Fogg
Department of Computer Science
University of Quuensland
St Lucia, QLD 4067
Australia

Brian Garner
Department of Computer Science
Deakin University
Geelong, VIC 3217
Australia

Jack Greig
Department of Computer Technology
Chisholm Institute of Technology
PO Box 197
Caulfield, VIC 3145
Australia

Gopal K. Gupta
Department of Computer Science
James Cook University
Townsville, QLD 4811
Australia
(gupta @sheila.jcu.oz)

Terry Halpin
Department of Computer Science
University of Quuensland
St Lucia, QLD 4067
Australia
(halpin@uqcspe.cs.uq.oz)

Thomas Hardjono
Department of Computer Science
ADFA
Canberra ACT 2600
Australia
(thomas@csadfa.cs.adfa)

Elizabeth Jane Haywood
Deptartment of Electrical Engg.,
Footscray Institute of Technology
Ballarat Road
Footscray, VIC 3011
Australia

Clifford Heath
Hewlett-Packard Australia
29 Ringwood st
Ringwood, VIC
Australia
(cjh@hpausla.oz)
(cjh@hpauslw.HP.COM)

John Hiller
Deptartment of Computer Science
University of New South Wales
P.O. Box 1
Kensington, NSW 2033
Australia

David Horton
Digital Equipement Corporation
12 Marney Street
Chapel Hill, QLD 4069
Australia

Chris Keen
Dept. of Elect. Engg. and Comp. Sci.
University of Tasmania
Hobart, TAS 7001
Australia
(cdk@tasis.utas.oz.au)

Alan Kent
Department of Computer Science
RMIT
124 La Trobe St
Melbourne, VIC 3001
Australia
(ajk@goanna.cs.rmit.oz)

Rao Kotagiri
Department of Computer Science
University of Melbourne
Parkville, VIC 3052
Australia

Godfrey Lance
Department of Computer Science
University of Bristol
UK BS8 1TR
(lance@compsci.bristol.ac.uk)

John K Lee
Department of Computer Science
University of Sydney
Sydney, NSW 2006
Australia

Ruddy Lelouche
Depatment d'Inforamtique
Universite Laval
Quebec
Canada G1K 7P4
(1170054@lavalvx1.bitnet)

Pearl Levin
Department of Computer Technology
Chisholm Institute of Technology
PO Box 197
Caulfield, VIC 3145
Australia

Tao Li
Department of Computer Science
Monash University
Clayton, VIC 3168
Australia
(tao@bruce.cs.monash.oz.au)

Qing Li
Deptartment of Computer Science
Australian National University
Canberra, ACT 2601
Australia
(qing@anucsd.oz)

Henry Linger
Department of Computer Technology
Chisholm Institute of Technology
PO Box 197
Caulfield, VIC 3145
Australia

Chee Chin Low
Department of Computer Science
RMIT
124 La Trobe Street
Melbourne, VIC 3001
Australia
(ccl@goanna.cs.rmit.oz)

Geoff Martin
Department of Computer Technology
Chisholm Institute of Technology
PO Box 197
Caulfield, VIC 3145
Australia

P. E. Martin
School of Information Sci. and Engg.
University of Canberra
PO Box 1
Belconeen, ACT 2616
Australia
(epm@ucisae.isae.uc)

John Mashford
CSIRO Div of Bld Cons. and Engg.
Graham Road,
Highett, VIC 3190
Australia
(johnm@dbrmelb.dbrhi.oz)

Ian Mathieson
CSIRO
Division of Information Technology
55 Barry Street
Carlton, VIC 3053
Australia

Ken J McDonell
Pyramid Technology Corporation
South Yarra, VIC 3141
Australia
(kenj@yarra.oz.au)

Vera Melisserators
Department of Computer Science
University of Adelaide
GPO Box 498
Adelaide, SA 5001
Australia
(vera@cs.ua.oz)

Fatma Mili
School of Engg. and Comp. Sci.,
Oakland University
Rochester, MI 48309-4401
USA
(milif@unix.secs.oakland.edu)

Mirka Miller
Deptartment of Computer Science
University of New England
Armidale, NSW 2351
Australia
(mirka@neumann.une.oz)

Tony Montgomery
Department of Computer Science
RMIT
Melbourne, VIC 3001
Australia
(aym@goanna.cs.rmit.oz)

Lazlo Nemes
CSIRO
Divion of Information Technology
55 Barry St
Carlton, VIC 3053
Australia

Pam Norton
Chisholm Institute of Technology
PO Box 197
Caulfield, VIC 3145
Australia

Kai O'Yang
Department of Computer Science
Monash University
Clayton, VIC 3168
Australia

John Olle
Department of Computer Science
Bendigo CAE
Bendigo, VIC 3550
Australia
(olle@greybox.bcae.oz)

Maria Orlowska
Deptartment of Computer Science
Univeristy of Queensland
St. Lucia, QLD 3083
Australia
(maria@uqcspe.cs.uq.oz)

Mike Papazoglou
Department of Computer Science
Australian National University
GPO Box 4
Canberra, ACT 2601
Australia

John Patrick
Deptartment of Computer Science
Deakin University
Geelong, Vic. 3217
Australia
(jon@aragorn)

Alison Payne
7/38 Durham Street
St Lucia, QLD 4067
Australia

Kerry Raymond
Key Centre for Software Technology
Deptartment of Computer Science
University of Queensland
St Lucia, QLD 4067
Australia
(kerry@uqcspe.cs.uq.oz)

Robert Redpath
Department of Computer Technology
Chisholm Institute of Technology
PO Box 197
Caulfield, VIC 3145
Australia

Brian Regan
Deptartment of ITQM
University of Newcastle
PO Box 84
Waratah, NSW 2298
Australia

Brian Retallick
Department of Computer Science
Bendigo CAE
Bendigo, VIC 3550
Australia
(retallic@greybox.bcae.oz)

G. Rochlin
Telecom,
GPO Box 249
Clayton, VIC 3168
Australia

Ron Sacks-Davis
Department of Computer Science
RMIT
124 La Trobe Street
Melbourne, VIC 3001
Australia
(rsd@goanna.cs.rmit.oz

Rod Simpson
Department of Computer Technology
Chisholm Institute of Technology
PO Box 197
Caulfield, VIC 3145
Australia

John Smith
CSIRO
Division of Information Technology
GPO Box 664
Canberra ACT 2601
Australia
(smith@csis.dit.oz)

Bala Srinivasan
Department of Computer Science
Monash University
Clayton, VIC 3168
Australia
(srini@bruce.cs.monash.oz)

Phillip Steele
Department of Software Development
Chisholm Institute of Technology
PO Box 197
Caulfield, VIC 3145
Australia

Phil Stocks
Department of Computer Science
University of Queensland
St Lucia, QLD 4067
Australia

James Thom
Department of Computer Science
RMIT
124 La Trobe Street
Melbourne, VIC 3001
Australia
(jat@goanna.oz.au)

Peter Wallis
Department of Computer Science
RMIT
124 La Trobe Street
Melbourne, VIC 3001
Australia

Max Warlond
Department of Computer Technology
Chisholm Institute of Technology
PO Box 197
Caulfield, VIC 3145
Australia

Wilson Wen
Department of Computer Science
RMIT
124 La Trobe Street
Melbourne, VIC 3001
Australia

Ross Wilkinson
Department of Computer Science
RMIT
124 La Trobe Street
Melbourne, VIC 3001
Australia
(ross@goanna.cs.rmit.oz)

John Zeleznikow
Department of Computer Science
LaTrobe University
Bundoora, VIC 3083
Australia
(johnz@latcs1.oz)

Wei Zhao
Department of Computer Science
Univerisity of Adelaide
Adelaide, SA 5001
Australia

Dan Zhou
Department of Computer Science
Australian National University
GPO Box 4
Canberra, ACT 2601
Australia

www.ingramcontent.com/pod-product-compliance
Ingram Content Group UK Ltd.
Pitfield, Milton Keynes, MK11 3LW, UK
UKHW061000120926
8556IPUK00032B/889

9 789810 202767